THE CO

Basset H

by MERCEDES

ILLUSTRATED

1965

HOWELL BOOK H

845 THIRD AVENUE

NEW YORK, N.Y.   1002

*To those who really care;
to whom the Basset of tomorrow
is more important than the wins of today
This book is respectfully dedicated.*

Tristan and Tristeuse, leading couple, Temporal and La Tentatrice, back couple, Artesien Bassets. The portrait from which this drawing was made was painted about 1875 by Charles Olivier de Penne (1831–1897).
Courtesy of *The Chronicle of the Horse*, Middleburg, Va.

Contents

Introduction

THE Basset Hound fancy has needed a book for a long time. I was happy when "Merce" told me she was asked to write one and more than willing to help in any way possible. Her years as a breeder, hunter, exhibitor, and obedience teacher qualified her to write on those subjects with authority. I was confident in her ability as a writer. She had done the breed's column for *Pure-Bred Dogs* for several years and published the Basset Hound Club of America's bulletin during my term as president of the club.

The contents of *The Complete Basset Hound* are facts collected and compiled by the author. She should be commended for a tremendous job and service to the breed. Only one who has true love for man's best friend could devote so much time and effort writing so that the rest of us could enjoy reading. She has tried to present the reader with the past and present history of all the varieties of the breed in every country in which it is known. The chapters on breeding, training, exhibiting, and field work are of great value.

May all who read this publication have a richer understanding of the breed. May we realize that the breed can only be as great as we, the Basset fanciers, make it.

JOHN N. EYLANDER

Acknowledgments

Without many wonderful people, there would be no book at all. To all of them, I wish to express my gratitude. I knew there was little reference material on the Basset and huge gaps in the history of the American bloodlines when I accepted the task of writing. There was a great need for a compilation of known facts, if nothing more, so that what was known would be accessible to all. What I did not know was that I would be invited to use books that were tucked away in private libraries so that I could compare the opinions of many authors. I also did not know that fanciers around the world would be eager to assist because they were just as anxious as we in America to see this book in print.

We must first thank Elsworth Howell who realized our need for such a book and expressed his desire to publish it if I would write it. It is impossible to thank adequately George Pugh of Xenia, Ohio, a judge who is wholeheartedly interested in any breed. His personal interests involve Obedience, the Springer Spaniels, Gordon Setters, Toy Manchester Terriers, and Bassets. When he learned of my un dertaking, he graciously threw open the doors of his private library where I found many old, out-of-print volumes that contained reference to the Basset. Here I was able to review information and form a theory on the origin of the breed. He loaned me his nearly-complete set of American Kennel Gazettes so that I was able to piece together the American bloodlines.

The officers of The Basset Hound Club of America were generous in their contribution. John Eylander, Norwood Engle, and Loren Free never tired of lengthy correspondence and discussions on pedigrees, pictures, and breeders. Darrielyn Oursler checked the club records. The secretaries of the regional clubs, for the most part, supplied the data on their clubs.

Many breeders were most helpful. Jean Sanger Look, especially, contributed a great deal of material and loaned pictures of many early Bassets. Clarence, "Clip," and Helen Boutell offered the scale drawing for the Standard chapter and a copy of the De Penne painting. Dr. & Mrs. Leonard Skolnick sent microfilm of French books. James S. Jones, Master of the Tewksbury Foot Basset Pack, volunteered to write the chapter on the packs in America. Alfred Bissell sent further information about the packs. Others sent pictures of them. Fred Carter assisted with the bloodlines in Canada. There were many more, too numerous to mention, who answered my plea for information and pictures. Mark Washbond, Chris Teeter, Richard Basset, Doris Hurry, and the Kenneth Eldridges were very helpful.

From overseas, help was given without restraint. George Johnston and Gerard Kemp of England supplied most of the material on modern Basset affairs in Great Britain. M. Hubert and M. Abel Desamy painstakingly translated my letters to them and sent the information on modern French Bassets as did M. Jean Rothea. Keith Goodwin contributed the Australian chapter. Peggy Blakeney wrote of the newly formed New Zealand club.

I am not schooled in the French language. Dr. Tryggve Baak of Waterville, Ohio, whose Bulldogs I handle, spent many hours translating the French writings. A friend, William Gravesmill, took some of the French correspondence to an associate at the Toledo Museum of Art where he is supervisor of music. Carolyn Wehrley, a commercial artist from Toledo, Ohio, offered to make the line drawings because she had taken a fancy to the breed.

It is impossible to thank all who offered so much. Nothing could have been accomplished without the help of my most severe critic, staunch supporter, and husband, Joe. We are deeply indebted to those who loaned their cherished photographs. Every little bit helped to make this a complete book. To all who contributed, even a small amount, the appreciation of the publisher, the author, and the Basset fanciers is gratefully acknowledged.

MERCEDES BRAUN
Curtice, Ohio

The author with Jenny Diver

1

What Is a Basset?

TECHNICALLY, he is a long, low dog of the scent-hound category, known for his pensive expression and easy-going manner. He was bred to hunt small game, and because this is his primary purpose, the following pages are filled with material concerning this function of the breed.

We must not forget, however, that it is the Basset's versatility that brought him fame. He is perhaps best known for the lovable nature which led him to be dubbed "the armchair clown." Do not be fooled when you see him sound asleep on his back or sprawled on his favorite chair (which he has taken away from you). Put a lead on this same dog, take him to a show, and he can give a polished performance with a "Don't you love me, Mr. Judge?" attitude that will command applause from the ringside. Take him to the field, and he can show you how a scent-hound should perform—over, under, and through rough ground, never tiring all day long.

At home, the Basset will assume his subtle manner of "ruling the roost." He refuses to accept the fact that he is a dog by devious methods. He can affect poor hearing when he doesn't want to obey or pretend to sleep so soundly that you do not have the heart to disturb him. But his alertness miraculously returns if you open the re-

1

frigerator door ever so stealthily. He is a built-in baby-sitter, an ideal family pet. A Basset needs firm convincing that his big, brown eyes will get him nowhere. But first convince yourself of this, if you can. He is smart enough to be very adept at playing dumb. He will do his best to outmaneuver you to gain his own way, and he will make you like it. You need only one Basset to fill the house with laughter, the woods with beautiful music, and the show with an approving ovation. Small wonder the breed has attained such popularity and owners readily admit, "I am owned by a Basset."

2

History of the
Basset Hound

THE origin of the Basset Hound is somewhat elusive. Until the writing of this book, I accepted the common belief set forth in most 20th century publications that the Basset Hound was a direct descendant of the St. Hubert Hound. The verity of this contention has been doubted since the uncovering of information in certain rare, old volumes. I shall present the facts I have discovered. The reader may draw his own conclusions, as I have done.

Though the many varieties of Basset Hounds are included in this book, we are chiefly concerned with the type that is known in America today. M. Jean Rothea, president of the Club du Basset Artesien Normand in 1964, states that since this was the line that produced the British Basset, and few other importations were made, we must conclude that the American Basset is descended predominantly from the Basset d'Artois, now called the Basset Artesien Normand in France. As you will read in the following pages, the Basset d'Artois had become nearly extinct at one time. Comte le Couteulx de Cantelue, Monsieur Lane, and a few other men were largely responsible for the revival of this variety. Genealogy before their time is of little importance to breeding programs though the early history is interesting. A letter from M. Abel Desamy, president of the Club du Griffon Vendeen, further substantiates and enlarges this theory: "Here is my personal opinion on the origin of the 'Basset Hound.' It is a descendant of the French Bassets 'le Couteulx' and 'Lane.' There are, moreover, common points between the 'Basset Hound' and our 'Artesien Normand.' M. Megin assures me that about 1880 the English (a certain Mr. Krehl) imported a Basset of M. le Couteulx (Fino) and several females (Gunera and Theo), next a Basset of M. Lane (Romano). These dogs took root and the English obtained their characteristic type; more heavy dogs, with head of a bloodhound. It is possible, evidently, that in order to establish this stock, one or the other called upon the ancestry of the Basset Ardennais (the Basset of St. Hubert). This remains to be proven."

One must bear in mind that prior to the later years of the Napoleonic era, all dogs lower than sixteen inches were called Bassets (*bas* meaning low-set) in France. Each province and each breed had its Basset. To ask a Frenchman for a Basset, without stating which variety, was like asking for a horse without indicating if it should be a race-horse, plow-horse, or cart-horse.

One must realize that terms, though they may fit *our* visualization of a dog, may not give us the description as it was in the mind of the writer. Words often do not compare with available pictures and data. For example, refer to the photograph of one of the earliest English imports, Sir Everett Millais's Model. While reading the delineation, one envisions great depth of muzzle, many folds of very loose skin, and great ear length. The dog in the picture, however, if compared to the modern American Basset, would be described today as having a snipey muzzle, a dry head, and short, heavy ears. In another publication, the Basset was said to be "broader in chest than a Bulldog" of that era, but he was certainly not broader than the Bulldog which is familiar to us today.

According to early writers, the original German Dachshund and the Schweisshund were indistinguishable from the Basset in structural characteristics though they were either copper-red or black-and-tan. Since the ancient origin of the Basset is of little value to a present-day breeding program, we will not go into the evolution of these hounds.

On the monument of Thothmus III, who reigned over Egypt

Sir Everett Millais's "Model."

taing Bassets with long bodies, short crooked legs, and owned by a French marquis. This variety had grand Otterhound heads with rough coats and were, undoubtedly, the type known as the Basset Griffon today. We will discuss the Griffon varieties in later chapters.

Most of the information on Bassets in modern books has been taken from the writings of English authors. Many of them admit openly that the true origin of the breed was not known to them. They knew only that the dogs were bred by M. le Couteulx and M. Lane. Sir Everett Millais was one of the earliest English breeders and writers. Others often referred to his theory. This in turn came from le Couteulx who believed that *all* French hounds were derived from the St. Hubert. He alludes to twelve different varieties of Bassets which appeared to have been known up to the time of the French Revolution. He concluded that, since all hounds had similarly shaped heads, long ears, and dewlap, they were related. Being certain that the Hounds of St. Hubert dated back to the eighth century, he theorized that all similar animals descended from them.

Sir Everett Millais further elaborated on this supposition by stating that the rickety-type Bloodhounds, descendants of the St. Hubert Hound, could have developed short, crooked legs. Millais believed that sportsmen who followed their hunting dogs on foot set to work breeding specimens with the shortest legs, and the Basset was the result. He was further convinced by the name, which he interpreted to mean "dwarf." However, Cassell's dictionary defines "bas" as "not high; low; lowered; inferior," depending on the context.

Sir Everett's theory is possible, though geneticists of today would call the process he describes selective breeding. They would attribute the formation of the legs to genetic makeup rather than to poor nutrition and rickets. If we accept the "direct descendant of the St. Hubert Hound" theory, we must suspect that these dogs carried genes capable of producing short legs which appeared in certain specimens when they were inbred. St. Hubert had taken dogs from the Rhone district in southern France to his abbey and kennels in the Ardennes province of northern France. We have previously ascertained that the Agasaeus, referred to by Oppian, had been sent to this district by the Roman Procurator Cynegii.

St. Hubert could have bred dogs that were approximately twenty-eight inches high but which were carrying short-leg genes.

A fact that is little known is that there was also a Basset of St. Hubert which was either shiny black or uniformly copper in color. Without perusal of possible records kept by the Abbots of St. Hubert, one cannot reach an indisputable conclusion about the origin of this type, but it seems feasible that St. Hubert took more than one breed to his kennel along the Belgian border. From the Agasaeus he bred the Basset of St. Hubert.

Undoubtedly, as later writers called upon the works of those before them, they neglected to realize that the St. Hubert Hound was a variety under the broader title of "Basset Hounds." At least, they failed to make the point clear. As time went on, there was confusion between the St. Hubert Hound and the Basset of St. Hubert.

The Bleu de Gascogne was another variety mentioned in early writings. This type was smooth-coated, heavily mottled, with longer ears than the St. Hubert. It was developed in the Gascony area along the Bay of Biscayne, east of the Rhone district. It is very possible that these dogs were also descendants of the Agasaeus.

Undoubtedly, fanciers of each district called upon the little Bassets along the Rhone, selected those best suited to their topography, and developed their distinctive types. The same breeding process would hold true for dogs of similar structure, known by different names, in other countries.

3

Modern Smooth Coats

IN 1887, Stonehenge wrote, "In France, about twelve distinct breeds of hounds are met with, including the St. Hubert, the smooth hounds of La Vendee, the Brittany Red Hound, the grey St. Louis, the Gascony, the Normandy, the Saintogne, the Poitou, the Breese, the Vendee rough-coated hound, the Artois, and the little Basset, coupled with the Briquet. Of these, the grey St. Louis is almost extinct, and all the others, with the exception of the Basset, may be grouped with the St. Hubert and the Red Hound of Brittany. . . . The varieties of the Basset are innumerable some being black-and-tan, and common throughout the Black Forest and Vosges, while the others are either tricoloured or blue mottled. The tricolour has lately been introduced into England in large numbers, having been first shown to the English visitors at the French show of 1863. . . ." He called upon the earliest French authority, De Fouilloux, to deal with the "Basset d'Artois," with which we are chiefly concerned, for a description of this dog: "The Artesien, with full-crooked fore-legs, smooth coats, brave, and having double rows of teeth like wolves." Stonehenge continued, "In the many political storms that have swept over France, carrying away her monarchial pageantry and the impressing ceremonies of the chase, many of that country's ancient breeds became almost extinct. Amongst them, the basset-hound fared a little better than its blood neighbors— the hounds of Artois, Normandy, Gascony, and Saintogne. Thanks to the sporting and patriotic instincts of the descendant of the old noblesse, Count le Couteulx de Canteleu, who spared neither trouble nor expense in his purpose, the smooth tricolour basset-hound of Artois has been preserved in all its purity. The breed was not revived; it had never died out, but it was necessary to search all over the 'basset' districts to find, in sportsmen's kennels, the few true typical specimens, and to breed from them alone. In these efforts on behalf of the old breeds he was greatly benefited by the valuable assistance of M. Pierre Pichot, editor of the 'Revue Britannique.' These are inseparably connected with the famous kennel of Chateau St. Martin, and hounds of Count Couteulx's strain are now as highly prized and eagerly sought for in England as in France. They are aptly described by the French writer De la Blanchere as 'large hounds on short legs.' " The remainder of this work is an account of their field work and standard.

George Krehl, one of the earliest English fanciers, wrote for Vero Shaw's *The Book of the Dog*, in 1881, ". . . The Basset par excellence, though, is the beautiful smooth-coated tricolour of Artois, and this is the type with its rich and brilliant colouring of black, white, and golden tan, its noble Bloodhound-like head so full of solemn dignity, and long velvet-soft ears, the kind and pensive eye, the heavy folds of the throat, the strange fore-limbs, the quaint and medieval appearance—this is the type, I say, that will stand first in the estimation of an intelligent dog-loving public. The type will always be associated with the name of Comte le Couteulx de Cantelue, and all the Bassets at present (1881) in this country (England) are descended from, or are direct importations from, his celebrated kennel. To this Nobleman, inspired with a hereditary love of the chase and all its accessories, is due the credit of, in a manner, resuscitating this breed, which twenty-five years ago, by careless rearing and the freakish crosses that Continental sportsmen affect, had become well-nigh extinct. The Count has been kind enough to supply me with the particulars of that period. Observing the growing scarcity of good and pure tricolour Artesien Bassets, he set about to do for them what he had already accomplished for other ancient and moribund breeds of Gaul. He

11

started to find a pair of true and pure specimens to revive the breed. After purchasing some thirty dogs, he at last acquired a grand dog, Fino (the first of the name), in Artois, and a lively bitch, Mignarde, in another part of the country. Their produce were true and level to their parentage, showing no signs of throwing back to misalliances; the pups only differed in being more or less crooked, as is still the case in modern litters. The Count continues that he bred in and in to perfect the breed, and that his dogs were sturdy and vigorous enough to permit this means. Ten years later he endeavoured to find another stud-dog for new blood. His huntsman travelled the North of France through to find one, and the experiment made with a superb Basset that he bought in the Saumur, having produced yellow pups, he destroyed them and continued to rely on his own strain. The Count, in his description of the head, lays great stress upon the occipital protuberance, which he calls 'la bosse de chasse'; the head long, narrow and thin in the muzzle, the ears very long; the head of the dog being much heavier and stronger than the bitch's. He gives about four inches for the height of the crooked legs. Colour, tricolour, sometimes ticked with black spots. He goes on to say that some of them have more teeth than dogs usually have, and that many have the 'bec de lievre' i.e. the lower jaw a little shorter than the upper. He states that two of the best bitches in his pack have this formation of the jaw.

"Of the dogs chosen for the coloured plate, Jupiter shows most of the Bloodhound type head; the bitch Pallas is but little short of perfection, and it was the eulogistic description of her qualities in 'The Field,' when she won at Brussels, that induced the writer to find her out in France, and buy her and her mate, Jupiter. Fino de Paris, the third dog in the picture, is demi-torse; he is own brother to Mr. Millais's Model, which is full-torse. He was, until I purchased him from the Jardin d'Acclimation, Paris, the stud-dog of Europe; and Count Couteulx considers him a 'particularly good and pure stud-dog, a perfect specimen of the breed, low on the legs, very strong, well-knit loins, and head typical of the breed, long and thin.' "

Mr. Krehl's article is very interesting. I suggest you compare his description with the copy of this picture of Jupiter, Pallas, and Fino de Paris.

Jupiter, Pallas, and Fino de Paris.

During this period, Monsieurs Couteulx, Masson, and Lane bred from the same original stock, but each got different results. In 1881, M. Louis Lane, of Francqueville, near Boos, exhibited several large, strong, heavy-boned hounds with a decided family likeness. The head was of good length, the ear long, but the faces lacked the Bloodhound character and expression that was seen in the Fino de Paris type. The Lane hounds became very much in demand when the two Couteulx types were much inbred and in need of an out-cross.

To better understand the difference in types, let us elaborate on them. There were eventually two Couteulx types, Fino de Paris and Termino (or Masson):

Fino de Paris Type

COLOR. Rich tricolor, harepie, lemon and white. The markings were even and brilliant, the tan deep, the black saddle-shape on the back running into tan on the buttocks.

COAT. Thick, strong, and, at times, crimped even to coarseness; stern, feathered.

HEAD. In those unallied to the Termino hounds, flattish; ears set high and small; skull domed. In those containing Termino blood, the head was large, well shaped, ears hung low and of good size, with well-developed flews, nose slightly inclined to Roman.

EYE. Dark, sunken, and showing a prominent haw.

BONE. Good; in those not too closely inbred, massive.

LEGS. Torses (full crooked), demi-torses (half crooked), droites (straight).

GENERAL APPEARANCE. A fine hound, a powerful physique.

EXAMPLES: Fino de Paris, Fino V, VI, Pallas II, Fresco, Forester, Merlin, Clovis, Eve, Texas Fino, Wazir, Aryan, Laelaps, Fancy, Fiddler, & Flora.

Termino or Masson Type

COLOR. Tricolor (light), lemon and white, harepie, blue-mottled. The tricolor was far less briliant than the Fino de Paris type, the tan not so rich, the back distributed in uneven patches over the body, frequently ticked or blue-mottled.

COAT. Short and fine; no crimping.

HEAD. Domed, though in many of the best specimens this was not apparent.

NOSE. Strongly Roman and finer than the Fino de Paris hounds.

EARS. Hung very low and immensely long.

FLEWS. Well marked.

EYE. Sunken, dark, hawed.

BONE. Somewhat light, except in one or two specimens.

LEGS. Torses, demi-torses, droites with an inclination to height.

GENERAL APPEARANCE. A fine, upstanding hound, well put-together, and of high breeding.

EXAMPLES: Termino, Guinevre, Bellicent, Bourbon, Chopette, Zues, Beau, Beauclerc, Narcissus, Colinette, Blondin, Desia.

It would be well to understand how the difference in Couteulx types came about. In the following table of production, C indicates Couteulx's Fino de Paris type, M is for Masson or Termino type.

Fino de Paris (C) ex Trouvette (C) produced Mignarde (C)
Fino de Paris (C) ex Mignarde (C) produced Finette (C)
Termino (M) ex Finette (C) produced Guinevre (M)
Fino de Paris (C) ex Guinevre (M) produced Bourbon (M) & Fino V (C & M)
Fino de Paris (C) ex Ravende II (C) produced Fanfaro (C)
Fanfaro (C) ex Theo (M) produced Vivien (C & M)

Although Guinevre and Theo were bred from Fino de Paris stock, on the dam's side, they were quite different from Fino de Paris, or any other hound from Comte Couteulx's kennels. They resembled Bellicent, a hound from M. Masson's kennels, which is proof that this peculiar type is indigenous in his line. They must have resembled their sire, which belonged to M. Masson.

Guinevre was mated with Fino de Paris. Had she proved true to common rules of breeding, she should have given birth to his type. She did not; her pup, Bourbon, resembled the Masson dogs. Fino V was similar to his sire but carried some of his dam's qualities.

Bourbon was mated with his aunt, Theo, and produced Chopette, a bitch excelling even her sire in points which made him so different from his brother Fino V.

Vivien was very weak Masson, or Termino, type. She threw both types which ever way mated, and threw in her own, as in the case of Jupiter, a poor type-producer.

Fino de Paris was bred from brother and sister. His pedigree before his grandparents is unknown. Termino as a sire was more prepotent, stamping the character of his family against odds in favor of Fino de Paris.

Lane Type

COLOR. Light tricolor, lemon and white, harepie with ticking.
COAT. Short and thick.
HEAD. Domed, large and coarse, lacking Bloodhound expression.
EARS. Long, heavy, broad, hung low.
EYES. Light.
FLEWS. Well-marked.
LEGS. Torses.
BONE. Enormous.
GENERAL APPEARANCE. A very big, heavy Basset; coarse and clumsy, with enormous chest development.
EXAMPLES: Romano II, Gavette, Blanchette II, Champion, Bavard, Chorister, Hannibal.

An interesting piece on field workers was written by "Wildfowler" in 1879: "He is the slowest of hounds and his value cannot be overestimated. His style of hunting is peculiar, inasmuch that he will have his own way, and each one tries for himself; and if one of them finds, and 'says' so, the others will not blindly follow him and give tongue simply because he does as some hounds, accustomed to work in packs, are apt to do; but, on the contrary, they are slow to acknowledge the alarm given, and will investigate the matter for themselves." He further tells how they work in Indian file, "each one speaking to the line according to his own sentiments on the point, irrespective of what the others may think about it, each working as if he were alone." How true.

All of these writers go on and on about their experiences in the field. Some used field dogs for vermin-killing (badger, fox, etc.);

16

others employed them for pheasant shooting, woodcock, etc., while some were trained to retrieve from water. The most unusual use was for truffle-hunting. Many peasants employed the dogs' extraordinary scenting power to assist them in finding tubers. All the peasant had to do was dig the potato-shaped delicacy from the ground. How versatile can a breed get?

Others in France had begun to take a serious interest in the breed. M. Leon Verrier started his kennel of Bulins in 1874. M. Verrier wrote that his finest Bassets reproduced themselves no matter what. The ancestry of le Couteulx was in their background, though he had no proof. Pedigrees were not kept on record in these days.

M. Verrier was a great admirer of the Lane type but desired to escape its lighter coloring without loosing the type. He purchased the best dogs he could find. He attempted to breed dogs with straighter legs but had many disappointments because he never kept records of the lines of his brood bitches or of the studs he employed. M. Verrier later left the country of Bray and moved near Rouen where he had the opportunity to work more closely with M. Lane and M. Bardin. He bred Brin d'Or, a fine stud hound, to Revaude and Timbale I, and many fine hounds resulted: Ch. Musquetaire, Cocardas, & Merville II. Timbale is associated with Ch. Caressant, Chimere, Gouveneur, Indescrete, Ch. Megere, and Ch. Tenebreau. All of these dogs measured twelve to fourteen inches and had half-crooked legs, which M. Verrier had by then, decided, was an essential characteristic. He also found that it was very difficult to maintain this type of leg in breedings due to the variations in backgrounds. He felt that another important feature of the Basset was the roundness of the hindquarters and noted that many were becoming slack in this point because amateur breeders did not agree on the importance of this characteristic.

In the 1920s he wrote that most Bassets were crosses between the dogs of Gossalin, le Couteulx, Marchart, and his own, the best coming from crosses between Lane and le Couteulx.

M. Machart of Somme had beautiful animals related to the Lane and le Couteulx lines. The dogs were enormous in type, with large ears, deep dewlaps, and some of grey-badger color. After his death, most of Machart's best dogs were purchased by the Colonel de Champs and M. le Baron de Segonzac.

17

Another resident of Somme was M. Gosselin. His dogs were thought to be products of a cross with le Couteulx, though the type was altered. Unfortunately, he did not keep many records. In an attempt to establish type, he sent a bitch, Sonnaute, to another kennel in the area to be bred. In the account of this mating, no further information about the sire was given. The puppies resembled Machart's lines. They carried a small part of the Couteulx and de Briey characteristics, but were different in type. At the exposition of d'Amiens, there were representatives of M. Gosselin and M. de Guilbon, and the types were established as Sonnaute, Gosselin, and Machart.

At many shows in Paris, M. Hannoire exhibited dogs whose ancestry appeared to go back to M. le Couteulx.

M. Mallart was known as an exhibitor of Briquets d'Artois, but he also bred Bassets. According to Leon Verrier, they were of excellent type.

M. Baillet lived in Villenauxe and later moved to Rouen where he acquired the eagerness of other Basset breeders. He preferred the smaller dogs.

A frequent exhibitor in Paris was M. Segonzac. He showed Chs. Troubadour and Intendante with success, but as he crossed the different sizes and leg structures, his dogs lost the uniformity for which the earlier examples had been known.

Col. de Champs showed several dogs of excellent quality. His Hourvari gained a championship and was a dependable producer. Justice de Fremont was a daughter of Ch. Hourvari. This lovely bitch was owned by le Vicomte de Peufeilhoux who exhibited a few Bassets. Verrier judged her at de Lyon and awarded her the highest honors.

Dr. Leseigner bred some of his le Couteulx bitches to various studs. His dogs were solid, robust, and admirable in the field. Leseigner became well known because he conducted his own hunt, uncoupled eight or ten dogs, and handled them in this manner, himself, to high awards. They would drive any kind of game to be killed. A friend, M. George Pariset, whose dogs had the same origin as Leseigner's, adopted the same manner of field work.

These were the earliest French breeders. Though they kept no records and had little knowledge of genetic theory, they were dedicated in their work. By trial and error, eliminating undesirable producers, they established the individual types for which they became known. Several breeders joined their ranks by the 1920s, but most of the importations in the days when the Basset was introduced to England and America came from dogs that were bred by these gentlemen. If one considers the difficulties of communication and travel in those days, one can better appreciate the results of their efforts.

This brings us to the time of the first imports to Britain and the first recorded Bassets in the United States. The French continued to breed a more diminutive size than did the British and American fanciers. Further French history will be found in a later chapter.

Readers may find the first British Standard and comments upon it, in *British Dogs* written by Hugh Dalziel in 1879, most interesting:

Points of the Basset Hound

Head, skull, eyes, muzzle, and flews	15
Ears	15
Neck, dewlap, chest, and shoulders	10
Fore legs and feet	15
Back, loins, and hind quarters	10
Stern	5
Coat and skin	10
Colour and markings	15
Basset character and symmetry	5
	100

1. To begin with the HEAD, as the most distinguishing part of all breeds. The head of the Basset-hound is most perfect when it closest resembles a Bloodhound's. It is long and narrow, with heavy flews, occiput prominent, "la bosse de la chasse," and forehead wrinkled to the eyes, which should be kind, and show a haw. The general appearance of the head must present high breeding and reposeful dignity, the teeth are small, and the upper jaw sometimes protrudes. This is not a fault, and is called the "bec de lievre."

2. The EARS very long, and when drawn forward folding well over the nose—so long that in hunting they will often actually tread on them; they are set on low, and hang loose in folds like drapery, the ends curling, in texture thin and velvety.

3. The NECK is powerful, with heavy dewlaps. Elbows must not turn out. The chest is deep, full, and framed like a "man-of-war." Body long and low.

4. FORE LEGS short, about 4", and close-fitting to the chest till the crooked knee, from where the wrinkled ankle ends in a massive paw, each toe standing out distinctly.

5. The STIFLES are bent, and the quarters full of muscle, which stands out so that when one looks at the dog from behind, it gives him a round, barrel-like effect. This, with their peculiar, waddling gait, goes a long way towards Basset character—a quality easily recognised by the judge, and as desirable as Terrier character in a Terrier.

6. The STERN is coarse underneath, and carried hound-fashion.

7. The COAT is short, smooth, and fine, and has a gloss on it like that of a racehorse. (To get this appearance, they should be houndgloved, never brushed.) Skin loose and elastic.

8. The COLOUR should be black, white, and tan; the head, shoulders, and quarters a rich tan, and black patches on the back. They are sometimes harepied.

Dalziel's comments follow: "In refusing to accept the above as a correct description of any dog, I take strong exception to the dogma that 'the head is the most distinguishing feature of all breeds.' It is not so in either the Basset or Dachshund, both of which are more distinguished from other hounds by the disproportion between their length and height, than any other feature.

"Whether we take dogs, sheep, or cattle, the head as distinguishing breeds does not go far, but in marking groups, each including many breeds, it comes into prominence. But what are we to say of an animal constructed as Mr. Krehl does the Basset, opining, unintelligible terms, a prodigy from his inner consciousness or abortive imagination?

"What would a English MFH say to a hound whose ears are worth all the rest of his head, including nose? What can anybody say to a dog of any kind, unless it be a fancy toy, whose hide, tail, and ears make nearly half of him and are reckoned at one-seventh more value than all the rest of him, except head and a something undefined, and called character—which latter quality, it is hinted, if not distinctly stated, is only visible to a judge? Certainly a dog 40% nice seems best fitted for the tanyard.

"The fact is, the description is absurd, and can only be accepted as a caricature of any hound; and it seems to me impossible that the Basset Club, or at least, those members of it who desire to use the Basset for his legitimate work, can, on reflection, continue to accept it as the standard by which their hounds shall be judged: even if indisposed to criticise too keenly, they liberally give their own definition to the obscurities of its involved sentences."

These comments are priceless. They continue to apply. Again, I urge you to compare the description with the photographs of Model, Jupiter, Pallas, and Fino de Paris.

4

The Basset Hound
in America up to 1950

THE history of the Basset Hound in America dates back to a surprisingly early period. It is common belief that George Washington's diary indicates that his friend Lafayette sent these hounds to the United States after the Revolution. Undoubtedly, others were brought here in the company of the more prosperous immigrants who enjoyed the sport of the chase.

According to *The American Book of the Dog,* Lord Aylesford imported a brace by Jupiter in 1883 which he used for rabbit hunting on his ranch near Big Springs, Texas. This same year, Mr. Chamberlain purchased Ch. Nemours from George Krehl, Hanover Square, London, and brought him to Lawrence Timson's Maizeland Kennels at Red Hook, N.J. Nemours was whelped March 21, 1883, sired by Ch. Jupiter out of Vivien. The following Spring of 1884, Westminster Kennel Club made a class for the Basset Hound and Ch. Nemours made his bow to the American public, just one year after the Basset Hound Club of England was formed. He was shown at Philadelphia and the National Breeders Show the same year. In 1885, he was first at New Haven, Boston, and New York, gaining his championship at Boston in 1886.

Mr. C. B. Gilbert of New Haven, Conn. soon followed Mr. Chamberlain's and Lord Aylesford's interest in the breed. He imported Bertrand (by Bourbon) and Canace (by Jupiter) in 1885. From these he bred Jose and Juan.

The first Bassets registered with the American Kennel Club were Bouncer and Countess in 1885. Bouncer: 3234; male; sire, Major; dam, Venus; black, white, and tan; whelped, March 18, 1881; breeder, Pottinger Dorsey, Newmarket, Md.; owner, Colin Cameron, Breckerville, Penna. Countess: 3235; bitch; sire, Nero; dam, Lotta; whelped April 1880; breeder, E. S. Krecht, Germany; owner, B. F. Seitner, Dayton, Ohio.

In 1889, Charles Porter of Philadelphia introduced Babette, by Merlin, at the New York show. Porter later adopted the Upland prefix. Cornelius Stevenson's Chasseur, by Farmer, was also shown this same year.

It is interesting to note that, according to the *American Kennel Gazette* of 1916, Bassets were listed as a recognized foreign dog and one of the breeds not eligible for the Winners classes. By 1917, reclassifications were as follows: large dogs, medium dogs, small dogs, and cage dogs. Basset hound-smooth coat and Basset hound-rough coat, were under the heading of medium dogs.

Gerald Livingston made his first importation in 1921. His Kilsyth line became well known near his Georgia plantation and his home at Huntington, Long Island. It was an important contribution to the breed.

In 1925, Erastus Tefft exhibited Simillante at the Westminster show under Walter Reeves in a combined sex class. He, as did Livingston, drafted heavily on the Walhampton pack. In 1925, Musique, another of Tefft's bitches, was Best of Breed over Simillante and Livingston's Pandora and Crescent. Classes were divided this year. Livingston's Vanneur took the Open Dog class, defeating Runt, owned by Tefft, and Vanneur's kennel mates, Rattler and Rector.

During 1925 and 1926, Tefft imported Ch. Lavenham Pippin, 422999; Pippin's tricolor niece Walhampton Passion, 651344; Ch. Leader (a French import who was the granddam of Baillet's Brano and Trompette II); and Reveuse. Gerald Livingston imported the Walhampton pack leader, Walhampton Dainty, 476679; Eng. & Am. Ch. Walhampton Andrew; tricolored Walhampton Aaron, 478305;

and the French Baillet's Brano. Lewis Thompson imported Eng. Ch. Amir of Reynalton, 943437 and Walhampton Nicety, 943438 which were both tricolored. During this period Smith imported the French dogs Baillet's Trompette II and Fr. Ch. Baillet's Corvette, also known as Cornette. Caviar, 476677, Dalby Hall Drifter, 651342, Dalby Hall Diligence, 665043, tricolored Walhampton Abbot, 988268, Governor, and Tapageur De L'Hermite also came to this country in the 1925–26 period. Consuelo Ford imported tricolored Ch. Westerby Vintage, A339140. Another import of the era was Walhampton Lively, 478303, whelped July 21, 1918. She was grand-dam of Caviar and the first Basset owned by Loren Free of Bainbridge, Ohio, whose kennel was much later known by its Shellbark prefix.

The February 1928 issue of *Time* carried a picture of a Basset puppy, the youngest creature ever to appear on its cover up to that time. The puppy, from Gerald Livingston's Kilsyth kennel, bred from Int. Am. & Eng. Ch. Walhampton Andrew and Walhampton Dainty, helped to bring the breed before the public.

Few were exhibited during this period and for several years to follow. They appeared sporadically at shows. By 1928, the American Kennel Club reclassified Groups, and the Basset was listed as a Sporting dog. At the Atlantic City show, Walhampton Linguist was Best of Breed over kennelmates, Brookmead Merchant, Mixer, Medley, Mindful, and Minnow, all owned by Mrs. G. Sloane of Locust Valley, Long Island, N.Y. Winners gained three points, and Linguist gained his championship in the same year. The following year, the same entries, plus Brookmead Mullet, Mollie, and Walhampton Alice, all owned by the Brookmead kennels, were the only Bassets at several eastern shows including Westminster where Mixer captured the honors. W. Fritz introduced Smith's True Boy at the Detroit show. S. A. Mitchell, of Oyster Bay, N.Y., offered a litter for sale. Walhampton Alice, Brookmead Mixer, Medley, and Mullet gained their championships in 1929.

About this time, the Basset was selected for use in experiments dealing with inheritance of coat coloring. A few new names began to appear. F. A. Ostendorf exhibited his Broadaxe and Blaze in Ohio. H. O. Putnam entered Trompette Chief in the same area. At Detroit, in 1929, the following were seen: G. W. King's Maple Drive Concertone, Carmelita (Walhampton Aaron ex King's

24

Walhampton Lively, English import owned by Loren Free.

Patches) dam of the first Field Champion, and Bugler. W. Fritz entered King's Fan All, Baillet's Trompette II, and Maple Drive Maxim (Walhampton Aaron ex Corvette). E. Krahn exhibited Carry on Michigan, and H. L. Cotton showed Peggy Leach (Ch. Walhampton Andrew ex Belle of Kilsyth).

The following year Fritz purchased Carry on Michigan. Carl Nottke showed his puppy bitch called Nottke's Bonnett.

Carl Smith took over the Starridge pack in 1930. Names connected with this pack are Smith's Yankee Lad, Lavinham Pippin, Walhampton Passion, and Woelk's Brigadier.

Entries continued to be small and scattered. At most shows, all entries were from one kennel. Many championships were gained in this manner. Westminster had no representatives of the breed at the 1930 show. In 1931 and 1932, Marvey's Sam, owned by W. H. Attwood, was the only entry. G. M. Livingston's Kilsyth Broker was Best of Breed over his kennelmates, Bramble and Famous, in 1933. None were entered in 1934. At other shows in this era, a few names appeared. The Cheston Kennels showed Dalby Hall Dormouse, Kilsyth Freddy, and Kilsyth Felix at Boston. J. F. Freeland entered his Freeland's Tarzan, Judy, Ginger, and Dinah at Baltimore. In Pennsylvania, Mrs. W. N. Ely exhibited Mrs. Ely Binki and Kilsyth Bracelet. The Irish Hills prefix appeared at Flint, Michigan. At Delaware County, Pennsylvania, W. P. Klapp, of Radnor, Penna., showed Klapp's Queen, Joy, and Mable, and the Stockford Kennels exhibited Diamond Rosebank. Klapp entered Rebecca at Devon, Penna., showing against Lewis Thompson's Amir of Reynalton, Stanco Joan, and Stanco Koto, and the Stockford Kennel's Kilsyth Bracelet. Rebecca 784043 gained her championship in 1934.

There was a noticeable rise in activity between 1935 and 1940. Ownership was changed on several dogs. In 1935, no Bassets were entered at Westminster or Chicago, which was not yet known as International. Carl Nottke showed Smith's Red Powder, Maple Drive Perk, and Nottke's Capaneus who was sold to B. F. Chaney that year. Irish Hill's Candidate and Senator, plus Jigilo's Blondy were exhibited by W. Fritz. Thompson's entries were Stanco Koto, Weedy, Dagget, and Chuck. Maple Drive Scorch Smith was shown by T. E. Seavey, and Ann Levy brought out Irish Hills Troubadour. Al's Accurate, Woelk's Beauty and Judy, Al's Famous, Ancient, and

26

Chief of the North, plus Rentschler's Colonel were some of the notable dogs shown by Alfred Kannowski. Emil and Effie Seitz appeared with Hillcrest Poyntair. Carmon Klink showed Maple Drive Rhythm, Dare Devil Babe, Raven Duke, and Ring Leader. Roy Smith began exhibiting Michigan Maestro. O. A. Grigsby had Nottke's Venus. This was the year that Stanco Liz was whelped.

Fanciers had begun to take a keener interest in serious breeding. 1936 saw the formation of the Basset Hound Club of America. The group of organizers was comprised of the Alfred Bissells, B. F. Chaney, Harold Frazee, William Fritz, George Gregg, Carmon Klink, Alfred Kannowski, W. P. Klapp, Jr., James Lee, Ann Levy, Gerald Livingston, Carl Nottke, Emil Seitz, and Lewis Thompson. Appearances at shows were still infrequent. None at all were entered at Westminster in 1936.

In 1937, Kilsyth Frills took Westminster's Best of Breed over seven kennelmates. At Boston, A. R. MacDonald exhibited Smith's Armac Auldscout. Maple Drive Maxim, now owned by F. J. Brookhiser, took a Group placing. Smith's Buena and Woelk's Mike were exhibited by J. Chenoweth in Michigan, and G. B. Woods appeared in St. Louis, Missouri with Michigan Don.

The Basset Hound Club of America held the first trial in the United States at Hastings, Michigan, in 1937. Entered were: Hillcrest Charley Boy, Hillcrest Peggy, Woelk's Lady Peterson, Taylor's White Collar, and the Michigan Maestro. Emil and Effie Seitz had adopted the Hillcrest prefix which was later changed to Hartshead. Theirs was an important contribution to the American bloodline. Hillcrest Peggy became the first Field Champion.

Best of Breed at Westminster went to B. Lippincott's Raffer A170434 in 1938. The only other entry was his Fallowfield Thunderer. Detroit had a large entry and five points went to Agawa Judy owned by H. W. Langrill. The Harold Fogelsons came forth with Venus Black Mischief and Peg O' My Heart. They were to become famous under the kennel name of Greenly Hall. Kannowski entered Al's Empress, Bess, and Chief Topic. Nottke showed his Red Gracious and Al's Ancient. Grigsby exhibited Northwood's Babe and Nottke's Venus. Two new exhibitors appeared: H. D. Abbot, showing Smith's Red Actor at Cincinnati, Ohio, and T. C. Brown, with Boots at Chattanooga, Tenn. J. E. Lee took an interest in showing Wanadoga Wallingford in the Michigan area as did the Seitz's with

Ch. Mon. Philippe of Greenly Hall, result of one of the early breedings by the Fogelsons, of Maple Drive Marlin and Coquette of Greenly Hall.

Hartshead Debutante, Hartshead Blackboy, Hartshead Melodie, Hartshead Duchess, and Hartshead Beauty.

their new entries Hillcrest Fryball and Belle of Hillcrest. In the East, Livingston exhibited Kilsyth Frills and Freckles, while the Thompsons entered Stanco Flit, Chuck, Toby, Cocoa, and Molly of Lincroft. Fred Bayliss brought the famous Chausseur and Edwina. Edwina and her sister, Stanco Liz, were daughters of Walhampton Nicety ex Reddy II (Reddy I ex Kilsyth Brevity). Chausseur was a son of Maple Drive Maxim ex Topsy. Edwina and Chausseur produced Bijou Pearl, Rhinestone, and Moonstone of Banbury, and Kiernan's Mitz. Pearl was the dam of Pepper Comstock. Bred to Sears Saratoga, Stanco Liz produced Roxey, Bell, and Pearl Cumberland for her owner Charles Sears. Maygold Bebe and Bijou Amethyst of Banbury were her offspring by Kilsyth Banker. All of these dogs are pillars of the breed as you will see by referring to the production chart of Walhampton Nicety.

A field trial was held at Kimberton, Penna., in 1938. Note that the following were the same entries that were being shown: Stanco Chuck, Koto, and Dagget, Hillcrest Peggy, Chausseur, Maple Drive Trude, and Queen Ruby. Dr. J. P. Honey, of Danville, Ill., ran his dogs at the Michigan trial and began to take a keen interest in both the show and the field under the Honey prefix.

Production Chart of Walhampton Nicety

The following is a partial list of the offspring of Walhampton Nicety (Walhampton Grazier ex Walhampton Nicknack) when bred to the studs Eng. Ch. Amir of Reynalton (Amant ex Dignity of Lohair) and Ch. Reddy II (Reddy I ex Kilsyth Brevity).

Offspring of Nicety & Amir	Grandchildren
Music of Woodleigh	Fallowfield Reaper (ex Walhampton Abbott)
	Fallowfield Contralto (ex Walhampton Abbott)
	Fallowfield Thunderer (ex Walhampton Abbott)
	Stockford Lady (ex Walhampton Abbott)

Al's Chief of Geneseo

Honey Girl of Geneseo (ex Wally)
Bard of Geneseo
Al's Janet (ex Woelk's Beauty)
Hess's Bold Buccaneer
Al's Gretchen (ex Woelk's Beauty)
Hess's Dignity of Devonshire (ex
Walhampton of Kilsyth)
Al's Chief Topic (ex Snitzel)

Offspring of Nicety & Reddy II	*Grandchildren*

Edwina

Bijou Pearl of Banbury (ex Chasseur)
Bijou Rhinestone of Banbury (ex Chasseur)
Bijou Moonstone of Banbury (ex Chasseur)
Kiernan's Mitz (ex Chasseur)
Bijou Sapphire of Banbury (ex Chasseur)

Stanco Liz

Roxey Cumberland (ex Sears Saratoga)
Bell Cumberland (ex Sears Saratoga)
Pearl Cumberland (ex Sears Saratoga)
Maygold Bebe (ex Kilsyth Banker)
Bijou Amethyst of Banbury (ex Kilsyth Banker)

Nicety's Grandchildren and Some of Their Get

Fallowfield Reaper

Hartshead Pepper, Hartshead Masked Knight, Hartshead Duchess, Hartshead Huntsman, Hartshead Firegirl

Fallowfield Contralto	Ben's Black King
Fallowfield Thunderer	Pearl, Malone
Honey Girl of Geneseo	Red Musette of Belbay, Neleigh's Ada, Eingle's Red Tim, Lady Belle, Freckles of Belbay, Belbay Saddler
Roxey Cumberland	Arbter's Rose, Dapple Queen, The Bricker's Belle
Bijou Sapphire of Banbury	Bijou Rutile of Banbury
Bijou Rhinestone of Banbury	Basso of Banbury
Hess's Dignity of Devonshire	Reisers's Tusc-o-Sport
Pearl Cumberland	Bricker's Betty, Rex Cumberland
Al's Chief Topic	Al's Bonnie Girl
Kiernan's Mitz	Melancholy Baby, Simone of Greenly Hall, Duchess of Greenly Hall

New names appearing this year were: J. R. Bream, F. J. Brookhiser's Esseff Drivette, G. R. Davis with Smith's Princess Royal and Big Wager, all in the New York area. In South Carolina, J. W.

Beckman and M. C. Crowder showed Peco Black Ranger and Smith's Pennellas. T. W. Landskroener exhibited Pensfield Bess in New Jersey. An important name to appear was Friar of Woodleigh owned by F. B. Carter of Devon, Mass. H. W. Langro's Agawa Judy gained her championship in 1938.

There were 134 stud book registrations in 1939. By 1940, these registrations were up to 241. Irish Hills Senator, owned by James E. Lee of Battle Creek, Mich., gained his field title. He was the second Field Champion; the first male. Sixty hounds were run at this trial in Pottersville, New Jersey. Besides Senator, entries were: Mrs. A. W. Porter's Stockford Duke, James S. Jones's Westerby Dreadnought, L. Thompson's Stanco Boy, Dagget, Chuck, and Koto, Consuelo Ford's Bijou Pearl of Banbury, Bijou Opal of Banbury, Livingston's Kilsyth Baronet and Bright, Fred Bayliss's Lasha, and Al Michel's Queen. Queen took first in the all-age bitch class, and Al was an enthusiastic breeder for the next twenty years. A stake was introduced for packs comprised of three couples. Consuelo Ford offered the Banbury Cross Challenge Cup won by the Brandywine Bassets of Mary Mather's kennel. At Hastings, Mich., Dr. J. P. Honey's Maple Drive Marlin defeated his Honey's Andy, Seitz's Ch. Hillcrest Charley Boy, Roy Smith's Michigan Maestro, and Nottke's Ajax in a combined-sex all-age class.

Stud book registrations were 214 in 1941. The breed had only one representative at Westminster, Mrs. E. W. Mile's Belle Chanson of Neverland. Bassets appeared for the first time at the Chicago International show. Carl Nottke's Harvey Prince was Best of Breed over the Fogelson's Sir Guy and Promise of Greenly Hall, and J. E. Lee's Ojibwa of Wanadoga and Nottke's Venus. The Fogelson's campaigned under their Greenly Hall prefix, showing Glamour Girl, Count, Promise, Baron, Serenade, and Sir Guy. C. V. Bickelman purchased Count and entered him at Bucks County, Penna., together with his Bick's Luck, Parnee's Jasper, and Bassette's Royal Wager. Talla's Black Duke of Valhalla was shown at Ravenna, Ohio. M. A. Vance bought Bugle Ann of Greenly Hall which was exhibited at Dayton, Ohio. Sir Rusty Boy, owned by R. H. Beckman, was at Syracuse, N.Y.; C. J Carr's Red Bear was at eastern Ohio shows; and H. R. Morrison showed Prancer of Gogo in western Pennsylvania. Alf Kannowski's Al's Chief Topic and Fogelson's Glamour Girl of Greenly Hall were the only entries at Detroit. In the Delaware area, Porters showed their Upland Master, Fancy, and Fresh. Another important dog was whelped this year, Samuel Smith's Roxey of Cumberland.

This is the year that Lester Kelly, of Alexandria, Penna., introduced his Bassets to the ring. Among them were Kelly's Chief Hareman, Kelly's Kanjur, Kelly's Model Huntress, and Smith's Pantasota. Kelly later adopted the Neleigh and Belbay prefixes which gained fame. Kelly's Chief Hareman had gained his championship by Fall. Promise of Greenly Hall was also finished about the same time.

The war severely curtailed extensive travel in 1942. Only Upland Fresh, Master, Topsy, Beauty, Tattler, and Fancy from the Porters' kennels were shown at Westminster in a combined-sex class. Fresh was Best of Breed for five points. Ch. Promise of Greenly Hall, Ch. Duchess of Greenly Hall, plus W. A. Davis's Davis King and Queen were at International. The Banbury Bassets of Consuelo Ford were entered at Westchester and E. Newcomb showed Schlegel's Conesus at Rochester, N.Y. There were 202 stud book registrations.

The following year, 1943, the Fogelsons joined the Upland entries at Westminster. Ch. Promise of Greenly Hall was Best of Breed. Their Duchess was also entered against Porter's Upland Spot, Sue, Spook, Laff, Lucky, Fred, and Mike who was Best of Winners. Duchess appeared later that year at Plainfield, N.J., shown by her new owners, Mr. & Mrs. M. Lynwood Walton who became well-known through the years for their Lyn-Mar Acres line. The Upland dogs were victorious over Duchess at Bryn Mawr and Devon, Penna. She was shown to her championship in Wisconsin, Indiana, and Illinois. Ch. Promise of Greenly Hall took the high honors at Westminster again in 1944.

In 1946, Ch. Duchess of Greenly Hall was Best of Breed at this show. The Waltons had adopted the Lyn-Mar prefix and showed Joliecoeur, Future, and Maitri of Lyn-Mar. The Belbay kennel of Lester Kelly was represented by Envy, Ginger, Bubbles Debut, and Model Huntress who took the points.

More serious breeders joined the ranks as interest in the breed continued to grow. One of these fanciers was Mark Washbond who purchased Jacqueson of St. Hubert from the Fogelsons in 1946. He later purchased Rossita of Greenly Hall. From Ch. Duke of Greenly Hall and Rossita he produced Ch. Anthony of St. Hubert. Tony was brought out in May of 1949. By September he had gained his

Ch. Anthony of St. Hubert, first Basset to go Best in Show; owner-breeder, Mark Washbond.

```
                                                                    Smith's Red Pathfinder
                                            Ch. Kelly's Chief Hareman
                          Ch. Butz's Yankee Boy                     Smith's Pantasota

                                            Kelly's Jet Girl        Smith's Major Le Havre

        Ch. Belbay Design                                           Woelk's Pebble

                                                                    Maple Drive Trimmer
                                            Duke of Blackhawk
                          Pattern of Belbay                         Ch. Lady Cinderella
Ch. Belbay Xtra Handsome                                            Ch. Kelly's Chief Hareman
Ch. Belbay Chevalier                        Neleigh's Pennsylvania Lady
Ch. Mr. Cyclops of Belbay                                           Neleigh's Ada
Belbay Cloud
                                                                    Smith's Red Pathfinder
                                            Ch. Kelly's Chief Hareman
                          Ch.. Butz's Yankee Boy                    Smith's Pantasota

                                            Kelly's Jet Girl        Smith's Major Le Havre

        Ch. Belbay Treasure                                         Woelk's Pebble

                                                                    Smith's Red Pathfinder
                                            Ch. Kelly's Chief Hareman
                          Neleigh's Pennsylvania Lady               Smith's Pantasota

                                            Neleigh's Ada           Bard of Geneseo

                                                                    Honey Girl of Geneseo
```

```
Ch. Belbay Design and Ch. Belbay Winning Look were brother and sister

Ch. Belbay Treasure and Ch. Belbay Triumph were brother and sister
```

Pedigree of Belbay Xtra Handsome, Ch. Belbay Chevalier, Ch. Mr. Cyclops of Belbay, and Belbay Cloud.

championship with a Group I already on his record. It must be remembered that judges were still hesitant about their evaluation of the Basset because entries were still small and scattered. Something about this dog, however, caught their fancy, and they carried him to fame. He was seldom defeated as a Special and gained many Group Firsts. In 1952 he brought glory to the breed by capturing the first Basset Best in Show in the country at the Egyptian Kennel Club show. Mark attained his goal of producing approximately one litter a year and finishing one of each sex from each litter. He later dropped from competition, as did many other serious fanciers, when too many unconscientious breeders began commercializing at the expense of better breedings.

Samuel J. Smith of New Cumberland, Penna., became an active breeder in this period. He owned Roxey and Pearl Cumberland out of Stanco Liz ex Sears Saratoga, Peg Cumberland (Ch. Westerby Vintage ex Bijou Pearl of Banbury), Pepper Comstock, out of the same breeding, Sailor Comstock and his son, Prince Comstock, out of Bell Cumberland, a sister to Roxey and Pearl. Pepper was the dam of Duke of Greenhill. In the early days Sam Smith showed his dogs as well as ran them in the trials. The Cumberland type was very much like the Basset of the 1960s, playing an important part in American bloodlines.

In 1946, Norwood Engle purchased Dapple Queen from Smith. She was a red-and-white out of Roxey and Peg Cumberland. Queen was bred to Darwin's General, a son of Hartshead Pepper and Ch. Byrl of Lyn-Mar Acres. The litter consisted of five females and one male. The male died at the age of eight months. Engle's Peg, Lady, and Mitz were sold, Patsy and Belle were kept. He then purchased Belbay Xtra Handsome (Ch. Belbay Design ex Ch. Belbay Treasure), and with the help of Frank and Dorothy Hardy, showed him to his championship. Then Engle, and a friend, Dr. Hughes, repurchased Engle's Peg and bred her to Handsome. In 1952, this mating produced two males and two females which bore the prefix of En-Hu derived from the first two letters of both owners' names. One male, Reddy of En-Hu, was sold to Ruth Turner in California; the other, Sport of En-Hu, went to Mr. Hatton in Kansas. Both gained their championships. Reddy died in 1961. Jill of En-Hu was sold to Dr. Mahon of New Cumberland, Penna. Although her quality was as high as the others, her new owner showed her only once, preferring

Rose M, littermate of Trailer M, whelped 1946; breeder, Al Michel.

Queen Cumberland and a litter of puppies.

Roxey and Pearl Cumberland when they were puppies.

Ch. Belbay Xtra Handsome.

to keep her as a pet. In 1954, Chris Teeter bought Fanny of En-Hu, the first bitch in his kennel. Fanny gained her championship and fame as the dam of a long line of champions. Thinking Peg and Handsome could be bred again, all of the puppies had been sold. However, Peg died during her next whelping and all the puppies were lost. Her name will live on through the bloodlines of her famous offspring. Her sister, Patsy, was bred to Handsome and produced Ch. Engle's Primrose Patsy. Dr. Mahon was persuaded to breed Jill of En-Hu to Engle's Black Jack. The two female puppies, named Engle's Jenny of Nor-Mil and Engle's Jill of Nor-Mil, were sold to Chris Teeter. One of the males, En-Hu's Tick On, went to the western part of the country. Others in the Engle kennel were Rose M, litter mate to Al Michel's Trailer M, and Engle's Miss Mitzie, dam of Ch. Tulpehocken Trailer and granddam of Field Chs. Tulpehocken Til and Hepsy. There are twenty-seven field champions bearing the name of Engle breedings up to this time.

During the year 1946, three exhibitors appeared with the first entries at California shows. J. W. Robinson exhibited Robinson's Red Bird, Robinson's Gold Nugget, Black Knight, and the English imports Maytime, Moonlight and Maytime the Pudding. He had the only entries at Santa Cruz, Vallejo, and San Rafael. At Harbor Cities he had a competitor in the puppy class where A. Morris showed Belbay Quintina. Grace Greenburg of Camarillo, adopting the Belleau prefix, entered Belleau Adjutant, Belleau Jet, Kelly's Patches, Parker's Hi Watha, Neleigh's Skippy, sister to Neleigh's Pennsylvania Lady, and Belleau's Apagliacci. She had the only entries at Ventura.

During this year, Al Michel was showing Ben's Black King. Kelly showed Butz's Yankee Boy, Belbay Model Huntress, Kanjur, Envy, Ginger, Quaint, and Qualitee of Belbay. Fogelson's representative was Coquette of Greenly Hall. The Fowlers showed Buckeye Bill's Tomboy Tootsie and Victory Queen, Fowler's Franco, and Glenmaire's Red Bear Tongue. Waltons entered Maitri of Lyn-Mar (dam of Ch. Lyn-Mar's Clown), Furor, Lew Lee, and Queen-O-Trump. A dog named Luke, owned by the Barabon kennels, appeared in Seattle, Wash. Topsy of Westerfield and Thompson's Trailer were shown by the Thompsons while R. Bossard exhibited Thompson's Helper. Championships were gained by H. R. Morrison's Braggelonne of Belbay, Fowler's Buckeye Bill's Victory Queen, Fowler's Franco, and

Buckeye Bill's Tomboy Tootsie, Kelly's Butz's Yankee Boy, Envy of Belbay, and Kelly's Kanjur.

In 1947, Ch. Braggelonne of Belbay was Best of Breed at Westminster. Best of Opposite Sex went to Ch. Envy of Belbay. Hartshead Pepper took the points in a combined class of dogs and bitches including Soubrette of Lyn-Mar, Belbay Treasure, Hartshead Ginger, Belbay Triumph, Talmai, Model Huntress, Buckeye Bill's Victory Toddles, Thompson's Ginger and Trailer, Chanson of Lyn-Mar, and Al's Chief Topic.

During this year the Lyn-Mar kennels covered the shows in the vicinity of New Jersey and eastern Pennsylvania. Ira Shoop showed in Pennsylvania, as did Kelly with the Belbay breedings and E. W. Graham bearing the Stregraham prefix. One of this line was sent to J. Barringer in the Chicago area. At Louisville, Ky., C. S. Furio appeared with Shaw's Corky. In Michigan, R. F. Smith's Major and Queen Elizabeth competed with Melancholy Baby, all owned by Roy Smith. R. L. Wilson entered Davis King, Trim's Joy, Ruppert's Royal Ace, Forester of Belbay, and Belbay Casandra at Bremerton, Washington.

In California, J. W. Robinson and Grace Greenburg were joined by M. Carney who had purchased Belleau's Apagliacci, and Cordelia Skapinski (Jensen) with Gun Major of Belleau.

During this year, Maitri of Lyn-Mar, Belbay Triumph, Furor of Lyn-Mar, Hartshead Pepper, Stregraham's Patricia, and Robinson's Red Bird gained their championships.

This was also the year that Johnny Bose's name began to appear. Johnny's primary interest was in the field. Often missed is the fact that his Bose's Princess Patty was bred to Al Michel's Ben's Black King, producing Webb's Black Amanda, dam of Chs. Siefenjagenheim Lazy Bones, Dominoe, Calico, and Gremlin, all bearing the same prefix. Amanda's sister, Antoinette, was bred to the son of their brother, Adam. A female of this litter, Braun's Hootn' Annie, was the dam of Ch. Braun's Humpty Dumpty CD and behind other champions in the Braun's kennel.

Jean Sanger Look became interested in the breed at this time. She was the first to exhibit Bassets in North Carolina. Residing in Greensboro, Mrs. Look became an ardent fancier producing a long line of champions as well as attending the trials. Her name gave her an ideal prefix. Hers is an interesting breeding pattern to study. Four matings of Ch. Andre of Greenly Hall and Ch. Belbay Winning Look, sister of Belbay Design, produced Ch. Look's Choice, Pensive, Agreeable, Winning Streak, Handsome, Nice, and Bashful. All but Look's Bashful gained their championships.

Ch. Look's Choice sired Champions Millvan's Design, Millvan's Blondie, Millvan's Blissful, Millvan's Cherub, Jeffery of Forest Bay, Antique's Little Nutmeg, Byron of Brookville, Monsieur Beaucoup, and Best in Show-winning Long View Acres Blaze By.

Ch. Look's Handsome produced Ch. Rockingham Cooper King when bred to Rockingham Red out of Ch. Belbay Winning Look ex Ch. Belbay Triumph. He also sired Ch. Anastasia Hubertus, Ch. Miss Murgatroid of Elvalin, and Eulenspiegel's Deb Crescent.

Ch. Look's Pensive's offspring were Ch. Reluctant Rachel of Elvalin and Ch. Kathenette of Elvalin. Look's Bashful was bred to Ch. Millvan's Casper and produced Ch. Look's Good of Pioneer. Her offspring by Ch. Belbay Triumph were Chs. Look's Special, Smooth, and Fancy. She was also the dam of Ch. Hartshead Micky when bred to Ch. Hartshead Top Hit. Triumph and Belbay Winning Look produced Ch. Edelham's Queen Bess, Rockingham Red, and Rockingham Echoe.

Ch. Belbay Design and Ch. Belbay Winning Look were both out of Ch. Butz's Yankee Boy ex Pattern of Belbay. Yankee Boy was bred to Neleigh's Pennsylvania Lady when he sired Ch. Belbay Treasure and Ch. Belbay Triumph, purchased at the age of three by Jean Look. Triumph succumbed to cancer of the liver in 1957, at the age of ten years. This red-and-white dog had been one of the first Bassets handled by Dorothy Hardy. Winning Look died the following year of kidney failure.

Most of the aforementioned dogs were shown in the 1950s. Dr. and Mrs. Vincent Nardiello owned Choice who gained approximately 100 Best of Breed awards. The Nardiellos adopted the Millvan kennel name and had such notables as the Best in Show-winning Ch. Millvan's Deacon. The Elvalin prefix was used by Elva and Franklin Heckler. Mrs. Heckler carried on after the death of her husband in 1956. The Hubertus name, of course, belongs to the kennel of Frank and Dorothy Hardy who have contributed so much to the breed.

Late in 1947, Mrs. Walter P. Houchin took a serious interest in the breed. She obtained Belleau Jet of Little Gate from Mrs.

Ch. Look's Choice.

Ch. Look's Winning Streak.

Ch. Look's Handsome.

Look's Bashful.

Hartshead Red Dust (Hartshead Masked Knight ex Hartshead Firegirl). She and her brother, Hartshead Shadow, were used in breedings to combine the Hartshead and Look bloodlines.

Ch. Look's Pensive of Elvalin taking Best of Opposite Sex at Westminster in 1957. Her brother, Ch. Look's Choice, was Best of Breed.

Ch. Belbay Triumph.

Ch. Anastasia Hubertus and Dorothy Hardy.

Walter Monroe, who had brought her from the Belleau kennels of Mrs. Greenburg. All three ladies were active in Dachshunds. Mrs. Monroe's kennel prefix was Little Gate. Jet had been whelped in 1946, sired by Hess's Drum Major by Belleau Jet. The Houchins adopted the kennel name Jet Foret when they moved to New Lennox, Ill., in 1944, describing the large trees (black forest) surrounding their home. Millie's interest in the breed continued to rise. She was secretary-treasurer of the Basset Hound Club of America from 1954 to 1957 and became a breeder-judge.

Walter and Marjorie Brandt became interested in the breed in 1947. They purchased French Belle in Woonsocket, R.I., and hunted her for the following thirteen years. Soon after acquiring Belle, their affection for the breed prompted them to obtain Lulu's Patches and Lulu's Red from Matthew Moore of Windber, Penna. These litter brothers were out of Ridenhour's Sport ex Lulu Saddler. The Brandts were the pioneers of Bassets in Obedience. Though the instructor at the training club was not very encouraging, the dogs did respond to the work. Red was the first Basset to receive a Companion Dog degree, soon followed by Patches, which was the second. Meantime, the Bench Show beckened. Patches went on to a CDX and a championship, the first Basset in the country to hold all three titles. Lulu's Red was struck by a car while driving a rabbit across a road. The Brandts became serious breeders, gaining championships, obedience titles, and hunting. Walter was another to become a breeder-judge. His death in 1963 was mourned by fanciers throughout the country. To mention a few of the famous Abbot Run Valley Dogs, there were Alexander the Great, Abbot Run Valley Asa, Andre, Suzzette, Gem, and Rocket, and Driquire of Blue Hill. In 1957 Roger Fredette bought part ownership in Abbot Run Valley Rudy. From combinations of the Brandt-Fredette dogs came Ch. Ro-Fre-le-Reine de la Belle, Ch. Abbot Run Valley Prankster, and Ch. Abbot Run Valley Brassy (sire; Lyn-Mar Acres Top Brass).

The Westminster entry in 1948 included Darwin's Leander and Katrinka, Lyn-Mar's Glamour, Lyn-Mar's Charm, Lyn-Mar's Joliecoeur, Belbay Aaron and Treasure, Kilsyth Longfellow and Lucky, and Ira Shoop's Ch. Hartshead Pepper which took Best of Breed. Belbay Treasure gained her championship that year. Only eight males and females were entered in a combined stake at the trial in Jackson, Michigan, with Snowfall Shorty, Queen Elizabeth, and Melancholy Baby placing in that order.

In 1949, there were seven dogs and two bitches under Walter Reeves at Westminster. Ch. Hartshead Pepper repeated his win of the year before. Ch. Belbay Treasure was Best of Opposite Sex. Best of Winners went to Belbay Design, and Derbydach's Belle de Beaupre took the points in bitches. At the Brighton, Mich., trial, Snowfall Shorty, Trigger Triumph, Lucky Boy, Hartshead Bold Venture, and R. F. Smith's Major were run in all-age dogs, placing in the order mentioned. All-age bitches were Queen Elizabeth, Snowfall Sadie, Hartshead Melanie, Hartshead Peggy Again, and Meyer's Black Queen. The Dog Stakes at Dubois, Penna., in October were: Shebe's Mingo, Trigger Triumph, Lucky Boy, Graham's Ring, and Hartshead Bold Venture. Bitches were: Graham's Jill, Melancholy Baby, Shebe's Lady, Hartshead Melanie, and Hartshead Jet.

This brings us to the close of the first half of the 1900s when most fanciers participated in both show and field endeavors. Interest had steadily grown. New names appeared each year. One must keep in mind that this information was compiled from records of activities. It must be presumed that there were others attracted to the breed who did not enter into competition. One does have perceivable data, however, on the progress of the principal dogs and breeders who were the foundation of the American bloodlines.

5

The Basset Hound
in America after 1950

POPULARITY of the Basset began to grow by leaps and bounds. By the latter part of the decade, he was doomed to become a celebrity. I say, "doomed," because once a breed becomes so attractive that there is a great demand for it, there are those who breed for quantity, to supply this demand, with little thought for quality. Further degeneration is brought about by those who breed-up certain "winning traits" to the point of overexaggeration, caring nothing for utility. Others, desiring to have "the fastest dog at the trial," breed for lighter bone and more height, ignoring the fact that the dog was intended to be a *slow trailer*. Fortunately for the breed, there remain the sincere enthusiasts who concentrate their efforts to produce *good* Bassets that are both beautiful and useful.

In the Northwest, perhaps Richard and Evelyn Bassett are the best known of the pioneers. In 1950, they purchased Ch. Jones's Virginia Jim and Jones's Virginia Jean. Both of these dogs were bred by Franklin W. Jones of Fairfax, Va., from his Upland stock. Jim was entered in Obedience, eventually at a trial, and in conformation.

He gained his CD, the third Basset in the country to do so, but had no competition in conformation at his first nine shows. He was bred to Bonny's Cissy Sue (Hartshead and Greenly Hall bloodlines) and produced the grand old dog, Ch. Mattie's Quercus CD, the first Basset on the West Coast to capture a Hound Group. He later became the third in the country to go Best in Show. Quercus sired thirteen champions and was grandsire to many more. Jean was bred to Sir Hubert II, a double grandson of Ch. Hartshead Pepper, producing Ch. Bassett's Jody and Josephine. Among Jody's offspring were Ch. Bassett's Miss Wrinkles, dam of eight champions, and Ch. Bassett's Eloise, who was sold to Jean Dudley. Josephine was the dam of Ch. Bassett's Roustabout, who, upon retirement in 1961, had won seven Best in Show awards, and thirty-four Hound Group Firsts. By this time, Rousty had sired eight champions. In 1955, the Bassetts imported Rossingham Barrister who gained his championship in 1957 and was the sire of twenty champions.

Another dedicated enthusiast joined the breed in 1950, though he had been in "dogs" with his father, Ed, since 1924. John Eylander acquired Danny Boy from the Pine Gables kennels of Gerald and Leona Harding. He bought and finished Ch. Etalle of St. Hubert, owned Am. & Can. Ch. Hoosier Linda's Bonnie and Ch. Siefenjagenheim Calamity. Among his Field Champions were Bose's Initiative, Shellbark's Michie, Ed's Jo Jo, Olson's Mitzie, Little Lady Tammy, and Max's Happy Hunter. Ch. Eylander's Red Rose was sold to Milton Stringer of Algonac, Mich. "Rosie" was the dam of Am. & Can. Ch. Whistle Down's Commando and other fine dogs. Though, in time, both Ed and John devoted most of their efforts to field work, John continued to breed for the points desirable in the show ring believing that the show and field dog should be of one and the same quality. The present Standard was approved during his term as President of the Basset Hound Club of America and the groundwork was laid for Field Trial rules for Bassets.

The Lyn-Mar name had risen to great heights by now. Ch. Lyn-Mar's Clown (Kilsyth Lucky ex Ch. Maitri of Lyn-Mar) was Best of Breed at Westminster, in 1950–1953.

In 1950 and 1951, the trials were followed by the entries of the Hartshead kennel, Greenly Hall, Roy Smith, Claude Smith, Johnny Bose, Al Michel, Norwood Engle, Meyers, Snowfall kennel, and the Tulpehocken kennel.

Ch. Bassett's Josephine, Ch. Mattie's Quercus C.D., and Ch. Bassett's Jody.

Am. and Can. Ch. Bassett's Roustabout with owner-handler, Richard Bassett, under judge, Percy Roberts.

Am., Can., and Ber. Ch. Ike of Blue Hill, with breeder, Doris Hurry; owned by Barbara Hurry.

Am. and Can. Ch. Boozer of Blue Hill holds an American and Canadian Companion Dog degree; shown with breeder-trainer, Louise Eldridge.

Ch. Boozer of Blue Hill (Ch. Abbott Run Valley Rockett ex Carousel of Blue Hill), Ch. Guzzler of Blue Hill ("Boozer" ex Ellen of Blue Hill), and Ch. Aberjona of Great Oak (Ch. Ike of Blue Hill ex Glamour of Blue Hill).

By 1952, a Dachshund breeder, Doris Hurry, was so impressed with Ch. Lyn-Mar's Clown that she purchased one of his daughters, Lyn-Mar Intrigue, who gained her championship by the time she was a year old. Mrs. Hurry adopted the Blue Hill prefix. She is well-known for her home-bred champions, Miss Randolph, Fire Cracker, Carosel (who produced four champions in one litter), Daiquiri, Senator, Buccaneer, Ivy, Guzzler, and Intoxication, all bearing the Blue Hill name. American & Canadian championships were gained by Boozer of Blue Hill CD, and Cherry Blossom of Blue Hill, while the Canadian titles went to Imperial and Ivan who had five Best in Shows in Canada. Am. & Can. Ch. Boozer of Blue Hill was purchased as a young dog by the Kenneth Eldriges of Reading, Mass. Ken took an interest in conformation while Louise preferred Obedience work. Boozer was the first Basset to gain an Obedience title in both the United States and Canada as well as a championship. His son, Ch. Guzzler of Blue Hill sired Ch. Aberjona of Great Oak, the kennel name adopted by the Eldridges. Perhaps the most notable was Doris's Ch. Ike of Blue Hill. He was the first male Basset to gain a Bermuda championship; the first to carry a Bermuda, Canadian, & American title. Ike captured a Best in Show before he was a year old at the Basset Hound Club of Canada's First Specialty in 1961. Bred and handled by Doris, owned by her daughter, Barbara, Ike was the product of a mating of Ch. The Ring's Ali Baba ex Am. & Can. Ch. Cherry Blossom of Blue Hill.

In California, Ruth Turner had become interested in Bassets and purchased Reddy of En-Hu from Norwood Engle. Paul Nelson had also joined the Mac Carlisles, Bill Morris, and Cordelia Skapinski in that area.

The Brandts, Doris Hurry, and the Frank Hardys were joined in the East by the Joseph Kulpers, Isabel Holden, Janet Yontz, Gladys Clement, Jeanne Millett, Dr. Pierre Morand, and Mrs. L. P. Gillespie.

Ruth and Helen Fox, Harry Gill, Lester Webb, and the John Siefens became Midwest breeders in this period.

Webb's Black Amanda was purchased by the Siefens. She was out of the Johnny Bose litter of Ben's Black King ex Bose's Princess Patty. Siefen bred Amanda to Ch. Lyn-Mar's Clown (Kilsyth Lucky ex Ch. Maitri of Lyn-Mar). From this mating came such dogs as

Calico, Calamity, Dominoe, Gremlin, Glory Be, and Lazy Bones, all carrying the Siefenjagenheim prefix.

Queenie Wickstrom purchased Dominoe. He was bred to her Oakdale Sue (Lord Tietge ex Ferge's Gypsy Girl: breeders, Mr. & Mrs. Everett Ferge, Webster, N.Y.) and her daughter by Ch. Slow Poke Hubertus, Wickstrom's Cozette. From these matings, Queenie produced many fine Bassets, which in turn, threw quality. Dominoe was first shown in the East at the time the competition was high. His career began at the age of seven months, when he was shown in Puppy classes except at Westminster, where he finished at nine months of age. He had his first Best in Show at thirteen months of age. Ch. Siefenjagenheim Dominoe was used sparingly and only on very select bitches. His percentage of champion offspring was high, however. He was bred to bitches of dissimilar backgrounds, and he is considered one of *the* great sires.

In 1954, Chris Teeter, who was already a familiar figure at the shows, decided he wanted a pair of Bassets that could be top winners. With the help of Frank Hardy, he purchased Fanny of En-Hu, from Norwood Engle, and Slowpoke Hubertus. In the next nine years he finished fifty-one champions. Among the progeny of Pokey and Fanny, were: Chs. Long View Acres Frannie, Long View Acres Sweet Talk, Long View Acres Night and Day, Stringer's Napoleon the Beau, Long View Acres Smokey, and Long View Acres Venture On who was the eighteenth champion produced by Fanny. Only two of these eighteen were not sired by Pokey. Chris purchased Siefenjagenheim Lazy Bones from Siefen. He became the top winning dog in the country, siring fifty champions before his death in 1962. Among these was his daughter, Ch. The Ring's Banshee, bred by Bob and Mary Lees Noerr out of Ch. Lyn-Mar Acres Flirtatious (Ch. Lyn-Mar Acres Scalawag ex Duchess of Lyn-Mar). Banshee brought more fame to her owner's Long View Acres kennel by topping her sire's record. Another Lazy Bones son, Am. & Can. Ch. Rocky of Long View Acres took several Best in Show awards, sired Chs. Long View Acres Repeater and Belle Patty of Barlindall, and later gained Obedience titles for his new California owner.

Loren Free began to enter competition in 1954, though he had obtained the import, Walhampton Lively, in 1927 and soon thereafter added Abbott's Girlie and Starridge Partner. He campaigned Belbay General Sno-Sheen (Belbay Triumph ex Larghetto of Bel-

Ch. Sir Clarence of Queen Wicke, a fine example of father and daughter breeding (Ch. Siefenjagenheim Dominoe ex his daughter, Wickstrom's Dominelle).

Ch. Siefenjagenheim Dominoe.

                                                    Kilsyth Baronet

                              Kilsyth Lucky

                                                    Kilsyth Mitzie

        Ch. Lyn-Mar's Clown

                                                    Ch. Promise of Greenly Hall

                              Ch. Maitri of Lyn-Mar

                                                    Ch. Duchess of Greenly Hall

Ch. Siefenjagenheim Lazy Bones
Ch. Siefenjagenheim Dominoe
                                                    Kishacoquillas Trailer

                              Ben's Black King

                                                    Fallowfield Contralto

        Ch. Webb's Black Amanda

                                                    Duke of Greenhill

                              Bose's Princess Patty

                                                    Freckles of Belbay

Pedigree of Chs. Siefenjagenheim Dominoe and Lazy Bones.

                                                    Kilsyth Baronet

                              Kilsyth Lucky

                                                    Kilsyth Mitzie

        Lyn Mar's Actor

                                                    Ch. Promise of Greenly Hall

                              Ch. Maitri of Lyn-Mar

                                                    Ch. Duchess of Greenly Hall

Ch. His Lordship of Lyn-Mar Acres

                                                    Venus's Black Mischief

                              Ch. Duke of Greenly Hall

                                                    White's Jaconde

        Ch. Duchess of Greenly Hall

                                                    Chausseur

                              Kiernan's Mitz

                                                    Edwina

Pedigree of Ch. His Lordship of Lyn-Mar Acres.

Ch. Slowpoke Hubertus.

			Walhampton Lingerer
		Walhampton Abbot	
	Fallowfield Reaper		Walhampton Arabel
		Music of Woodleigh	Eng. Ch. Amir of Reynalton
Ch. Hartshead Pepper			Walhampton Nicety
		Duke of Rising Sun	Stanco Dagget
	Hillcrest Gigolette		Stanco Lady
		Maple Drive Murky	Walhampton Aaron
Ch. Slowpoke Hubertus			Peggy Leach
		Fallowfield Reaper	Walhampton Abbot
	Hartshead Huntsman		Music of Woodleigh
		Hartshead Firefly	Chausseur
Abigail of Woodleigh			Hillcrest Fyrball of Hartshead
		Ch. Duke of Greenly Hall	Venus's Black Mischief
	Glamour Girl		White's Jaconde
		Red Musette of Belbay	Ch. Kelly's Chief Hareman
			Honey Girl of Geneseo

Pedigree of Ch. Slowpoke Hubertus.

bay) to his championship. The field trials beckoned and Free began running his dogs. Among his field champions were: Eingle's Beckie, Queen Bee, Shellbark's Atomic Blue, Shellbark's Michie, Little Mac, and Kanode's Sally Nell. Beckie in turn produced more field champions, and by the '60s, Loren claimed every dog in his Shellbark kennel to be her descendant. The Eingle prefix was used by Clarence Eingle of Carey, Ohio, not to be confused with Norwood Engle of Pennsylvania,

We begin to see such names as the Buchers with the Warwick breedings, the Meadow Park prefix of the Wolfs, the King's Trojan Echoes line, the Julian Dexters with the Galway prefix, Bob and Mary Lees Noerr, Dorothy Shula, breeder, and Frank Inn, trainer of Cleo of television fame, the Robert Lindsays and their Lime Tree dogs, the Bob Ellenbergers, Ken Hirst, the Lester Cabbage's Southwind breedings, the Donald Batemans, Helen Boutell's Double B prefix, and many more, including your author's, within the next few years.

By 1957, Nancy Evans purchased Ferge's O'Conners Bugle from the Everett Ferges. The following had taken a Best in Show: Ch. Sport of En-Hu, Ch. Lenfield's Juliana, Ch. Lyn-Mar Acres Top Brass, Ch. Greenore's Joker, and Ch. Siefenjagenheim Lazy Bones.

Jean Look moved to East Randolph, N.Y., in 1958. Ch. Bassett's Roustabout went Best in Show, as did Ch. Millvan's Deacon, Ch. Rocky of Long View Acres, and Ch. Long View Acres Blaze By. By this time, Warwick Squire, Anastasia Hubertus, Double B's Ishmael, Hubertus Dark Josephine, and many others had gained their championships, including Chs. The Ring's Ali Baba, Arthur North, and Aleric out of the Noerrs's mating of Ch. Long View Acres Smokey ex Ch. Miss Linda Lovely of Elvalin.

It is impossible to include all worthy contributors and their dogs of this period. "Morgan" appeared on the Gary Moore television show, followed by "Cleo." The Basset was sold to the public. Improvement of travel and increasing numbers of shows brought more exhibitors into the ring. With the formation of regional clubs came an increase in field trials. Many fanciers found they could not devote enough time to both, so they followed whichever gave them the most pleasure. Among the organizers of the regional clubs are some of the most dedicated breeders who played such an important part

Ch. Belbay General Sno-Sheen.

Fd. Ch. Queen Bee with owner, Loren Free.

Ch. Long View Acres Smokey.

in the progress of the breed in this country. It is regrettable that space does not permit mention of all who offered so much.

It was not until 1964 that a Basset gained a dual championship. Dual Champion Kazoo's Moses the Great, owned by James and Patricia Dohr, earned his field title in 1963, a Canadian bench title the same year, and his American bench championship in 1964. "Moses" was bred by Ralph and Mary Jo Shields; whelped November 2, 1958, out of Ch. Casey of Kazoo ex Ch. Long View Acres Donna.

BEST OF BREED AT WESTMINSTER

Year	Dog	Owner
1884	Ch. Nemours	Lawrence Timson
1889	Babette	Charles Porter
	Chausseur	Cornelius Stevenson
(1917	Basset recognized and eligible for points)	
1924	Simillante	Erastus Tefft
1925	Musique	Erastus Tefft
1929	Brookmead Mixer	Mrs. G. Sloane
1930	None	
1931	Marvey's Sam	W. H. Attwood
1932	Marvey's Sam	W. H. Attwood
1933	Kilsyth Broker	Gerald Livingston
1934	None	
1935	None	
1936	None	
1937	Kilsyth Frills	Gerald Livingston
1938	Raffer	B. Lippincott
1939	Lady Cinderella	G. Gipolo & C. Straley
1940	None	
1941	Belle Chanson of Neverland	Mrs. E. W. Miles
1942	Upland Fresh	Charles Porter
1943	Ch. Promise of Greenly Hall	Mr. & Mrs. Harold Fogelson
1944	Ch. Promise of Greenly Hall	Mr. & Mrs. Harold Fogelson

Ch. Fanny of En-Hu.

Ch. Siefenjagenheim Lazy Bones.

Ch. The Ring's Banshee;
handler, Dorothy Hardy.

Ch. Lyn-Mar Acres Flirtatious with
handler, Alfred Murray; owned by
Robert and Mary Lees Noerr.

Am. and Can. Ch. Rocky of Long View Acres C.D.

1946	Ch. Duchess of Greenly Hall	M. L. Walton
1947	Ch. Braggelonne of Belbay	H. R. Morrison
1948	Hartshead Pepper	Ira Shoop
1949	Ch. Hartshead Pepper	Ira Shoop
1950	Ch. Lyn-Mar's Clown	Mr. & Mrs. M. L. Walton
1951	Ch. Lyn-Mar's Clown	Mr. & Mrs. M. L. Walton
1952	Ch. Lyn-Mar's Clown	Mr. & Mrs. M. L. Walton
1953	Ch. Lyn-Mar's Clown	Mr. & Mrs. M. L. Walton
1954	Ch. Greenore's Joker	Mrs. Michael Hanlon
1955	Ch. Lyn-Mar's Top Brass	Mr. & Mrs. M. L. Walton
1956	Ch. Siefenjagenheim Lazy Bones	Chris G. Teeter
1957	Ch. Look's Choice	Dr. & Mrs. Vincent Nardiello
1958	Ch. Siefenjagenheim Dominoe	Queenie Wickstrom
1959	Ch. Siefenjagenheim Lazy Bones	Chris G. Teeter
1960	Ch. The Ring's Banshee	Chris G. Teeter
1961	Ch. The Ring's Banshee	Chris G. Teeter
1962	Ch. Nancy Evans King Leo la Belle	Nancy Evans & James LaBelle
1963	Ch. The Ring's Ali Baba	Mrs. Frances G. Scaife
1964	Ch. Eleandon's Mr. Pinkerton	Mona Ball

INTERNATIONAL KENNEL CLUB— BEST OF BREED

Year	Dog	Owner
1941	Nottke's Harvey Prince	Carl Nottke
1942	Ch. Promise of Greenly Hall	Mrs. H. Fogelson
1948	Ch. Belbay Triumph	Belbay Kennels
1949	No entries	
1950	Ch. Belbay Design	Belbay Kennels
1951	Ch. Anthony of St. Hubert	Mark Washbond
1952	Ch. Anthony of St. Hubert	Mark Washbond

1953	Webb's Black Amanda	J. F. Miller
1954	Ch. Slow Poke Hubertus	Chris G. Teeter
1955	Ch. Siefenjagenheim Lazy Bones	Chris G. Teeter
1956	Ch. Siefenjagenheim Lazy Bones	Chris G. Teeter
1957	Ch. Siefenjagenheim Lazy Bones	Chris G. Teeter
1958	Ch. Siefenjagenheim Lazy Bones	Chris G. Teeter
1959	Ch. Bassett's Roustabout	Richard & Evelyn Bassett
1960	Ch. The Ring's Banshee	Chris G. Teeter
1961	Ch. The Ring's Banshee	Chris G. Teeter
1962	Ch. Peppy's Top Serenade of Shadbo	Ray & Beverly Knezevich
1963	Ch. The Ring's Banshee	Chris G. Teeter
1964	Ch. Eleandon's Mr. Pinkerton	Mona Ball

THE BASSET HOUND CLUB OF AMERICA SPECIALTY

Year	Dog	Owner
1960	Ch. The Ring's Brunhilde	M. L. & Robert Noerr
1961	Ch. Lyn-Mar Acres Top Brass	Lyn-Mar Kennels
1962	Ch. Lyn-Mar Acres Bally Hoo	Lyn-Mar Kennels
1963	Ch. Jesse James of Eleandon	Nicholas & Marcia Polizzi
1964	Ch. Hunting Horn Noah	Charles & Priscilla Gillespie

Ch. Huey of Cypress, son of Mon Philippe of Greenly Hall and sire of Ch. Gladstone of Mandeville.

Ch. Double B's Veronica; handler, Helen Boutell, and Ch. Eleandon's Mr. Pinkerton; handler, Frank Hardy; judge, Col. Julian S. Dexter. Mr. Pinkerton was Best of Breed at Westminster in 1964; Veronica was Best of Opposite Sex.

Ch. Jesse James of Eleandon, handled by Paul Saucier; John Eylander presenting trophy.

Ch. Tannenbaum's Funtastic, a top winner on the West Coast in 1963 and 1964; breeder-owner-handler, Lucille Barton; judge, Alva Rosenberg.

6

The Basset Hound
Club of America

A group of fanciers set about to form the Basset Hound Club of America in 1936 at a gathering in Detroit, Mich. The records show the following as charter members: Mr. & Mrs. Alfred Bissell, B. F. Chaney, Harold R. Frazee, William Fritz, George C. Gregg, Carmon Klink, Alfred E. Kannowski, W. P. Klapp, Jr., James E. Lee, Ann Levy, Gerald M. Livingston, Carl Nottke, Effie Seitz, and Lewis Thompson. The Constitution and By-Laws are dated July 18, 1938, executed by Cathryn A. Burton, James Fornary, and George R. Simanek in Racine, Wisc.

It was some time before the breed became popular enough to warrant the formation of smaller groups, called "regional" clubs, under the jurisdiction of the "parent" club. In 1947, Bill Morris, an enthusiastic Californian, undertook to organize breeders in that area, but it was not until 1951 that his efforts matured. In attendance at the first meeting of the Basset Hound Club of California were: Mr. & Mrs. Mac Carlisle, Mr. & Mrs. Gill, Mr. & Mrs. Robert Hicks, Mr & Mrs. Don Lowe, Mr. & Mrs. Bill Morris, Paul Nelson, the Walter Rowleys, and Mrs. Cordelia Skapinski (Jensen). After reorganizing in 1953–54, the club became known as the Basset

Ch. Gladstone of Mandeville.

Dual Ch. Kazoo's Moses the Great, the first to gain the title.

Hound Club of Southern California. It was then recognized by The American Kennel Club and the parent club. Another of the earlier groups was the Dal-Tex Basset Hound Club of the Dallas, Texas area.

During the next few years the popularity of the breed increased. As it did, several regional clubs were organized in various areas. In the East, New England fanciers, Walter Brandt, Frank Carter, Mrs. L. P. Gillespie, Wallace Balsewicz, Joseph Allen, Dr. Ruth Strong, Mrs. John Hurry, the Joseph Kulpers, Isabel Holden, Mrs. Gladys Clement, Frank and Dorothy Hardy, Jeanne Millett, Dr. Pierre Morand, and Janet Yonts formed the Pilgrim Basset Hound Club in March 1953.

Midwest fanciers A. Ruth Fox, Glenden Stephenson, Queenie Wickstrom, Robert Finnerty, Chris Teeter, Charlotte King, Milton Stringer, Helen Fox, Liguori Britain, Lauretta Daly, Eugene Dembicki, Marjorie Shimantowski, and Virginia Webb organized the Basset Hound Club of Greater Detroit.

In 1955, at the home of Norwood Engle of Hummelstown, Penna., the Susquehanna Basset Hound Club was started by Norman Bucher, Al Michel, Dorothy Bowers, and the Engles.

Within a few months Mrs. Margaret Walton called together several couples to establish the Rancocas Valley Basset Hound Club in their section of Pennsylvania. Among those present were the Samuel Hamlins, John Bodkins, Truman Smiths, George Brightenbacks, and the Wendall Crams.

The Northern California Basset Hound Club came into existence this same year. Their first Specialty show was in 1958. With jackrabbits for quarry, they held the first field trial for Basset Hounds west of Chicago in 1959.

1957 saw the formation of several clubs. Arthur Coutcher, Mr. & Mrs. R. J. Mahaffey, Norma Clark, Mr. & Mrs. McChesney, and the Mischlichs organized the Basset Hound Club of Colorado. The name was changed to Timberline Basset Hound Club in 1962.

The Western Michigan Basset Hound Club was set up under the direction of John Eylander, his father, Ed, Ralph & Beatrice Seamon, Harold Campbell, William Hays, Bruce Beam, Charles Burrell, Peter Waltz, Roy Ingram, Ronald Race, Bonnie Ingram, Arlie Syers, Clark Elliot, James Knight, Tom Barr, Ralph Frein, Aloise and Virginia Michalski, Mike Verwys, and M. Witt.

64

In eastern Pennsylvania, Robert Taber, Mr. & Mrs. Joseph Navar, Mr. & Mrs. John Streeter, Mr. & Mrs. Robert Matthews, Mr. & Mrs. John Nehre, and Joseph Oliviere founded the Valley Forge Basset Hound Club.

The Kentuckiana Basset Hound Club was organized through the efforts of Joe Miller, John Helm, Clinton Kaelin, Graham Roth, Virginia Brinsteel, Eddie McWilliams, John Pellerin, Delbert Mulhall, and Alvin Blair.

In the Chicago area Mrs. Walter P. Houchin, Donald Bateman, Ruth Bateman, and Bestor Coleman were among the first to form the Fort Dearborn Basset Hound Club.

In 1959, the Potomac Basset Hound Club was accepted after changing its name from Congressional. The Long Island Basset Hound Club held a Sanctioned Match, one of its first events.

During the early years, the Basset Hound Club of America held its annual meeting and field trial at Holland, Michigan. In 1959, the site was moved to Lebanon, Penna. It held its first Specialty in conjunction with the annual meeting and trial in 1960. Before that time, the parent club Specialty was held in conjunction with the International Kennel Club show in Chicago.

Under the guidance of Mr. & Mrs. Robert Lumma, the Lawrence Seilers, the Russel Schroeders, and the William Kinslows, the Gateway Basset Hound Club was formed in Missouri in 1960.

Later in 1960 the Basset Hound Club of Maryland was organized by Bill & Joan Tittsworth, Shirley & George Mueller, Eleanor Stewart, Joe VanderVeken, and the Carl Kohlhepps.

By 1963 several more clubs were being organized and sought recognition. Among them, in upstate New York the Patroon Basset Hound Club was formed by the Clifford Warrens, Michael Maxons, L. J. Elmores, Robert Kellers, Roland Coles, John Lennon, Joel Hill, and Oscar Mosher. The northwest fanciers organized the Basset Hound Club of Oregon. The Basset Hound Club of San Diego came into existence in California, and another, the Golden Gate Basset Hound Club was in its infancy.

The purpose of the Basset Hound Club of America is to guard the interests of purebred Bassets. It holds field trials and shows. The BHCA was responsible for the revision of the show Standard in 1964. It undertook to establish separate rules and running order for Basset trials this same era. In October, the annual meeting, election of officers, specialty show, and field trial are held. Any regional club that has the facilities for these events may apply to host them in their area so that the annual affair may be moved about the country. The BHCA publishes a news magazine every other month to keep the members throughout the country informed of events in all areas.

THE BASSET HOUND CLUB OF AMERICA OFFICERS 1935 TO 1964

Year	President	Vice-president	Secretary	Treasurer
1935–36	William Fritz	Emil Seitz		Carl Nottke
1937	Emil Seitz	Otto Grigsby		Carl Nottke
1938	Emil Seitz	Harold Fogelson		Carl Nottke
1939	Emil Seitz	Consuelo Ford		Carl Nottke
1940–44	Consuelo Ford	Melvin Freeman		Effie Seitz
1945–50	Roy Smith	Dr. J. P. Honey		Claude Smith
1951	Claude Smith	Harold Fogelson		Roy Smith
1952–53	Claude Smith	Johnny Bose		Roy Smith
1954–55	Johnny Bose	Norwood Engle		Millie Houchin
1956	Leslie Kelly	Chris Teeter		Millie Houchin
1957–58	Johnny Bose	Chris Teeter	Effie Seitz	Donald Bateman
1959–60	Dr. D. Wahl	Norwood Engle	Dorothy Shula	Effie Seitz
1961–62	Paul Kulp	Norwood Engle	Elizabeth Phillips	Julian Dexter
1963–64	John Eylander	Norwood Engle	Darrielyn Oursler	David Feron
1964	John Eylander	Norwood Engle	Mercedes Braun	Donald Bateman

7

The Standard

A Standard is a word picture of the ideal dog in any breed approved by the American Kennel Club. It describes the characteristics that set one breed apart from the other. The goal of the breeder should be to produce dogs as nearly perfect as possible. Judges are duty-bound to use the Standard as their guide in making awards.

The present Standard for Basset Hounds was accepted by the American Kennel Club in early 1964. Revisions had been made, as recommended by the Basset Hound Club of America, to clarify the old Standard and make stronger emphasis on the utility of the breed.

The Basset's versatility has been a threat to his quality since the days when the ladies of the French Court found his medieval quaintness amusing and took him into their chambers. He enjoys his role of an "arm-chair clown." But, lest he be doomed to degeneration by over-emphasis of singular points, the purpose of the breed must forever be kept foremost in mind.

The Basset was bred to be a slow, deliberate trailer, endowed with great physical stamina. The Standard describes such a dog if, and only if, *each* point is carefully considered. Once his loose skin, heavy bone, long ears, etc., become so exaggerated that they interfere with his work in the field, he is no more Basset-type than his light-boned, leggy counterpart. The fundamental principle, upon which the description of the ideal Basset is based, is the breed's utilitarian value. Also included must be characteristics unique for the breed though many of these are advantageous to him in his work. Let us discuss them point by point. One must remember it is difficult to draw up a Standard that is complete and concise. Lengthy descriptions are frowned upon. Therefore, the picture is not always clear to the novice.

The A.K.C. Standard for the Basset Hound

GENERAL APPEARANCE: The Basset Hound possesses in marked degree those characteristics which equip it admirably to follow a trail over and through difficult terrain. It is a short-legged dog, heavier in bone, size considered, than any other breed of dog, and while its movement is deliberate, it is in no sense clumsy. In temperament it is mild, never sharp or timid.

AUTHOR'S COMMENT: There's not much elaboration necessary here. Heavy bone, followed by "in no sense clumsy," should rule out the slobs that cannot make it around the show ring, let alone spend a day in the field. As for temperament, perhaps *"should* never be sharp or timid" would have been better. There are several bloodlines that have produced many timid dogs. There is always an excuse why this one or that one has been "ruined." But when we see too many relatives with the same shy tendencies, it is hard to close our eyes and say it is not inherited. I am not referring to the young dog making his initial public appearances and finding himself a bit unsure in all the new occurrences. These dogs usually warm up to a few people who are strangers even though they seem a bit wary of some.

HEAD: The head is large and well proportioned. Its length from occiput to muzzle is greater than the width at the brow. In over-all appearance the head is of medium width. The skull *is well domed, showing a pronounced occipital protuberance. A broad flat skull is a fault. The length from nose to stop is approximately the length from stop to occiput. The sides are flat and free from cheek bumps. Viewed in profile the top lines of the muzzle and skull are straight*

68

and lie in parallel planes, with a moderately defined stop. The skin over the whole of the head is loose, falling in distinct wrinkles over the brow when the head is lowered. A dry head and tight skin are faults.

AUTHOR'S COMMENT: Since many, apparently, never read beyond the description of the head, perhaps one of the most important revisions for the new Standard was made in the first paragraph. The old Standard described the skull as being narrow. What was meant was that the skull was narrow in proportion to its length. The tendency grew to breed for wind-splitting appendages that reminded one of an inverted ice-cream cone, and certainly not in balance with the desired broad body. It is amusing to refer to pictures of the Bassets from the era when the original Standards were worded. It would be difficult to find an American Basset that is quite so dry or has such a shallow muzzle, though they were described as having an abundance of loose skin and wrinkles, great depth of muzzle. One must conclude that these words were used to depict the Basset as opposed to other dogs of that time. We continue to use the same terms though our visualization of their meaning is different. Elasticity and wrinkle prevent punctures of the skin in dense undergrowth and, supposedly, abet the scenting organs. Does it necessarily follow that the "dog with enough loose skin for two" is the better Basset? At least, "dryness" is not listed as a *serious* fault.

The muzzle is deep, heavy, and free from snipiness. The nose is darkly pigmented, preferably black, with large wide-open nostrils. A deep liver-colored nose conforming to the coloring of the head is permissible but not desirable.

AUTHOR'S COMMENT: You will ask, if a light nose is not desirable, why is it allowed? Many breeders want a Standard to fit *their* dogs. In order to gain acceptance of more important points, a few minor ones were conceded.

The teeth are large, sound, and regular, meeting in either a scissors or even bite. A bite either overshot or undershot is a serious fault.

AUTHOR'S COMMENT: A close fitting of the front teeth of the upper jaw over the front teeth of the lower jaw is a scissors bite. The upper teeth protrude over the lower in an overshot bite, and when the lower teeth extend beyond the upper, the bite is referred

stop too prominent; snipey muzzle

broad, flat skull; high-set, heavy ear

GOOD HEADS   POOR HEADS

to as undershot. It is common knowledge that dentistry can be used, in some instances, to alter the set of the teeth, creating an illusion of a scissors bite. However, by carefully checking the set of the jaw-bone, such an alteration can be detected. Structure of the jaw is an inherited factor and should be considered as such in breeding. We are to be plagued with bad bites. Stonehenge, in 1887, referred to the works of De Fouilloux, describing the Basset d'Artois as having double rows of teeth like wolves. In this same period, the Counte le Couteulx de Canteleu wrote that "some of them have more teeth than dogs usually have, and many have the 'bec de lievre' or the lower jaw a little shorter than the upper." Two of the best bitches in his pack had such a formation of jaw. The early Standard of the Basset Club (Great Britain) stated that this was not a fault. The American breeders must be vigilant if we are to rid ourselves of this vexation.

The lips *are darkly pigmented and are pendulous, falling squarely in front and toward the back, in loose hanging flews. The* dewlap *is very pronounced. The* neck *is powerful, of good length, and well arched.*

AUTHOR'S COMMENT: The sentences on lips and dewlap are self-explanatory. What is "good length" in reference to the neck? It is such an important item in the make-up of the Basset, and yet has never been strongly emphasized. The British dog may lack our tremendous rib and depth of brisket, but it has maintained a beautiful, long, well-arched neck, so important to elegant carriage of the head. It should be of sufficient length to allow the dog to drop his nose to the ground without breaking gait. Unfortunately, the entry that trots around the show ring, looking adoringly at its handler, is a "ringside pleaser." No Basset looks his best when aping a carpet sweeper. However, I firmly contend, part of the evaluation of gait should include a few steps with the nose dropped to the ground. It takes correct length of neck, plus a well-balanced body, to move true in this position, an important feature of Basset "type."

The eyes *are soft, sad, and slightly sunken, showing a prominent haw, and in color are brown, dark brown preferred. A somewhat lighter colored eye conforming to the general coloring of the dog is acceptable but not desirable. Very light or protruding eyes are faults.*

The ears *are extremely long, low set, and when drawn forward, fold well over the end of the nose. They are velvety in texture, hanging in loose folds with the ends curling slightly inward. They are set far back on the head at the base of the skull, and, in repose, appear to be set on the neck. A high set or flat ear is a serious fault.*

AUTHOR'S COMMENT: A prominent haw is one thing; a scoop-shovel to collect debris is another. The low-set ear is to be long (as opposed to other breeds) enough to wrap around the end of the nose. The longer the better? This author maintains that, though it may be amusing to see the dog trip over his *excessively* long ears, good judgment dictates that this interferes with his work.

FOREQUARTERS: The chest is deep and full with prominent sternum showing clearly in front of the legs. The shoulders and elbows are set close against the sides of the chest. The distance from the deepest point of the chest to the ground, while it must be adequate to allow free movement when working in the field, is not to be more than one-third the total height at the withers of an adult Basset. The shoulders are well laid back and powerful. Steepness in shoulder, fiddle fronts, and elbows that are out, are serious faults.

The forelegs are short, powerful, heavy in bone, with wrinkled skin. Knuckling over of the front legs is a disqualification.

The paw is massive, very heavy with tough heavy pads, well rounded and with both feet inclined equally a trifle outward, balancing the width of the shoulders. Feet down in pastern are a serious fault. The toes are neither pinched together nor splayed, with the weight of the forepart of the body borne evenly on each. The dewclaws may be removed.

AUTHOR'S COMMENT: Approximately two-thirds of a Basset's weight is borne by the frontquarters. This portion of his body is all-important. The shoulders are well muscled, with shoulder blades very long, forming a right angle with the upper arm. The entire assembly should be placed far enough back to cover the lowest point of the breastbone. Most of the faults of feet and legs stem from a too-short shoulder blade. The sternum bone should be felt. It is easy to be deceived by fat that only appears to be a prominent sternum. If the shoulder is placed back far enough, and the chest is broad enough, the upper arm, of necessity, is slightly curved when viewed from the front. It follows the curve of the rib to the lower part of the forearm, with the wrist straight, terminating in a massive, but compact, paw that turns slightly outward. Quality of feet can be

72

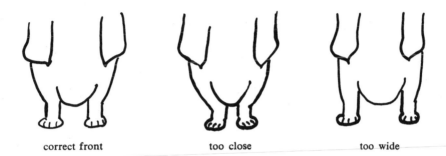

correct front   too close   too wide

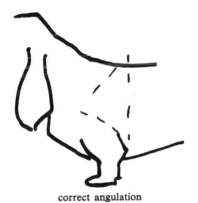

correct angulation

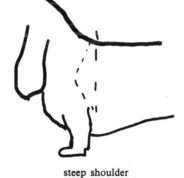

steep shoulder

checked by examining how the pads are worn. It is best to evaluate the frontquarters while the dog is "at ease." A smart handler can hamstring them to give the appearance of a good front. On the other hand, a novice dog will often lean into the hand of its handler and distort what may be a good front. Another successful appraisal can be made by requiring the handler to lift the dog under the neck and "drop" it. Much can be seen by the way it gaits.

BODY: The rib structure is long, smooth, and extends well back. The ribs are well sprung, allowing adequate room for heart and lungs. Flatsidedness and flanged ribs are faults. The topline is straight, level, and free from any tendency to sag or roach, which are faults.

AUTHOR'S COMMENT: Most back troubles stem from a short rib-cage. There should be little space from the last rib to the hip, leaving a very few lumbar vertebrae without some support. The rib should be as wide as the shoulder and two-thirds to three-quarters as deep as the height at the withers, which when considered as a unit, add up to powers of endurance. A topline that is level to the last rib, with a very slight rise over the loin, ending in a slightly rounded croup is very different from a roach back. Simple engineering principles tell us that a long topline must have a reasonable amount of arch to take up the shock, lest we doom our breed to slipped discs, etc.

HINDQUARTERS: The hindquarters are very full and well-rounded, and are approximately equal to the shoulders in width. They must not appear slack or light in relation to the over-all depth of the body. The dog stands firmly on its hind legs, showing a well let down stifle with no tendency toward a crouching stance. Viewed from behind the hind legs are parallel, with the hocks turning neither in nor out. Cowhocks or bowed legs are serious faults. The hind feet point straight ahead. Steep, poorly angulated hindquarters are a serious fault. The dewclaws, if any, may be removed.

AUTHOR'S COMMENT: Equally as important as the front, the hindquarter must be correct to propel the heavy body. A Basset is no better than his running gear. The term "well-bent stifle" often bewilders the neophyte. The angulation between the femur and pelvis is approximately 90 degrees. When the hocks are set at a right angle to the floor, viewed from the side, they are well behind the dog and show a distinct curve of the stifle. The distance between

good rear   cowhocked   too close

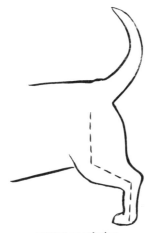 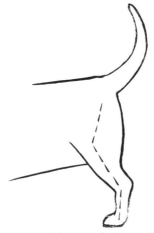

correct angulation   insufficient angulation

the hock joint and the foot is short. When viewed from the rear, they are to be parallel with each other and almost straight down from the broad, well-muscled rump. The term "crouching stance" should not be applied to obviously inexperienced dogs, especially puppies, that are merely "coming unglued." A good judge will patiently attempt to correctly evaluate the hindquarter while the handler may assist by gently rubbing the undercarriage to encourage the dog to stand. Actually, much can be seen, regarding structure, by the way the dog "sinks."

TAIL: The tail is not to be docked, and is set in continuation of the spine with but slight curvature, and carried gaily in hound fashion. The hair on the underside of the tail is coarse.

AUTHOR'S COMMENT: The tail should be of sufficient length to provide good balance with the length of the dog. It should be very thick at the base tapering to a white tip to be seen in the field. A thin, willowy tail is not in balance with the body, nor is one that is too short. It should not be carried "ring-tail" or "squirreltail" fashion, just gaily up, curving slightly forward. The underside is bushy but not silky and feathery.

SIZE: The height should not exceed 14 inches. Height over 15 inches at the highest point of the shoulder blades is a disqualification.

AUTHOR'S COMMENT: The average Basset ranges from 12½ inches to 13½ inches at the withers. A 12½ inch dog would weigh between 55 and 60 pounds. In order to be in correct proportion, a height of 15 inches would require at least 90 pounds of weight. It should be obvious that the best size would be around 13 inches.

GAIT: The Basset Hound moves in a smooth, powerful and effortless manner. Being a scenting dog with short legs, it holds its nose low to the ground. Its gait is absolutely true with perfect coordination between the front and hind legs, and it moves in a straight line with hind feet following in line with the front feet the hocks well bent with no stiffness of action. The front legs do not paddle, weave, or overlap, and the elbows must lie close to the body. Going away the hind legs are parallel.

AUTHOR'S COMMENT: Movement cannot be emphasized too strongly. It is the most important means of true appraisal. With the exception of checking the bite, sternum, rib, and pads, a good judge should know how a dog is "put together" by the manner in which he moves. He can hardly be expected to "flit about like a gazelle;" he's not built like one. His manner should be deliberate, determined, full of drive, and give evidence of exceptional endurance. Though he may have a slight bounce when he really "gets going," he must in no sense be clumsy. A dog with a "hitch" in the hip or shoulder should never be considered for an award. Even though it may be temporary, let him do his winning if, and when, he gets over it.

COAT: The coat is hard, smooth, and short, with sufficient density to be of use in all weather. The skin is loose and elastic. A distinctly long coat is a disqualification.

AUTHOR'S COMMENT: The coat is a most controversial subject. We must keep in mind that it must give protection from the weather. Dogs quartered out of doors in winter often develop a dense, slightly wiry coat. One should not be able to see the skin easily when running one's hand against the fur. But, just how long is a "long coat?" This may be better answered if re-worded to, "What is a long coat?" A long coat is soft, silky, and feathery like a Setter coat, with ear fringes and feathers on the legs and tail. The outer body coat is soft and silky, inclined to waviness. If one keeps the texture in mind, he will not be confused between a "long-coat" and a good winter coat. It would be out of the question to penalize a dog for a coat that is capable of protecting him in severe weather. The clippers will be taken to a few "long-coats" and they will get by, but this will not help when it comes to producing puppies. Mother Nature will give us such coats until all the carriers of these genes are weeded out. The loose and elastic skin will roll rather than puncture in dense cover. However, nothing says that it must be "two sizes big."

COLOR: Any recognized hound color is acceptable and the distribution of color and markings is of no importance.

AUTHOR'S COMMENT: The tyro might inquire what is meant by any recognized hound color. Bassets are black and brown with white undercarriage, paws, tail tip, and possibly around the neck or on the muzzle (tricolor)—or brown and white in the same places. The shade of brown varies in either case from deep mahogany to lemon and is described accordingly, red being the intermediate hue. Open-marked is applied to either tricolors or brown-and-whites when the coat is basically white, on the back, with large patches of color as opposed to solid color. There are varying amounts of white on the muzzle, neck, and legs. Though I have seen it, none is desired on the ears. The distribution of markings is of no importance unless one considers the effect to the eye of the viewer.

DISQUALIFICATIONS: Height of more than 15 inches at the highest point of the shoulder blades.

Knuckled over front legs.

Distinctly long coat.

AUTHOR'S COMMENT: Now, how does all this concern us as lovers of the Basset Hound? With the exception of the purely distinctive breed characteristics, every requirement of the Standard is justifiable on the basis of the Basset's ability to spend a day in the field in slow, determined pursuit of game. You will note, for the most part, the serious faults deal with points that concern his work. We want to improve him, not by exaggerating any of the requirements of the Standard, but by striving for the perfect combination and balance of the characteristics as stated in the Standard. He is not the result of breeders' fads, nor is he the result of whims of judges. A Basset is a working hound, ideally suited for his task which he truly enjoys.

It should be the aim of Basset Hound breeders to avoid such over-emphasis of any point of the Standard as might lead to unbalanced exaggeration.

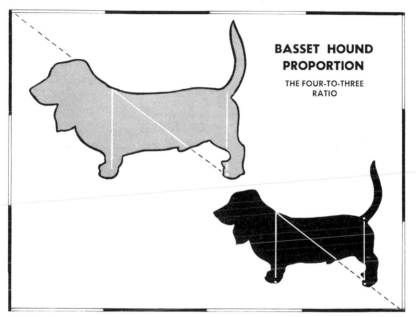

BASSET HOUND PROPORTION

THE FOUR-TO-THREE RATIO

A well-proportioned Basset is built in a four-to-three ratio: the height at the withers is approximately three-fourths of the measurement from withers to tail. The silhouettes illustrate the proportions of a Basset measuring 14 inches at the withers compared to those of a Basset measuring 11 inches.

8

Breeding and Raising
Better Bassets

T OO much time, money, and hard work are involved to breed for anything less than the best. Judge the sire by his get when bred to bitches of different bloodlines. Will he be compatible with your bitch? Does he consistently throw certain traits, either good or bad? These are the questions that must be answered before you decide. His winning record is no proof that he will produce quality, though the name might help to sell a few puppies. Often, breeders in the know would not use the current winner if his service were offered free, while they seek a comparatively unknown dog whose bloodlines they value.

There are many excellent books on Genetic Theory. However, since little research has been done with Bassets, a brief resumé of pertinent information may be of help. The term DOMINANT applies to the effect produced by one gene, showing in half the family of a parent having it, and usually appearing in every generation. RECESSIVE traits are commonly overshadowed by DOMINANT. The recessive effect requires two genes, one from each parent, to show, and it usually appears in every second generation.

For this reason, it is important to evaluate the characteristics of the grandparents of a contemplated litter. Though the effect may not show in the sire and dam, it may be transmitted to the offspring if it is in both maternal and paternal grandparents. Some of the foremost characteristics of the Basset are so thoroughly implanted that they show even though they are genetically considered RE-CESSIVE. Note, however, such items as "long hair" in the following list of RECESSIVE traits. This accounts for the sudden appearance of such a coat in the offspring of apparently "smooth coat" sire and dam whose parents were also apparently "smooth coats." Enough "long coat" genes were transmitted, even though hidden, to show when mutual genetic makeup was used.

We need not concern ourselves as much with the undesirable characteristics that appear listed as DOMINANT. They will be seen if they are being carried. Dominant traits include: normal head, course hair, wavy hair, short tail, stub tail, high style hunting, dewlap, short legs, long nose. Recessive traits include: narrow head, fine hair, straight hair, long hair, long tail, low style hunting.

To plan your mating, check carefully into the makeup of your bloodlines, considering brothers, sisters, grandparents and their littermates, as well as the immediate sire and dam. Decide upon the source of the desirable traits and increase the bloodlines carrying them. At the same time, eliminate the carriers of the undesirable. It is best to introduce new genes gradually lest there is a complete hodgepodge caused by too many possible combinations of genes. Line breed until these genes are firmly established. Always select sound animals for breeding stock. Never breed one with a glaring fault. It may not appear in the immediate offspring, but it will be around to plague your stock at some later date.

Bassets are, genetically, a deviation from normal structure. Nature tends toward the normal and punishes overemphasis of abnormalities by producing monstrosities, thus extreme care must be exercised. Breeding a good Basset is a challenge, second only to establishing a good Basset bloodline.

Count the days to establish the proper time for mating. It is more successful to breed when the color of the menses begins to lighten. Better still, mate when the stud and bitch indicate they are ready. Then continue mating every other day until the bitch's desire is gone. This will vary with individuals.

The actual mechanics of mating may be a bit more difficult. In fact, it can be downright backbreaking. The following method is quite successful. Two people are required. Place the bitch either across the knees of one person, or across a block that is "belly" high. This person also keeps her from struggling, nipping, or whatever she may decide to do. The second person handles the male. He is allowed to mount her and is then assisted with the "steering," guided from side to side until he hits his mark. At this time, the bitch is grasped by the stifles and held back against him, he is pushed forward, and held until copulation takes place. Often a young male must be encouraged to allow such assistance. After the first few times, he soon learns to expect your help. After copulation is assured, gently remove the support, allow them to get comfortable (usually end to end) and speak reassuringly, especially to a nervous bitch. Continue this until the job is done. It makes for easier work in the future. Copulation may last from ten minutes to over an hour, so do not be alarmed.

Pre-natal care consists only of proper nutrition and adequate exercise. Calcium is added to the bitch's diet during the last three weeks. She will be more comfortable if fed two meals a day. Accustom her to her draft-free whelping box in advance. To be, or not to be with the mother at the time of whelping is always controversial. Most Bassets are less nervous when you are there to reassure them. Many are slow whelpers. If you are with her, you will know if she is just slow or if she is having trouble.

Each puppy will arrive in its own membrane. This must be quickly removed. The cord is cut about two inches from the puppy's navel. Hold it head down and rub with vigor (it will not come out of its skin). When it is dry, and squalling, give it back to mama, unless she has too many to handle. In the event that a puppy appears but cannot be dislodged, grasp it gently but firmly and rotate it until it pops out. Above all, do nothing to upset the dam. She is better off alone than disturbed by a flustered, would-be assistant.

For your own convenience, you will undoubtedly prefer heated quarters in winter. However, an air-tight box equipped with a 100-watt electric bulb enclosed in a fireproof container is sufficiently warm even in very cold weather. You may prefer a heat lamp. If so, be certain it is not too near nor too hot. When puppies are cold, they cry and try to burrow under each other. If they are quiet, except when hungry, they are warm enough.

Continue to feed the dam calcium and nutritional foods until the puppies are weaned. The first food is offered puppies soon after the eyes are open; a mixture of pablum and milk. Thoroughly soaked, softened kibble or meal gradually replaces the pablum. Puppies should be completely weaned at the age of six weeks though they need the companionship of their littermates for another two weeks. Vitamins are very important at an early age if the puppies are to develop good bone. A multiple-vitamin such as is given to babies should be started at three weeks of age. Beef, cottage cheese, and cooked eggs are excellent sources of nutrition in addition to milk and a high-quality kibble. The importance of proper nutrition cannot be stressed too strongly. A Basset requires as much, if not more, bone-making food than any other breed.

Training

Personalities are developed from the first few days of a puppy's life. The first sixteen weeks are all important. Suggested reading is *The New Knowledge of Dog Behavior,* by Clarence Pfaffenberger (Howell Book House). A dog that has "learned how to learn" can be taught anything within reason. The responsibility lies with the breeder. By the time he leaves the kennel, a puppy should understand NO, COME, and GOOD BOY (or GIRL). The tone of voice is all-important. He learned COME for food and affection. NO was shouted at him when he misbehaved, and he was told he was GOOD when he was just that. Any breeder who cannot bother to teach these fundamentals has no business raising dogs.

Success with housetraining depends on the determination of the owner. The more effort that is put into it, the quicker it is accomplished. Paper-training is not recommended. Common sense will dictate that, after he learns to eliminate on a paper and cannot find one on the floor, he is apt to jump on your favorite couch to use the paper he sees lying there. Puppies usually "go" after

Basset puppies at ten days.

Basset puppies at three weeks.

naps and meals. Spend a few days watching for him to "hunt a spot." This is your cue to take him out, wait until he does his job, praise him lavishly, and return him to the house immediately. If he is to be allowed to play outdoors, bring him in first, and then put him out to play. He must associate going out with his toilet duties. It does no good to scold him for accidents unless he is caught in the act. Then shout NO and rush him out. A few days of doing nothing but watching the pup for indications of the need to relieve himself are well spent. The more accidents he is allowed to have, the longer it will take to train him, and he won't learn if his owner is too lazy to teach him.

Physical Condition

First of all, good diet is all-important. Second is adequate exercise. A Basset is a massive animal. He needs well-toned muscles, not sloppy fat. Only by running and romping will he develop the muscles that are necessary to prevent problems with joints bearing his heavy weight. Muscle tone and control are essential. Allow puppies to learn to jump up on things, and then back off, gradually increasing the height in accordance with their ability. Muscle coordination is insurance against injury, provided the skeletal structure is proper in the first place. Good length of rib and deep joint-sockets are necessary. I am not suggesting that the dog will never sustain an injury. After all, a human can turn an ankle while walking down the sidewalk. I am merely saying that well-developed muscles not only make him a more beautiful animal, with good shoulders, apple-round rear, and all the other desirables, but will help to keep him from being a Basset which is forever "on three legs."

Always lift a Basset with two hands, one under the front-quarter and the other under the hind-quarter.

General Health and Care

Vitamins, good food, and exercise are not enough. All dogs must be kept free of internal and external parasites if they are to be healthy. Never attempt worming with patent medicines. See your veterinary to determine the kind of worms, if any, and the

How to lift a Basset puppy.

Basset puppy at eight weeks.

proper medication to administer. See him, also, for external problems.

Loose stools, temperature, excessive discharge of the eyes, dull coat, listlessness, or coughing are warnings that veterinary advice should be sought.

Many problems can be avoided with a small amount of care. Have your Basset vaccinated against distemper, hepatitis, and leptospirosis. Should the "dog down the street" be reported "sick," give yours a booster shot.

Cleanliness of bedding and runs is absolutely essential to good health. Cedar chips, added to the bedding, discourage fleas.

Excessive bathing removes the oil from the coat. Daily brushing will remove most of the dirt. Better than a brush, is a hack-saw blade. The skin is held taut with one hand, while the blade is used to rake from neck to rear with the other. Dead hair and dirt are dislodged leaving the coat clean and glossy.

Ears should be cleaned weekly. A simple, economical method is suggested. Fill the ear with a dropperful of mineral oil. Massage a few seconds to loosen wax. Remove oil with a piece of absorbent cotton or soft cotton cloth wrapped around the finger. Do not probe too hard as it irritates the delicate membranes.

Nails must be kept short. If they click on the floor, they are too long. Clipping is a simple matter if done weekly from puppyhood. Lay the dog on his side and talk gently to him. Few will object if they are used to it. However, once they are allowed to raise a fuss, trouble begins. Straddle him if need be, get an assistant, or do anything necessary to convince him that he *must* allow this to be done. Be patient. Praise him when he settles down. He will soon learn that it really isn't so bad after all. If done weekly, once the nails are short, only a few strokes of a coarse rasp are needed. Teach him to roll over on his back, between your legs, with his head in your lap. Most Bassets love this position. Make it fun; rub his tummy. File from the top of the nail downward. KEEP THOSE NAILS SHORT, but do not cut into the quick.

The eyes may be rinsed with the same boric acid solution used by humans if they are slightly irritated. Your veterinarian will supply you with ointment if needed.

Remove tartar from the teeth occasionally. A professional scraper may be purchased, but, a tough thumbnail will remove most of it, with less possibility of cutting the gums. Give him large bones or dog biscuits to chew. They help to keep the teeth clean.

Less than half an hour each week will keep him in good condition. It can be "fun-time" if he has been sensibly trained.

9

The Basset in the
Show Ring

DOG shows are the medium by which comparisons are made, awards bestowed, and the official "go ahead" given on the breeding potential of dogs. The merits of the dogs are judged against the breed Standard. Theoretically, the dog which conforms most closely to the Standard for its breed is awarded the highest honor. The opinion of different judges will vary according to their different interpretations of the Standard. Until the breed is uniform, one cannot expect judging to be uniform, but, without dog shows, there would be no uniformity at all. Each breeder would develop his line according to his own taste and purpose. The frequent official public rating provided by the shows, plus the rivalry among breeders seeking acclaim, affords the incentive to breed for continual improvement of quality.

A beautiful show dog does not just happen. His career begins at the time his mother is bred to the male most consonant with her bloodline. The male's sire and dam are undoubtedly the result of the same kind of selective breeding. He is chosen because his conformation is most akin to that of the ideal dog described by the Standard, though there is no "perfect" dog. His personality indicates that he would enjoy a career in the ring.

From then on it is a matter of management. His nutritional needs are met to insure development of good bone, teeth, and coat. He is lead trained at an early age. In the early stage, this is play. He may balk either by sitting, rolling over, jumping straight up in the air, and/or yelping as though he were being beaten, or he may trot along nicely. If he objects, he is coaxed with food, kind words, or any other means that encourages him to take his first steps on lead. Praise is lavished upon him when he complies. He is allowed to have his own way as long as he walks at first. Gradually he is taught that he must walk nicely alongside. This is done with short tugs on the lead. If he pulls forward, he is jerked back. If he is behind, he is tugged forward. As soon as he is in the proper position, he is reassured with words and a tone that tell him he is doing the right thing. Then he is taught to walk on both sides of his handler so that the judge can see him at all times. The handler must avoid getting between the dog and the judge. The judge tries to evaluate the gait of the dog. He is taught how to execute a turn to reverse directions. The handler stops, turns toward the dog, switches the lead to the hand that is on the side the dog is also on, at the same time turns the dog around, and they are off in the opposite direction to that in which they have been going before the turn. Time after time this procedure is repeated until they can make the maneuver with graceful coordination. The dog knows that he is to walk on the same side of his handler as is the hand that holds the lead. He is trained to stand when the handler stops. This is not easy. The Basset prefers to sit, roll over, or crawl in the instructor's lap. But, with patience, his teacher stops, turns toward him, places one hand under the muzzle and the other under the hindquarters and tells him "stand." When the dog stands quietly for even a short period, he is praised. When he misbehaves he is told "no" rather gruffly, and the act of standing him is repeated again. Eventually he understands that he is to stand when his trainer stops. He is eager to please because he is praised for his good behavior. It is necessary for him to learn that he must remain standing quietly while the judge looks at his teeth, feels his shoulders, ribs, pushes on his back, and checks his testicles. He may forget many of these things his first time in the ring. Experience makes him a polished performer.

At some time, his trainer has learned how to pose a Basset from watching exhibitors who were winning with theirs. He has watched other breeds being shown, too. He has observed those in the Group ring. He realizes that, for a dog to look his best, he must be presented well. Dog and handler must be a team in order to paint a pretty picture. He has noted that the front legs of a Basset are placed so that they are straight down from the shoulder and well under the dog when viewed from the side. From the front, no daylight shows between the leg and the chest. The feet are as straight forward as structure permits. The hind legs are set so that the hocks are straight up and down when viewed from the side or the back. The head is held in such a manner that the arch of the neck is shown, the nose held slightly downward to reveal expression. The topline is as level as possible. The tail is held lightly from behind to form the proper curve. Practice before a mirror may help the trainer to perfect the best technique. By doing this, he can see just how he and the dog will look to the judge. It takes only a few minutes every day until he and the dog are a team that can match all others.

At an early age, the show dog is taught the fun that lies ahead when one gets in the car. He is introduced to a crate so that he does not mistake such confinement as punishment. He is taken to strange places among strange people to learn that here he will gain new friends. He is proud that his beauty and good behavior bring glances and words of admiration. He becomes a "ham."

He stands on a table for his daily brushing, his weekly nail trim, and ear cleaning. The clippers and scissors for his whiskers are introduced at an early age so that when he must be trimmed for a show, he knows what to expect. He is not a born showman; he is made one.

So, you would like to show your Basset, too. If the quality is right, all you and your dog need is training. It takes practice. Begin now. Write the American Kennel Club, 51 Madison Ave., New York, N.Y., for the free booklet, "Rules Applying to Registration and Dog Shows." It defines the different types of shows and classes. Familiarize yourself with all the rules. Contact your nearest kennel club; there you will find further assistance. Although the members may not know the fine points of a Basset, they do know about dog shows and will be willing to help you. They hold frequent training classes which will be of great value to you. If you are fortunate enough to have a Basset club in your area, by all means, join it. Club members at either organization will assist you in obtaining entry forms, referred to as "premium lists," and will explain how to fill in the proper information to be sent to the show superintendent two weeks prior to the show. A few days before the show, you will receive a ticket, identification slip for your dog, and a schedule of the time of judging. You will be more at ease if you attend a show with someone who is entered, preferably before you actually enter. Do not be ashamed of your lack of knowledge, however. Every exhibitor has his "first time out."

At the age of six months, a dog may be entered in a show where points toward a championship are gained. There are, however, "matches" where younger puppies and novice exhibitors may enter for practice, gaining knowledge in an informal atmosphere at a very small cost. These shows serve the further purpose of informing club members about the mechanics and procedure of putting on a show.

There are six classes from which to choose when making entries. A dog over six months of age, and still under twelve months, may be entered in the Puppy, Novice, American-bred, or Open Classes. Bred-by-Exhibitor class may be entered if the owner is also the breeder. After the dog reaches the age of twelve months, he may be entered in any of the classes except Puppy class. Once he has won three first prizes in Novice class, a first prize in Bred-by-Exhibitor, American-bred, or Open class, he is no longer eligible for the Novice class, nor is a dog that has gained points toward his championship. To enter the Bred-by-Exhibitor class, a dog must be owned wholly or in part by the person or by the spouse of the person who is the breeder or one of the breeders of record. It must be handled in the class by the owner, or a member of the immediate family of the owner. The purpose of the class is to honor the breeder-exhibitor. It is a prestige class. In Open, you will find the experienced dogs, shown by experienced exhibitors, vying for points. You will hear often that you have to be in the Open class to win. This is not necessarily true. Granted, the points are usually awarded to a dog from this class if he is of high quality, beautifully groomed, in top condition, and shown well. Many Best of Winners awards have been taken from the Puppy class, however. Ch. Braun's Humpty Dumpty CD gained all but his first two points (taken from the Puppy class) from the Bred-by-Exhibitor class. You do not have to be in Open to win. I would advise, though, that a new exhibitor enter the Novice and American-bred classes only a few times for experience. After that, he should show in the Puppy class as long as the dog is within the age limit, the Bred-by-Exhibitor class if he is eligible, or in the Open class.

Another false rumor is that Obedience spoils a dog for the show ring. On the contrary, the "Stand-Stay" exercise is very helpful, and the one problem that can arise from this practice, heeling only at the left side, is easily solved. Use a show lead for show training, gaiting him on both sides, and a slip-chain for obedience work. He will learn the difference.

In grooming your Basset, first make certain his nails are short. This task should be done weekly, anyway. The night before the show, a more professional appearance can be obtained by filing from the top downward with a heavy rasp. This instrument may be purchased at a hardware store. A nail file for this purpose is also available at pet shops. A touch of oil or vaseline will make the nails glossy. Next, ears must be clean. Then the whiskers on the muzzle, cheeks, and eyebrows should be removed with scissors or clipper. Pull the skin taut so that the whiskers stand out to insure close clipping. Scrape tartar from the teeth. Round off any straggly hairs at the tip of the tail. Trim excess hair from the paw to give it a neat appearance. It is not necessary to bathe the dog completely unless he is really dirty. Wash the white parts with the same quality shampoo you use for yourself. Tincture of green soap is excellent. Rub any black parts with a damp terry washcloth. White chalk powder may be brushed into the damp white hair if it is off-color. When the dog is dry, be certain all the powder is removed by vigorous brushing, for the dog would be disqualified if it should chalk off in the ring. A hack-saw blade is the best tool for removing loose hair from the coat, and the skin must be held taut while the dog is raked in the direction that the hair naturally lies. A hound glove (a mitt equipped with fine wires or bristles in the palm) is an excellent last-minute aid. There is nothing like a final rubdown with the hands to make a good coat shine.

One can invest in many expensive items of equipment, but few are necessary. A crate is worthwhile. It affords protection from injury while riding, and at unbenched shows, provides the dog with

Ch. Braun's Humpty Dumpty C.D., finished from the Bred-by-Exhibitor Class, winning under judge Herbert Cahoon.

a place to relax. He can be groomed on top of it. If it is wire, it can be used on the bench at this type of show. At benched events, dogs must remain in their assigned stalls for the duration of the show except when they are being groomed, for one hour prior to the judging, when they are being judged, or for fifteen-minute periods while being "exercised." Unless you use a wire crate, you will need a collar and chain that can be fastened to metal loops in the stalls to confine your dog at benched shows.

There are two preferable types of show-leads. One is flat-braided nylon about one-half inch wide. The other is a light chain collar with a nylon lead. These items are available at the equipment stands at shows. A can of foam cleaner, turkish towels, a hack-saw blade or hound glove, a pan for water, and a lead are the most necessary items to take to the show. Paper dishes for food and water are usually provided by one of the dog food companies.

Try to get your dog to move his bowels before leaving home. Often the best-trained are the most difficult to convince at the show that it is permissible to perform such duties in the given place called the "exercise ring." Do take him there before judging time. Try to get him to relieve himself, and praise him for it. He will soon learn what is expected. Should you have considerable difficulty in getting him to move his bowels, a suppository helps. At least, try to avoid accidents in the ring. If, after doing your best, a misfortune occurs, do not let your embarrassment reflect on your handling. It happens to the most seasoned, this goes without saying, but the conscientious professional tries desperately to avoid such scenes because they reflect on his reputation.

A bit of liver or some other goodies may help to keep the attention of your dog. There is often an abundance of such things scattered on the ground or floor by those before you. A hound with a nose is sure to be aware of them. He is more apt to gait unhampered if he knows he will receive them from your hand at the proper time.

When you arrive at the show, settle down somewhere. If it is benched, you put your dog in the stall immediately. At unbenched shows, you will find space in the grooming area. Check the ring assigned to you. Be ready when the judge is ready to start Bassets. Often the judging is later than the time listed on the printed schedule. There is no point standing at ringside with your dog until it is necessary. When Bassets are called, get your armband (this has your dog's number on it and is worn on the left arm) from the person who is assisting the judge, the "ring steward." When your number is called, and you enter the ring, show as though you believe you have the best dog and intend to win. Your own mental attitude carries through to the dog. *Smile!* The whole idea is to present a pleasing picture. Poise is the fundamental attribute. Save your nervous breakdown until after the judging. Do, whether you win or lose, be gracious . . . you'll be back again someday.

If you find *you* cannot "take" it, and your dog is good enough, hire a professional handler. He gets paid for his know-how. He learned how to train, to groom to be aware of what certain judges look for in a dog and how they want them presented. But remember, the amateur with a good dog can win just as often as the professional if he has taken the time and trouble to school himself. Very few exhibitors are fortunate enough to come from a show-dog family. Handling dogs is a skill that must be learned. Almost everyone starts out a novice. Your author remembers well the days of stumbling around the ring. It takes determination to learn by observation and practice. You CAN do it. Keep informed of any changes in rules governing dog shows. They do change from time to time. Changes are published in the official magazine published by the American Kennel Club.

Now, go ahead and enter a show. There is so much enjoyment in winning with your "pride and joy." If you lose, there's always the next time. The show-bug will bite; you will know you are crazy, but you'll have lots of company.

While at the show, watch the dogs in the Obedience ring. Bassets are very dependable workers if trained properly. Many have gained a Companion Dog degree which is awarded for Novice work. A few have difficulty attaining the next degree, Companion Dog Excellent, because Bassets are not natural jumpers and jumping is part of the test. Obedience work is very enjoyable. If it appeals to you, read a good book on the subject and enroll in an Obedience training class. By 1964, approximately one-hundred-eighty Bassets had gained a Companion Dog degree, thirty-two a Companion Dog Excellent degree, and eleven had attained a Utility Dog degree.

10

Basset Hounds
in the Field

THE Basset has a natural instinct to hunt. It merely takes opportunity and experience to cultivate this desire, though some are more eager than others.

In style, they are slow, careful, and deliberate. If unsure of themselves, they may check back at their starting point and take up the track again. Unless trained otherwise, most of them prefer to run as individuals. It is not uncommon to see them work Indian file. Often they do not honor another's signal of a find, but prefer to seek their own, each talking to his own line in his own particular manner. Early writers often stated that they did not believe the Basset would make a pack dog nor would he work as a brace. We have since accomplished both through training and selective breeding.

In selecting a puppy, the nosey one usually matures with more incentive than the lazy one. To assist in training, scents may be purchased and dragged. An old rabbit skin is full of scent. The best training, however, is right in the field. By taking the Basset for walks where the game can be found, and allowing him to

Dover, Ohio, field trial 1951, Dog Stakes. L to R: Bose's Bass Bawl, Engle's Ace, Snowfall Shorty, R.F. Smith's Major, and Trigger Triumph.

Dover, Ohio, field trial 1951, Bitch Stakes. L to R: Queen Elizabeth, Melancholy Baby, Hartshead Jet, Meyer's Black Queen.

stumble onto his quarry, he will soon learn. Praise him highly when he makes attempts at tracking. It is not wise to let him trail by sight too often.

At first, he may track only a few feet and return to you. Be patient. Give him plenty of time to know that you will not depart without him. Go with him. Encourage him to seek the track again. Each time he will go a bit farther. If you are fortunate enough to shoot a rabbit, let it lay. Let the dog know the thrill of finding what he has been tracking. Praise him highly so that he learns that this is what you wish him to do.

A young dog may make many mistakes. If he has the will to do it, he will profit by his mistakes. Do not expect too much during the first year or two. Age and experience make the sharp hunter.

Hunting with a Basset is not limited to the rabbit. He will work on other game if you prefer. Bassets were used on all small game and birds in the early days in France.

I would like to recount a tale of one of our first bench champions. He was a mature dog when we purchased him. Being novices in the show ring, we did not know how to show off his better qualities. It took approximately a year to finish him. The following hunting season, we decided to allow him to accompany us in the field. His first time out, while the other dogs were busy in search of game, he followed on my heels waiting for me to break a path in the weeds. We were disdainful of his field work, but because we loved him, he was allowed to tag along on the next day. Soon he was venturing a few yards around me. One day he lifted his head, sniffed the air a few times, made several leaps forward, and put up a pheasant. From then on, this was his method. Since we had several good rabbit dogs, but no good bird dog, we never attempted to train him otherwise. Although his style was highly unorthodox, we valued him highly, and shot many birds over him before his untimely death at the age of five.

A hunting dog, to be of value, must work to please its master on the game that inhabits the territory and is prized. Given the opportunity and encouragement, a Basset can be trained to seek almost any small game.

The true joy of owning a Basset is to hear the air resound with his bell-like voice. The will is there. It is up to you to nurture it and know the joy of seeing him at his intended work.

11

Field Trials for Basset Hounds in America

BASSET HOUND field trialing is a great and wholesome sport for both young and old and is growing steadily in popularity. The first licensed trial in the United States was held in 1937 by the Basset Hound Club of America soon after its formation. Now trials are either given by the parent club or by one of the regional clubs under the approval of the parent club.

Rules governing the conduct of AKC licensed trials are contained in a manual referred to as "The Red Book," formally titled "Rules Applying to Registration and Field Trials." A current copy may be obtained by writing to The American Kennel Club, 51 Madison Avenue, New York, N.Y.

Field Trials are defined as follows:

"A MEMBER FIELD TRIAL is a F. T. at which championship points may be awarded, given by a club or association which is a member of The American Kennel Club.

"A LICENSED FIELD TRIAL is a field trial at which championship points may be awarded, given by a club or association which is not a member of The American Kennel Club, but which has been specially licensed by The American Kennel Club to give the specific field trial designated in the license.

"A SANCTIONED FIELD TRIAL is an informal field trial at which dogs may compete but not for championship points, held by a club or association, whether or not a member of The American Kennel Club, by obtaining the sanction of The American Kennel Club."

Clubs also hold "Fun" trials. These are excellent aids for the novice dog or novice field-trialer. They are an easy, informal means of gaining the experience necessary for rough competition.

Trials usually occupy a two-day weekend. They may be expanded to three days when the need arises. Stakes are normally provided for Derby dogs, Open All-age, and Champions. Open stakes are usually divided by sex at licensed trials.

A DERBY dog is a male or female whelped on or after the first day of January of the year preceding that year in which the field trial is run.

OPEN ALL-AGE stakes are for all that have not yet gained a championship. They may be divided by sex if so stated in the premium list and/or entry form. If, however, the premium list or entry form states that the stakes are divided by sex, and thereafter when the entries are received it is found that there are less than six entries of each sex in any stake, that stake shall be combined and run with both sexes in a single stake, but no stakes which the premium list or entry form states are to be divided by sex shall be combined into a single stake under any other circumstances.

Championship points are awarded to hounds placing first, second, third, and fourth only in Open All-Age stakes. They are awarded on the following basis: one point to the winner of the first place for each Basset Hound actually starting in the stake. The following fractions of points are awarded through fourth place for each dog starting: one-half point to the winner of second place; one-quarter point to the winner of third place; one-eighth point to the winner of fourth place. However, points shall be awarded to Basset Hounds placing second, third, and fourth only in the event that there are fifteen or more actual starters in an Open All-Age stake. In order to be recorded a field champion, a Basset Hound must have won championship points in at least two licensed or member club Basset Hound field trials and must have placed first in at least one

Open All-Age stake. At present, the total number of points required is forty.

CHAMPION stakes are open to Field Champions of Record. This stake is comparable to the Specials class in the show ring. The honor of the win, or the prize offered, is the incentive.

The stakes of a licensed or member club trial may be run as brace stakes on rabbit or hare and are open only to purebred Basset Hounds.

Provisions are made for Pack stakes consisting of two, four, or eight couples on hare, though this stake is not usually utilized at the trials. Additional non-regular stakes may be run if so specified in the premium list and/or entry form.

A club must apply to The American Kennel Club for leave to hold a field trial. The application must state the day, or days, upon which the club desires to hold the trial. The location must also be given. Each club which has held a field trial in any one year has first right to claim the corresponding date for its succeeding trial. Regional clubs must also apply to the Parent Club for permission. Should the Parent Club unreasonably withhold permission, the Regional club may request a hearing at The American Kennel Club. If the application is approved by the board of directors of The American Kennel Club, the applying club then selects a committee of at least five members and the Field Trial Secretary, premium lists are prepared and submitted, and, if approved, sent to prospective entrants.

Closing time for entries is stated on the premium list. Usually, this immediately precedes the running of the stake. A drawing is held to determine the running order of the dogs. The first and second names drawn are the first brace, third and fourth names are the second brace, and so on. In the event that there is a single dog left at the last drawing, the judges will later select a dog that has previously run in the stake to be the running mate for the single.

There are two judges. Judges are not required to obtain licenses. The club may submit the name of any reputable person in good standing at The American Kennel Club. The club, of course, considers the capability and popularity of a judge when making the selection. Judges may run dogs in any stake they are not judging.

Others actively engaged in the trial are The Trial Chairman,

Trial Secretary, Field Marshal, gallery, handlers, and braces of dogs. The Trial Chairman is responsible for the initial plans. The Trial Secretary must attend to the "paper work" and reports. The Field Marshal instructs the gallery and handlers as to conduct in the field. The gallery consists of persons who are not currently engaged in running a brace. Their duty is to follow the instructions of the Field Marshal and put up a rabbit. This becomes quite a sport in its own right. The person kicking up the quarry calls "Tally-Ho" and directs the judge to the spot. It gets to be a contest among the gallery for the most "Tally-Hos." The gallery forms a line under the direction of the Field Marshal. They proceed forward, beating the brush, kicking clumps of weeds, until someone kicks out a rabbit and calls "Tally-Ho." The line is stopped and expected to stand quietly. The judges go to the spot indicated. The running brace is brought forth by their handlers, put on this place, called the "line" and turned loose. The judging of their tracking ability begins. Handlers are allowed to follow the dogs but may not interfere or assist unless the judge so instructs them. The dogs are expected to follow the path of the rabbit closely and not give tongue falsely. They are, however, expected to claim the rabbit by opening-up (barking) on the track.

When the judges feel they have properly evaluated the hounds, the dogs are called in and the procedure is repeated for the next brace. Should the judges feel the brace did not have a fair chance, they may call for as many rabbits as they feel necessary. All the braces are run once in what is called the first series.

After this, the best running dogs are called back to be run again in second series. It is left to the discretion of the judges as to which dogs shall be run again and in what order they are to be braced. They may call for as many series as they deem necessary to evaluate the merits of the dogs before awarding their placings.

Judging and running are a bit more difficult than may seem. Sometimes a rabbit does not emit scent. Weather conditions are an important factor in tracking. It is not uncommon to see the dogs come through, hot on the track, some distance to the left or right of where the rabbit passed. The wind may carry the scent far off course. The judge must consider all of these things.

Once the dogs are off and away, the gallery takes a break. Some watch the dogs as far as possible. Others relax, grab a smoke, tell stories, and rest their weary feet. They keep a watchful eye and open ear to estimate the value of the run. Occasionally, an oft-run, tired, and frightened rabbit will hop right into the midst of the gallery. It is the duty of all present to remain as quiet as possible so the running hounds are not distracted. It takes a good dog to continue his work unmindful of the surroundings. Since the judging continues all day, except for a lunch break, some of the gallery may drop out, while late arrivals may join. In either case, one must exercise care while joining and departing, being alert for hounds and rabbits, lest a run be spoiled.

Though the field trialers take their wins seriously, the atmosphere at the trial is one of congeniality. Perhaps it is a part of being close to nature or perhaps because trialers are the kind of people who enjoy the little things in life.

The only requirement in wearing apparel is comfort and protection. Any jacket, boots, and pants that will serve the purpose are acceptable. Nobody cares how you are dressed. The women do not sport the latest coiffures. At meal time, the white linen table cover and fine china may be missing, but the food is always delicious. The rest rooms are often the outdoor variety. Sleeping accommodations may be anything from the clubhouse, camp trailers, trucks, and cars to the luxury suite at a nearby hotel. Who sleeps? After endless miles of walking back and forth through stubble-fields, woods, and ditches, trialers spend most of the night spinning yarns. Everyone seems intent on spending every minute in having a good time. When the trial is over, they return home blistered, scratched, and weary, to anxiously await the next event.

The big difference between a hunting Basset and a trial dog is that the hunter is expected to seek out his own game .while the trial dog must run the particular rabbit that his handler indicates. If you are planning to enter trials, keep this in mind. The dog will be led to the line on a leash. He will be expected to run on various types of terrain and with strange bracemates, so accustom him to them during his training. One must realize that at a trial there will be strange people, dogs, and confusion all around, but one's dog will be expected to claim his line and run it. John Eylander, who has had years of experience at the work, offers a hint of help: wear the same clothing for training that you wear to the trial. Your dog will have more reassurance that he is doing what is expected

Field Champions Taber's Solo Sue, Navar's Ears, Navar's Snapper, Navar's Jolly, Navar's Heather, Navar's Jill, and Navar's Ginger.

Field Champion Stakes winners at the 1964 Nationals on October 9: l. to r.: Eugene Beldean with Fd. Ch. Aquino's King Kong; John Eylander with Fd. Ch. Max's Blue Echo; Harold Campbell with Fd. Ch. Campbell's Bit O Gold; Fd. Ch. Olson's Samanthe, owned by Eugene Beldean, handler unknown.

DuBois, Pennsylvania, field trial 1949. L to R: Graham's Jill, Melancholy Baby, Shebe's Lady, Hartshead Melanie, and Hartshead Jet.

of him. It may seem unimportant to you, but remember, Bassets are truly creatures of habit in any form of behavior.

BASSET HOUND FIELD CHAMPIONS—1938 through 1964

1. Field Ch. Hillcrest Peggy—Maple Drive Jigilo ex Maple Drive Carmelita
2. Field Ch. Irish Hill's Senator—Starridge Pol ex Trompette II
3. Field Ch. Bijou Rutile of Banbury—Ch. Westerby Vintage ex Bijou Sapphire of Banbury
4. Field Ch. Queen Elizabeth—Maple Drive Marlin ex Cook's Bonnie Best
5. Field Ch. Hartshead Jet—Hartshead Masked Knight ex Hartshead Firegirl
6. Field Ch. Perry's Marigold—Hartshead Trigger II ex Bose's Melicent Hepsy
7. Field Ch. Pounder II—Field Ch. Bose's Royal Knight ex Malone
8. Field Ch. Bose's Royal Knight—Duke of Greenhill ex Bose's Melicent Hepsy
9. Field Ch. Yoder's Sally Belle—Reiser's Tusc-O-Sport ex Baker's Judy Ann
10. Field Ch. Tulpehocken Peg—Maple Ridge Sandie ex Field Ch. Perry's Marigold
11. Field Ch. Eingle's Becky—Smith's Major Tempo ex Al's Bonnie Girl
12. Field Ch. Bose's Neil Theron—Duke of Greenhill ex Bose's Melicent Hepsy
13. Field Ch. Bose's Exploress—Bose's Dapper Dan ex Field Ch. Yoder's Sally Belle
14. Field Ch. Arrowhead Jody—Belbay Cloud ex Lord's Majorette
15. Field Ch. Long John Silver—Lord Tietge ex Todle's Peggy
16. Field Ch. Bose's Dusty Scarlet—Duke of Greenhill ex Bose's Melicent Hepsy
17. Field Ch. Behney's Bill—Shaw's Brownie Prince ex Field Ch. Eingle's Becky
18. Field Ch. Bose's Alethia—Field Ch. Bose's Neil Theron ex Field Ch. Yoder's Sally Belle
19. Field Ch. Miss Mitzie—Rex Cumberland ex Princess Pat Sport

Field Ch. Bose's Whirlwind with Art Shaeffer.

Field Ch. Eingel's Beckie with Loren Free.

20. Field Ch. Bose's Snowflake—Bose's Dapper Dan ex Field Ch. Yoder's Sally Belle
21. Field Ch. Bose's Speedy—Field Ch. Bose's Neil Theron ex Field Ch. Yoder's Sally Belle
22. Field Ch. Germann's Darky Dot—Smith's Yankee Lad ex Kincaid Dash
23. Field Ch. Newton's Black Jackolyn—Kanode's Buck Shot ex Jule
24. Field Ch. Queen Bee—Roisterous Rambler ex Veraestau Mabel
25. Field Ch. Shellbark's Atomic Blue—Smith's Yankee Lad ex Black Judy
26. Field Ch. Bose's Shag—Ch. Siefenjagenheim Lazy Bones ex Ch. Bose's Whirlaway
27. Field Ch. Bose's Karen—Bose's Black Bruno ex Bose's Solo
28. Field Ch. Bose's Bashette—Field Ch. Bose's Speedy ex Bose's Peggy II Express
29. Field Ch. Jensen's Black Boy—Trigger Triumph ex Lady Beth
30. Field Ch. Olson's Mitzy—Olson's Mr. Zip ex Field Ch. Bose's Snowflake
31. Field Ch. Taber's Solo Sue—Tulpehocken Shorty ex Creole Baby
32. Field Ch. Olson's Rocky—Olson's Mr. Zip ex Field Ch. Bose's Snowflake
33. Field Ch. Holly Hills Duffy—Holly Hill First Knight ex Dare's Lady
34. Field Ch. Tulpehocken Hepsy—Ch. Tulpehocken Trailer ex Field Ch. Perry's Marigold
35. Field Ch. Tulpehocken Nifty—Tulpehocken Duke ex Tulpehocken Millie
36. Field Ch. Olson's Daddy Long Legs—Olson's Mr. Zip ex Field Ch. Bose's Snowflake
37. Field Ch. Oak Shadow's Sloppy Joe—Duke of the Woodlands ex Lemieux's Ula
38. Field Ch. Susque-Hanna—Engle's Trailer Chief ex Engle's Minnie Pearl
39. Field Ch. K-Y Colonel—Engle's Ace ex Fetherolf's Cyclone
40. Field Ch. Bash's Sabrena Sue—Engle's Brown Prince ex Bose's Solo

Field trialers taken in 1955: Leonard LaFollette, Loren Free, Al Michel, Norwood Engle, Stephen Free, and Kenneth Engle.

Field Ch. Mac's Gentle Majesty with Pat Malone.

41. Field Ch. Shellbark's Michie—Jody of Airline Acre ex Field Ch. Ingram's Beauty
42. Field Ch. Aquino's King Kong—Bose's Ura Prodigy ex Olson's Little Fly
43. Field Ch. Tulpehocken Sadie—Tulpehocken Red Boy ex Field Ch. Perry's Marigold
44. Field Ch. Bose's Initiative—Field Ch. Bose's Whirlwind ex Bose's Starette
45. Field Ch. Fetherolf's Fun and Frolic—Black Raider ex Fetherolf's Arvilla
46. Field Ch. Shellbark's Little Mac—Bose's Jo Mac ex Hartshead Royal Jet
47. Field Ch. Tulpehocken Til—Ch. Tulpehocken Trailer ex Field Ch. Perry's Marigold
48. Field Ch. Wheaton's Sam—Osage's Lord Built Well ex Bell of Baytru
49. Field Ch. Irle's Cleopatra—Cook's Killbuck Chief ex Darwin's Nutmeg
50. Field Ch. Campbell's Black Jack—Field Ch. Jensen's Black Boy ex Bose's Triumphette
51. Field Ch. Hamlin's Torpedo—Ch. His Lordship of Lyn-Mar Acres ex Clorox of the Coral
52. Field Ch. Ingram's Beauty—Red Man of Belleawood ex Bose's Triumphette
53. Field Ch. Bose's Whirlwind—Bose's Bass Bawl ex Malone
54. Field Ch. Navar's Ears—Field Ch. Behney's Bill ex Navar's Joy
55. Field Ch. Navar's Heather—Tulpehocken Shorty ex Engle's Xmas Cheer
56. Field Ch. Navar's Snapper—Warwick Lochinvar ex Engle's Xmas Cheer
57. Field Ch. Germann's Albertino—Lad ex Dark Bula
58. Field Ch. Jackie Jo Jan—Red Man of Belleawood ex Bose's Triumphette
59. Field Ch. Otto Irenaeus—Darwin's General ex Nacy's Margarita
60. Field Ch. Ric-Mar's Fenian—Ch. Erwin's Copper Duke ex Pet-Tom's Spring Beauty
61. Field Ch. Olson's Samanthe—Olson's Mr. Zip ex Field Ch. Bose's Snowflake

111

Field Ch. Ed's Jo Jo.

Field Ch. Campbell's Black Jack and Field. Ch. Bose's Initiative with owners, Harold Campbell and John Eylander.

62. Field Ch. Ed's Jo Jo—Field Ch. Bose's Royal Knight ex Field Ch. Miss Mitzie
63. Field Ch. Mac's Gentle Majesty—Sammy Joe McDonald ex Bose's Stardust
64. Field Ch. Olson's Tommy Lee—Olson's Mr. Zip ex Field Ch. Bose's Snowflake
65. Field Ch. Beacon Tulpen Duke—Tulpehocken Duke ex Beacon Beauty Rose
66. Field Ch. Oak Shadow's Apache—Ingram's Red Trailer ex Richard's Suzie Q
67. Field Ch. Aquino's Socrates—Field Ch. Olson's Rocky ex Olson's Little Fly
68. Field Ch. Bash's Spring Fury—Bose's Pepper Pot ex Bose's Solo
69. Field Ch. Campbell's Bit-O-Gold—Jody of Airline Acre ex Luckey Huey Delila
70. Field Ch. Navar's Jolly—Tulpehocken Shorty ex Engle's Xmas Cheer
71. Field Ch. Mr. Bassinger—Ehrig's Spotted Ace ex Field Ch. Bose's Exploress
72. Field Ch. Navar's Jill—Field Ch. Navar's Jo Jo ex Jill's Winona
73. Field Ch. Navar's Ginger—Field Ch. Behney's Bill ex Navar's Joy
74. Field Ch. Shellbark's Memory—Field Ch. Shellbark's Atomic Blue ex Field Ch. Eingle's Beckie
75. Field Ch. Navar's Jo Jo—Tulpehocken Shorty ex Engle's Xmas Cheer
76. Field Ch. Tulpehocken May—Tulpehocken Duke ex Tulpehocken Millie
77. Field Ch. Rosie's Bill—Hartshead Sportsman ex Rosie's Ed's Miss Mitzie
78. Field Ch. Kanode's Sally Nell—Shellbark's Rambler ex Field Ch. Queen Bee
79. Field Ch. Hoosier's Zealous Zipper—Ch. Colorado ex Hoosier's Liza Jane
80. Dual Ch. Kazoo's Moses the Great—Ch. Casey of Kazoo ex Ch. Long View Acres Donna
81. Field Ch. Little Lady Tammy—Field Ch. Ed's Jo Jo ex Eylander's Pretty Patti

82. Field Ch. Rider's Black Beau—Russet Jewel ex Field Ch. Fetherolf's Fun & Frolic
83. Field Ch. Paul's Kate—Engle's Ace Red Man ex Ida
84. Field Ch. Kraemer's MoJo—Appleton Acre Black Duke ex Nitnore
85. Field Ch. Mathew's Rusty Red—Kanode's Buck Shot ex Martin's Daisy May
86. Field Ch. Max's Happy Hunter—Fiddlefoot ex Eylander's Blue Moon
87. Field Ch. Bash's Black Dahlia—Engle's Brown Prince ex Bose's Solo
88. Field Ch. Fouse's Cindalee—Field Ch. Olson's Rocky ex Fouse's Cinda Lou
89. Field Ch. Trenary's Smokie—Field Ch. Bose's Neil Theron ex Holly's Sassy
90. Field Ch. Campbell's Cindy Lou—Field Ch. Campbell's Black Jack ex Field Ch. Campbell's Bit-O-Gold
91. Field Ch. Olson's Torena—Field Ch. Hoosier's Zealous Zipper ex Olson's Tiny
92. Field Ch. Jake's Rose—Engle's Ace Red Man ex Ida
93. Field Ch. Germann's Fish Eye—Lad ex Dark Bula
94. Field Ch. Bellow's Star—Field Ch. Bose's Speedy ex Field Ch. Germann's Darky Dot
95. Field Ch. Hoeger's Molasses—Cook's Killbuck Chief ex Darwin's Nutmeg
96. Field Ch. Beacon Tick Tock—Tulpehocken Duke ex Beacon Beauty Rose
97. Field Ch. Ingram's Little Ann—Eylander's Blue Ace ex Ludlow's Miss Freckles
98. Field Ch. Navar's Ripple—Holly Hill's Basil Duffy ex Navar's Joy
99. Field Ch. Queen Toby—Warwick Lohengrin ex Happy Queen Carmel
100. Field Ch. Campbell's Jill—Campbell's Black Jack ex Ed's Royal Miss
101. Field Ch. Ed's Block Buster—Eylander's Danny Boy ex Miss Mitzie
102. Field Ch. Max's Blue Echo—Eylander's Blue Afton ex Max's Happy Hunter

12

Packs of Basset Hounds in America

THERE are at the present time eight registered packs of Basset Hounds in the United States. James S. Jones, Joint Master of the Tewksbury Foot Bassets, Gladstone, N.J., has been kind enough to write the following history of them:

"The first organized hare hunting, by a pack of Bassets in this country, was carried on, I believe, by Mr. Gerald Livingston, who hunted his Kilsyth Bassets in the vicinity of his house at Oyster Bay, Long Island, in the late nineteen-twenties and early thirties. Since there were no indigenous hare on Long Island, Mr. Livingston stocked the country with Jack rabbits brought in from Kansas, and with hare imported from Central Europe. This was a private pack completely supported by the Master. His hounds came mostly from Capt. Godfrey Heseltine's famous Walhampton Pack which was, in its turn, the first pack in England to hunt hare in an active fashion over an extended period of years. (The Walhamptons were active from 1890 to 1914 except for several periods of a few years while their owner was away from England on military service.)

"Mr. Livingston's Kilsyth Bassets made one of their last public appearances at the Eastern Field Trials of the Basset Hound Club of America which were held at Gladstone, N.J. in 1940. On that occasion, three-couple packs were hunted on Jacks in open grazing country. The mounted judge was Josiah Child, Master for many years of the Waldingfield Beagles of South Hamilton, Mass. Pack entries included: Brandywine Bassets, Lenape, Pa., Miss Jane Mather, Master; Kilsyth Bassets, Oyster Bay, L.I., Mr. Gerald Livingston, Master; Bijou Bassets, Old Chatham, N.Y., Mrs. Consuelo U. Ford, Master; Mr. and Mrs. "Pinkie" Thompson's Bassets, Red Bank, N.J.; the Rowe House Bassets of Pottersville, N.J., Percy Chubb & James S. Jones, Joint Masters. From this entry list, you can see that there were several other packs, in addition to Kilsyth, which hunted hare or Jacks in the Eastern States in the period between World War I and World War II.

"Mr. & Mrs. Alfred Bissell had their Stockford Bassets hunting a country outside Wilmington, Delaware. This pack is still in existence.

"Miss Mather's pack hunted cottontail rabbits in the country of her father's Brandywine Foxhounds at Lenape, Chester County, Penna.

"Mrs. Consuelo U. Ford's well-known Bijou pack was descended in part from imports from Dr. Eric Morrison's Westerby Bassets which were kenneled at that time at Great Glen in Leistershire, England. The country around Old Chatham, in New York State, which Mrs. Ford hunted was very rough and hilly with long hard winters. Nevertheless, she very gamely put on regular meets for quite a few years, hunting the local rabbits and some imported Jacks, and with her hunt staff turned out in very smart brown velvet jackets. Mrs. Ford was very largely responsible for the great success of the BHCA 1940 Eastern Trial.

"Mr. & Mrs. Thompson's pack, like all the others of the period before World War II, was privately owned. They started it when they lived near Geneseo in western New York State. Later, when they moved to Rumson, N.J., they were fortunate to be in an area where there were some native European hare. This was the registered country of the Monmouth Co. Harriers. It had formerly been hunted in the twenties, by the Navasink Beagles of which W. Strother Jones and Edward Hurd were Joint Masters. The hare in Monmouth County are descended from those imported from Europe in 1890 or so by Mr. Pierre Lorrillard and released at his nearby Rancocas Stud Farm at Columbus, N.J.

"In the years 1939, 1940, and 1941 Mr. Percy Chubb and the author hunted a small pack, the Rowe House Bassets, in the outer portions of the country of the Vernon-Somerset Beagles in Hunterdon and Somerset Counties in New Jersey, by permission of their Master, Mr. R. V. N. Gambrill. Our hounds consisted of drafts from the Westerby and from Mrs. Ford. We had some good sport and lots of fun hunting native hare and Jacks until the war put a stop to all activities. In 1941 these hounds were given to Mr. Carrol Basset and Mrs. Marion Dupont Scott of Montpelier, Orange County, Virginia.

"The first post-war II pack to become active were the Timber Ridge of which Charles R. Rogers is the founder and first Master. He is still in office. These hounds hunt outside Baltimore, Maryland, in the country of the Green Spring Valley Foxhounds. They are the first publicly supported subscription pack of Bassets in the United States and the first pack to be recognized and registered by the National Beagle Club which is the governing body for the organized packs of Bassets.

"The Timber Ridge have developed a large and enthusiastic following. They have no native hare or Jacks, so they do the best they can hunting rabbits and grey foxes in their very attractive open countryside around Hampstead, Maryland. In 1963, they retired the cup for five-couples of Bassets at the Bryn Mawr Hound Show having won this class five times.

"The next post-war pack to appear on the scene were the Tewksbury Foot Bassets, started by Mr. Harlburton Fales II and myself as a small private pack in 1951. Our foundation stock came from Mrs. Ford, the Westerby, and from Mrs. Walton of Mt. Holly, New Jersey. In 1953, Mr. Richard V. N. Gambrill died and the country he had hunted with his Vernon-Somerset Beagles became vacant. It is an open farming and grazing area lying in Somerset and Hunterdon Counties in New Jersey. Over the years, it had been pretty well stocked with European hare and Kansas Jack rabbits. At Mr. Gambrill's death, the Tewksbury Foot Bassets were reorganized as a publicly supported subscription pack to take over the vacated area. The hounds were "presented to the country" by Mr. Fales and myself and we remained on as Joint Masters. Mr. Louis Starr was the first Chairman of the Hunt Committee. Mrs. James

Casey, Mr. Gambrill's daughter, was elected Secretary and Mrs. Charles B. P. Van Pelt, Treasurer. Mr. Fales and I are still in office as Joint Masters and we were joined in 1959 by Mr. James Cox Brady, Jr. We maintain about thirteen couples of Bassets and try to breed about three litters of puppies every second year. Our season begins the first of August and ends on April 1. We hunt early in the morning until the third week in October which is the start of our "regular season" during which the advertised meets are held on Sunday afternoons. We have some 150 subscribers. Sunday "fields" average about forty people.

"We compete annually at the Bryn Mawr Hound Show held at Malvern, Penna., in June and in the two and four couple Basset division at the National Beagle Club Field Trials held at Aldie, Virginia, in early November. Our T. F. B. Elmer '54, out of Ch. Lyn Mar Clown ex Grim's Unity, was Champion Basset Hound at Bryn Mawr for six consecutive years, and has been quite widely used at stud.

"Among the most pleasant features of our season are the joint meets held from time to time with the various adjacent packs of Beagles or Bassets. For example, on each alternate year we are invited to hunt the country of the Ardrossan (formerly Treweryn) Beagles near Philadelphia and on the off year they visit us. To finish our season, for the past ten years, we have been invited to hunt the brown hare at Thornedale, Millbrook, Duchess County, N.Y., by the invitation of Morgan Wing, Jr., the very active Secretary of the National Beagle Club, and Master of the Sandanona Beagles. At various other times, we have visited, or been visited by, the Buckram Beagles of Long Island, The Timber Ridge Bassets, the Poona Bassets, and the Little Prospect Beagles. Often, on these occasions, the home pack hunts in the morning and the visiting pack hunts after lunch the same day.

"I've noted above that the National Beagle Club is the governing body for all packs of foot hounds in the U.S. New packs are inspected by a committee and first registered and then, when fully established, they are 'recognized.' A map showing the boundaries of the country is placed on file and the hunt livery and roster of staff are placed on the official list. New packs cannot be started within or near the boundaries of existing packs without sanction from the National Beagle Club Committee.

"In addition to Timber Ridge and Tewksbury, it is nice to note that the following six new packs have been added to the list in the past ten years.

"The Poona; Joint Masters, Kent and the late Adele Leavitt of Fraleigh Hill Farm, Millbrook, Duchess County, New York. This small, but in its time, active family pack is now unfortunately disbanded. In previous years, however, in their old-gold livery, they carried off many ribbons at Bryn Mawr and Aldie. They won the five-couple class for packs at Bryn Mawr in 1958 and the present challenge trophy for this class is presented by Mr. & Mrs. Leavitt in memory of their daughter. Kent Leavitt is currently the 'Basset representative' on the National Beagle Club Committee. He takes an active interest in the field trial grounds at the Institute at Aldie.

"The Bridlespur Bassets are affiliated with the Bridlespur Hunt, run for many years by the Adolph Busch family near St. Louis, Missouri. This is a subscription pack and the joint Master and Huntsman is Mr. Clarkson Carpenter, Jr. They show good sport on cottontail rabbits to an enthusiastic field and compete with success at Aldie each year.

"The Somerset Bassets: At Montpelier Station, Orange County, Virginia, near the famous home of ex-president James Madison, are the kennels of this pack which shows great sport on cottontail rabbits to an enthusiastic following under the leadership of their Master, Mrs. James H. Andrews, Jr., and her genial huntsman, Melvin Poe.

"The Skycastle Bassets: a private pack of partially rough-coated hounds which hunt rabbits and show sport to the neighbors of Mr. John Streeter of Chester Springs, Pennsylvania. Mrs. Elizabeth Streeter takes an active part in the management of this pack. They compete extensively at local field trials.

"Ashland Bassets; Warrenton, Virginia: This very workmanlike private pack is in a sense an offshoot or descendant of some Bassets which Mrs. Amory S. Carhart, the present Master, had in conjunction with the late Mr. "Babe" Gibb in 1941. They hunt rabbits in the country of the Warrenton Hunt and compete successfully at the Aldie Field Trials.

"The Coldstream Bassets: The newest addition to the roster of Basset packs is the Coldstream under the joint Mastership of Mr. & Mrs. Joseph J. McKenna of Media, Pennsylvania. They also hunt rabbits in the former country of the Rose Tree Foxhounds and have, in a very short time, developed a good looking level pack. On their first appearance at the Bryn Mawr Show, in 1964, they accounted for the class for entered dog hounds and followed this up by winning the important five-couple pack class.

"I don't want to conclude this article without mentioning the fact that in the past fifteen years almost all the active hunting packs of Bassets in England have seen fit to use a harrier or beagle outcross in order to obtain a more quickly responsive and active hunting hound. Col. Eric Morrison, founder and now ex-Master of the Westerby, took the lead in this movement and he claims that some thirteen packs are now hunting hounds descended from his Westerby strain which he started cross breeding in 1946. These cross-bred hounds are referred to as 'English Bassets,' the term 'Basset' being reserved for the pure bred variety.

"In April of 1964, I had the pleasure of hunting with a pack of English Bassets, the West Lodge Hare Hounds, in Hertsfordshire. They are a partially rough coated, lemon and white, fifteen inch pack, with only mildly crooked legs. They handle and hunt extremely well and have a very good cry and great drive.

"I quote below part of a letter which I sent in 1959 to the Editor of "The Field" in London, commenting on this development in England especially as it relates to hunting with Bassets in the U.S.: 'Dear Sir: As joint master of one of the four active packs of Bassets in the United States, I was very interested to read your May 14, 1959 article by Miss Jane Buckland on the subject of the recent crossing of this breed in England with harriers, beagles, etc., and the resultant discussion as to an appropriate name for the cross-bred product.

'In this country the need for such an out-cross has not been felt even with the active hunting packs. I believe the reasons for this include the following:

'a. In the hare hunting countries we do not have frequent fields of deep plough, ditches, stone walls or thick hedges. The fields are grass and the fences are post and rail or three strands of wire which presents no problem to a pack of Bassets.

'b. The central European hare which we hunt, and which are native since about 1925 in our own country in New Jersey, are of considerable stamina and what you, in England, would call a good scenting day comes only once or twice per season! Fortunately it is not expected that we kill very often! With two or three herds of fifty deer or more a common sight on any hunting day, it is a help not to have foot hounds running at too great a pace.

'A pack of the larger cross-bred type—such as the two hounds Doctor (now Col.) Morrison sent us in 1952—would get clean away from us in this relatively wooded deer infested area. Incidentally, these cross-breds were exported to us, unseen, in response to a request for a couple of Bassets similar to a very fine orthodox dog-hound puppy which I'd gotten from Dr. Morrison in 1938. This bears out well the point made by both Miss Keevil and Mrs. Rawle that the name question should be settled to avoid confusion and further misrepresentation! I fully sympathize with the desire to have a smarter more active pack and to kill more hare but we stick to the orthodox type of necessity. Incidentally, they are said to run 'one field in five' slower than a pack of 15-inch Beagles and manage to give most of our good runners a more than adequate workout!

'Lastly, I feel that there has been no tendency in America to look for an out-cross to another breed because the number of Bassets in the country did not have to be cut down drastically during the second war as was done in England. A. K. C. figures show 21,555 Bassets registered in the U.S. during the years 1953–1958 inclusive. The growth has been rapid—from 1,300 in 1953 to 7,000 in 1958. I believe, the English number registered in 1953 was considerably less.'

"The above letter indicates why, in my opinion as of 1964, the American packs will all stick to the 'pure-bred' strain and not find it necessary to attempt any cross-bred experimenting. Even on this basis the breeding of a good hunting level pack is an ambitious undertaking. We all have a good way to go yet before anyone achieves this goal!"

Alfred E. Bissell supplied the following about his Stockford pack, the only pre-war pack which is still active in 1964: "In the early 1930's I started a pack of Beagles and my wife started a pack of Bassets. Being over 60, I had to give up the Beagles as they became too fast for me." Mr. Bissell bought his first Basset from Gerald Livingston. In 1932, the Kilsyth strain of Livingston's was the only pack known to Bissell. The Bissells then imported dogs from the Eastington Park Bassets of Mr. de Lisle Bush in England and Colonel Morrison's Westerby pack. They later imported dogs of the Grims line owned by Miss Peggy Keevil. Mrs. Bissell was the first Master of the Stockford Bassets. She hunted them twice a week and won many prizes at the shows. The pack was given to Mrs. Andrew Porter at the start of the second world war and returned to the Bissells in 1946. For the next ten years they were hunted regularly. It was always a private pack with no dues and by invitation only. Mr. Bissell says, "Now I take them out when I feel like it and have no fixtures. We had volunteer Whips, personal friends, children, and now grandchildren—no horses allowed but I now have golf-carts for the infirm." Jack rabbits are imported from New Mexico each September. These, with the native ones left over from the previous year, usually provide a good hunt.

The staff consists of the Master, or Joint Masters, Secretary, Whippers-in, and Huntsman. The people participating in the hunt are called the Field. Customs observed are: close gates; roll under fences, if possible, or climb near a post; move quietly near stock; stand still when hounds are close by; don't overrun hounds at check; exercise care when smoking in field; stand still and point with cap or handkerchief when quarry is viewed; do not shout. The following is a brief glossary of hunting terms: *drag*, artificially laid scent; *draw*, exploration of likely hiding places of quarry; *field*, those hunting; *full cry*, musical chorus of hounds running their quarry; *hold hard*, stand still; *lift hounds*, moving hounds to new covert; *line*, the line traveled by the quarry; *mark*, the spot quarry was last viewed; *mark to ground*, hounds indicating quarry has gone to ground (technical kill); *pack*, term for the working unit of hounds; *quarry*, animal being hunted; *tail hounds*, hounds running some distance behind the pack; *tally-ho*, the call made when quarry is viewed; *worry*, hounds fighting over quarry killed. Signals are given by horn.

NATIONAL BEAGLE CLUB LIST OF ACTIVE PACKS OF BASSETS WITH REGISTERED COLLARS—1964

Name of pack	Established	Master	Kennel
Ashland Bassets	1960	Mrs. Amory S. Carhart	Warrenton, Va.
color of collar—green, hunting pink piping			
Bridlespur Bassets	1958	Clarkson Carpenter, Jr. & Samuel W. Mitchell	
color of collar—robin's egg blue, scarlet piping			Defiance, Mo.

Coldstream Bassets   1962   Mr. & Mrs. Joseph McKenna, Jr.,   Media, Penna.
     color of collar—oxford gray, scarlet piping
Skycastle Bassets   1949   John W. Streeter   Chester Springs, Pa.
     color of collar—crimson
Somerset Bassets   1959   Mrs. James N. Andrews, Jr.
                                   & Mrs. Worth Koopman   Somerset, Va.
     color of collar—yellow, purple piping
Stockford Bassets   1932   Alfred E. Bissell   Fairville, Pa.
     color of collar—green, gold piping
Tewksbury Foot Bassets 1950   James S. Jones, Haliburton
                                   Fales II, & James Cox Brady, Jr.   Gladstone, N.J.
     color of collar—robin's egg blue
Timber Ridge Bassets   1947   Charles R. Rogers   Hampstead, Md.
     color of collar—old gold, blue piping

The Tewksbury Foot Basset Hound Pack.

123

The Timber Ridge Basset Hound Pack.

The Coldstream Basset Hound Pack.

Louisa Neilson.

13

The Basset Hound in Britain

I T is impossible to give a detailed account of the breed's history in the British Isles without taking up the whole book. It is a fascinating history, not surprising in a unique breed, and worthy of closer study. However, space permits only a sketchy outline of the main events and the people involved. Much of the information about the twentieth-century breeders was written by George Johnston of Wigton, Cumberland, England.

Despite the proximity of France, it was not until the late 1800s that the first Basset Hounds were introduced into Great Britain. In 1866 M. LeComte de Tournon presented some to Lord Galway. They had been bred by M. LeComte Couteulx de Canteleu and were the smooth-coated Artois variety. Lord Galway eventually passed them on to Lord Onslow. In 1874 Sir Everett Millais imported Model who was exhibited the following year. Model was the first Basset to appear on the show bench in Britain. He was from the Couteulx kennels. This fine hound attracted much attention which resulted in many more joining the ranks of Basset fanciers.

In a letter to Mr. Croxton-Smith dated 1894, Sir Everett related that, due to a scarcity of the Basset at the time he imported Model, he bred this dog with a good-sized Beagle bitch. In 1877 he showed second generation hounds that were not distinguishable from Bassets. He gave up this strain when the Earl of Onslow imported a couple named Fino and Finette from Couteulx in 1877. Model was bred to Finette giving Millais his first purebred Basset bitch in lieu of a stud fee. She was named Garrenne. Lord Onslow kept her brother Proctor. From then on Millais began breeding in earnest. He was a true amateur and never sold a hound, preferring to give them to interested people. Isabel was produced from a union of Model and Garrenne in 1878. Lord Onslow's Fino was bred to Isabel. George Krehl imported Fino de Paris in 1880. With these the fanciers were able to guarantee the first Basset class in England at Wolverhampton this same year.

During these years Lord Onslow's kennel was under the care and management of Mr. T. Pick. He had been breeding a hound he imported named Juno. Millais referred to her as the most prolific Basset ever in the country though hardly the best. Her union with Proctor produced Cigarette. This hound was made famous through her daughter Medore who was bred to Fino VI producing Champions Forester, Fresco, Merlin, and Flora. Millais had a share in the breeding of Proctor. Cigarette was bred by Lord Onslow, Medore by Herbert Watson, Ch. Bourbon, Fino V, and Fino VI by George Krehl. F. B. Craven was the breeder of Ch. Forester, Fresco, Merlin, and Flora. Fresco died on his way to the Spa show. Merlin died in Melbourne, Australia, in 1892, having been sent there to found the Melbourne Basset Hound Pack. Forester and Flora were in Millais kennels. By 1886 the breed had prospered enough to find an entry of 120 hounds at the Aquarium show in London. The leading breeders had formed the Basset Hound Club two years earlier. Sir Everett later severed connections with the club because he believed it was not advancing kennel interests. Prior to this he had presented Mr. Arthur Croxton-Smith with a couple who were the parents of Champions Welbeck, Wensum, and Wantage.

By 1886 a difference in genetic makeup could be seen in the hounds. Fino de Paris had a pronounced bloodhound-type head, heavier bone and build, thicker coat, and richer coloring than did George Krehl's four hounds secured from Lord Onslow. The latter were straighter in leg and shorter in ear. Though Model and Fino de Paris were brothers they and their progeny were not similar in type. Model and Fino were not bloodhound type. The mating of Guinevere and Fino de Paris in 1882 produced Fino V and Bourbon. The problem of the two types of Couteulx hounds was discussed in the previous chapter. Fino carried the Fino de Paris type. Bourbon took after his dam with lighter color, finer bone, thin skin and coat. This was the only litter Guinevere produced before her death. The best specimens thereafter date back to these two hounds.

In 1894 Sir Everett Millais resolved that twenty years of inbreeding had caused the Basset to deteriorate. The general mass of hounds had become below average in size. There was increasing difficulty in breeding and rearing them. Barrenness was becoming prevalent. When reared they succumbed to distemper in a most alarming manner. It was his opinion that French imports were far inferior to the English strains. Fresh blood from this source would be no benefit, thus a cross breeding was inevitable.

He chose to cross with the Bloodhound because the Basset head should closely resemble it. His experimental work with Beagles had previously proved that the return to Basset formation in legs was only a matter of one or two generations. Only the question of color remained a problem.

The first cross was between the Basset hound Nicolas, a son of Ch. Forester, and the Bloodhound bitch Inoculation. The puppies were produced by the method now known as artificial insemination. Twelve were born. They were nearer the Basset anatomy than the Bloodhound but all took after the dam in color.

The next cross was between Ch. Forester and his half-Basset granddaughter Rickey, a product of the first cross. Six puppies were tricolor, one black and tan, all of Basset anatomy.

Dulcie, one of this ¾ Basset and ¼ Bloodhound litter, was bred to the Basset named Bowman. The next cross was between a Dulcie-Bowman female and the Basset Hound Guignol. Of the six puppies born, four were tricolor, one lemon and white, and one black-and-tan. It was impossible to distinguish them from purebred Bassets.

Millais opined he had attained his purpose. The offspring of the four great sires, Fino de Paris, Fino V, Fino VI, and Forester, for the most part had not equalled the size and bone of the parent. By the use of the Bloodhound cross, both third and fourth generations were comparative in size to Forester.

The influence in the American bloodline will be seen in the pedigree shown of Walhampton Ferryman, sire of Walhampton Andrew and Alice. From these descended such dogs as Maple Drive Murkey, Walhampton Aaron, Peggy Leach, Maple Drive Jigelo, Field Ch. Hillcrest Peggy, Ch. Westerby Vintage, Chausseur, Hartshead Masked Knight, Smith's Red Bear Tongue, and many more. Ada was half Bloodhound, and the great-granddam of Ferryman.

Partial Pedigree of Walhampton Ferryman

<pre>
                                                Sandringham Zero

                        Walhampton Merryman

                                                Mimi

Walhampton Ferryman

                                                Walhampton Farmer

                        Walhampton Freda

                                                Capt. Levans Music

                        Walhampton Maizie

                                                Ada (half Bloodhound)
</pre>

Other leading breeders at this time were Mrs. C. C. Ellis, Mr. Loet, Mr. Krehl, Mr. Kennedy, and Mr. Muirhead. At the turn of the century, the Basset was very strongly positioned and firmly established in Britain. Probably no other imported breed had such a sound foundation and this has surely had a lasting effect on the breed. The first fanciers were people of means and were able to buy the best hounds France had to offer.

In the early 1900s the principle breeders were Croxton-Smith, Mrs. Ellis who owned Chs. Zena, Paris, and Forester, Mrs. Walsh who had Ch. Bowman, and Mrs. Lubbock with her notables Locksley and Maid Marion. Mrs. Mabel Tottie had a strong kennel in Yorkshire that housed rough and smooth Bassets including Ch. Louis le Beau, Solomon, Napoleon II, and Chs. Puritan, Priscilla, and Pervance, and Tambour. The brothers Godfrey and Geoffrey Heseltine began to breed and hunt the Walhampton pack which became famous for decades. Their convictions were strong regarding the breed. Major Godfrey Heseltine later wrote that his brother,

Lt. Col. Christopher Heseltine, O.B.E., and he, joint Masters of the Walhampton Basset Hounds, resigned their membership in the B. H. C. because in spite of a rule passed by the club "that no unsound hound should be awarded a prize," judges continued to be appointed who disregarded this rule by giving top honors to hounds which were unsound and badly built in body and legs. These judges were accused of giving priority to dogs whose heads most closely resembled bloodhounds', encouraging breeders to produce animals for the sole purpose of obtaining this point. The by-product of such a practice was the alarming weakness of the rest of the breed's conformation.

The Masters of Basset Hounds formed an Association about 1910. These fanciers kept hounds for hunting the hare. Lord North was President, the Hon. W. F. North, his son, compiled a stud book. Only hounds affiliated with the association were permitted to be entered in the stud book. North never completed compilation. In 1926 Major Heseltine produced the first volume.

This period was the crest of the wave for Bassets. H.R.H. Queen Alexandra was a regular exhibitor. Her Sandringham hounds were both rough and smooth. Sandringham Bobs, Babil, Dido, Vero, Vanity, and Weaver were all prominent in the show ring. In 1924 the Brancaster prefix of Miss Adams came to the fore. She based her kennel on Walhampton Zilla. At the same time, Mrs. Forester-Rawlins combined Dandie Dinmont Terriers and Bassets under her Potford prefix. Her Potford Ragout was used as a model for a Danish porcelain statuette of a Basset. Miss Adams bred Rob Roy and Rosabel of Reynalton first shown by Mrs. N. Elms in 1929. She also had a large kennel of Beagles and Bloodhounds and a fine stud of Arab horses. Another horse lover was Mrs. Edith Grew who established her Maybush kennel prior to the 1930s.

From 1900 to 1932 the Walhamptons had been steadily growing stronger. They bred judiciously and brought their pack to perfection for the show bench and for hunting. They believed that no Master should be entirely satisfied if he would continue to improve his pack. Godfrey Heseltine was a regular correspondent with leading French breeders. He made a series of three importations. The last occasion was 1920 when he introduced Meteor and Pampeute. The merging of English and French bloodlines was successful and resulted in a long line of famous hounds: Chs. Walhampton Andrew,

1923, Gratitude, 1925, Ambassador, 1928, and Lynnewood, 1931. Heseltine considered Nightshade to be the best Basset he had ever known. Overseas breeders made use of the fine Walhampton bloodlines. Among those exported to the U.S.A. were Chs. Walhampton Andrew and Linguist, Walhampton Ferryman, Walhampton Alice, Walhampton Abbot, Walhampton Dipper, and Walhampton Lawless. For over thirty years the Heseltines reigned supreme, until their untimely death in 1932 resulting in the dispersal of the pack.

Mrs. Elms and Mrs. Grew purchased some of the dogs at the dispersal sale. From then until the outbreak of World War II their kennels were all powerful. From two of her purchases, Walhampton Nightshade and Walhampton Lynnewood, Mrs. Elms bred the Reynalton hounds Ch. Orpheus and Venus, and from the same strain Chs. Monkshood, Minerva, Narcissus, and Amir whom she exported to the United States. She judged several times and always supported the Basset classes at major shows. At Crufts, in 1935, she entered no fewer than sixty Bassets, Beagles, and Bloodhounds. She had the secret of producing hounds of substance and great bone which continued to be known as the Reynalton influence.

Mrs. Edith Grew had the breed since childhood. Her Maybush hounds were well known. Among the Walhamptons she purchased were Ch. Walhampton Ambassador, the period's top Basset, Walhampton Nicknack, and Walhampton Grazier. These hounds were the ancestors of her Chs. Pigeon, Partridge, Patience, and Plover. Other good hounds bred by her were Maybush Mallard, Martha, Puffin, and Marcus. Marcus was exported to America. Mrs. Grew seemed to be dogged with misfortune in breeding dogs. It was doubly sad when the outbreak of war prevented her campaigning Maybush Musket, her favorite hound, reckoned to be the best she had ever bred.

The war saw the closing of many kennels and severe reductions in every breed. Only thirteen Bassets were registered in 1939, and seven in 1940. Mrs. Grew and Mrs. Elms managed to breed a few hounds during these dark years and the breed still had a nucleus at the cessation of hostilities. Advancing years, however, prevented the two brave old ladies from breeding many dogs so the task of reconstructing the breed fell on the shoulders of Miss Peggy Keevil.

New blood was unobtainable in Britain and the introduction of outcross blood was a prime necessity. Miss Keevil purchased three hounds from France, all tricolors. They were Ulema de Barley, 1946, bred by M. Mallant; Aiglon des Marriettes, 1951, from Mme. Raulin; and Cornemuse de Blendocques bred by M. Leduc. All were fine hounds and accomplished the rejuvenation of the breed. Ulema was a prepotent sire in France. He had the most influence on British Bassets, siring some grand hounds which included littermates Chs. Grims Westward and Whirlwind. Aiglon was litter brother to France's top sire Azur Des Mariettes. He too sired some good hounds. The bitch Cornemuse could not have such an apparent influence as the dogs but nevertheless played her part. These hounds, with those Miss Keevil already had, refounded the breed in Britain. By the early 1950s it was in a healthy, if not numerous, position. The Grims kennel of dual purpose was winning on the bench and hunting successfully. From the kennel have come an impressive list of champions: Chs. Grims Wishful, 1940; Grims Warlock, 1946; Grims Doughnut, 1947; Grims Waterwagtail, 1949; Grims Useful, 1950; Grims Wideawake, 1951; Grims Willow, 1951; Grims Whirlwind, 1954; Grims Westward, 1954; Grims Gracious; and Grims Vapid. Just as the Walhamptons dominated things in their day, the Grims did in the 1950s and 1960s.

In the early 1950s the breed gradually crept out of the shadows. In 1953 Mrs. Angela Hodson was chiefly responsible for forming the Basset Hound Club. The original club had been disbanded in 1921 owing to a split between the show bench and hunting fraternities. Mrs. Hodson had the Rossingham kennels and was first Secretary of the reformed club. She was most fortunate in having Ch. Grims Willow in her kennel. This fine bitch bred Champions Rossingham Amber, Rossingham Badger, U.S. Ch. Rossingham Barrister and Rossingham Blessing, India Ch. Rossingham Brocade, and Rossingham Cosy. Amber and Badger in turn produced more champions. The Rossingham line had plenty of size and length, good bone, and quality.

Among the first to support the new club was the old stalwart Mrs. Grew. She was still keen though no longer breeding dogs. It was a sad blow when she passed away January 23, 1963.

Another to join the ranks was George Johnston who had owned some Reynalton hounds in 1939. He and his son, George Jr., disbanded their well-known kennel of Dandie Dinmonts and began breeding their Sykemoor Bassets. Rossingham Amber became a champion in their hands and was behind almost every Sykemoor hound. Mr. Johnston Sr. died in 1958 but his son kept the kennel going and bred Int. Ch. Sykemoor Blossom, Ch. Sykemoor Aimwell and Wiza. He exported many hounds that became champions in other countries. In 1959 he imported a young French hound named Hercule de L'Ombree. The Basset Hound Club purchased Lyn-Mar Acres Dauntless from the U.S.A. These two hounds proved useful outcrosses and produced winning progeny. Another addition to the already available American lines in Britain was Int. Ch. Bold Turpin of Blackheath imported by Mesdames McArthur-Onslow and Kewley. All three were fused successfully and were a decided advantage to the breed.

One of the last available Reynalton stud hounds was owned by Mrs. Wendy Jagger. With him and the Grims hounds she built up her noted Fochno kennel. Ch. Grims Whirlwind was her popular stud hound. Trumpeter of Reynalton was a valuable link with the past. Whirlwind sired Chs. Fochno Trinket and Trooper. This perfectly matched blue-mottled pair were virtually unbeatable and won many Brace classes. Trooper sired champions in the Grims kennel. Trinket produced winning puppies. Fochno stock founded kennels in Australia, Italy, U.S.A., and India.

The Townsons and their Kelperland prefix were also well known in Bloodhounds. Their Rossingham Badger was the first to attain the high honor of Best of Opposite Sex in Show at Windsor in 1958. He was the pillar of the kennel appearing in the pedigrees of most Kelperland hounds including Chs. Kelperland Artful and Baneful, Kelperland Blazer, and others. Their Bloodhound, Ch. Kelperland Scarcity, was reckoned to be one of the best ever bred up to that time.

Mrs. Hodson relinquished the post of Club Secretary which was filled by Mrs. Margaret Rawle of Minehead. Despite being a busy farmer's wife, she still found time to look after the interests of the club and her Barnspark hounds. She owned two Grims champions, Gracious and Vapid. From these were produced Ch. Barnspark Rakish, Vanity, Rollick, Rustic, Charity, and Teddyboy. Her export, Barnspark Loyalty, was a winner in Scandinavia and Barnspark Rambler gained a championship in the area.

Another great supporter and regular exhibitor was Mr. John Evans and the Stalwart hounds. He also had a celebrated kennel of

Ch. Fochno Trinket, a Crufts winner, with owner, Mrs. Wendy Jagger. Sire, Ch. Grims Whirlwind; dam, Sykemoor Gossip.

Ch. Grims Whirlwind, considered one of the top sires in England.

Bulldogs. With Grims blood and American bloodlines he bred Ch. Stalwart Debbie, exported to Italy, Stalwart Anna, Hardy, Hopeful, Blazer, and many others. Keen on the working side, he whipped-in for the Basset Hound Club Working Branch and organized many meets. Mr. Evans also managed West Lodge Hare Hounds for Lionel Woolner. This pack was bred from Bassets, Beagles, and Harriers. A type was established that reproduced itself and proved ideal for fast hunting.

One cannot give a complete resume of all the British kennels. Those mentioned are the oldest. Hounds from them can be found in many pedigrees. Their stock was used to found other kennels in Britain and abroad. It would be only fair to give mention to some of the later kennels which became ardent supporters. In Scotland were the Crochmaid dogs owned by Mrs. McArthur-Onslow and her daughter Mrs. Kewley. Mrs. McKnight had the Chantinghalls. The sole Irish kennel to the time of this book was Ballymaconnell operated by Mrs. Bridgham. The Harraton kennels of Messrs. Frost and Bell, Dalewell belonging to Mrs. Beard, and Robert Varon and Mr. Ghent's Highpeak were in the north and midlands of England. In the southern area were the kennels of Breightmet owned by Mrs. Baynes, Fredwell by Mrs. Wells, Mrs. Hunt and her Hunters-brook hounds, Mrs. Matthews carried the Hardacre prefix, Mrs. Rowett-Johns the Wingjays, and Mrs. Seiffert had the Maycombes. There were the Cornmeade breedings of W. W. Wells and the Appleline hounds of Mr. & Mrs. Douglas Appleton. Mrs. M. Nuttall bred from the Grims line. Stalwart Carol bred to Janvrins Dasher, both descendants from this line, produced Fivefold Chipmunk which was exported to the U.S. and acquired by your author. Gerard Kemp of Surrey became active and adopted the Buzbuz affix. His experience as a reporter for the "Daily Mail" made him the logical editor of the Basset Hound Club newsletter. His young wife, Sheila, took an active interest in the club's Working Branch.

Almost a century after the first Bassets were introduced into Britain, the breed registration for the year exceeded 800. Mrs. Seiffert was the Basset Hound Club Secretary, and the membership exceeded 300.

The Working Branch is the hunting group of the club and is discussed in the next chapter. The Basset Hound Club awards Working Certificates to hounds which prove themselves able hunters.

To become a bench champion a hound must win three Challenge Certificates under three different judges. Challenge Certificates are offered for competition by the Kennel Club at Championship shows, one for Dogs and one for Bitches. A judge is entitled to withhold any award if he does not feel the quality is good enough. Champions can compete with the other hounds. The winners of the various classes are called back to compete against other class winners of their own sex. Best Dog and Best Bitch receive Challenge Certificates. They then compete against each other for the Best in Show award.

Ch. Dreymin Appeline Coral, daughter of Grims Lager (Lyn-Mar Acres Dauntless ex Grims Glamour) ex Appeline Dawn (Int. Ch. Crochmaid Bold Turpin of Blackheath ex Appeline Serious). Both grandsires were U.S. imports.

Int. Ch. Sykemoor Blossom by Sykemoor Garnet (Trumpeter of Reynalton ex Ch. Rossingham Amber) ex Sykemoor Jealousy (Ch. Grims Whirlwind ex Sykemoor Gossip).

SIZES OF EARLY BRITISH BASSETS

	Onslow's NESTOR	Onslow's FINO	Millais's MODEL	Millais's GARRENNE	Ch. BOURBON	BLONDIN	BERTILLE	THEO
age	3	4½	7½	2½	4½	2½	3	8½
weight	39	39	46	38	40	35	33	35
height at shoulder	14	13	12	9¼	12	12	11	13
length nose to croup	36	33	32	29	35	33	33	35
girth of chest	24	24	25	24	25	23	22	22
girth of loin	22	23	21	16	19½	19½	19	19½
girth of head	15½	16½	17	13	15	14	14	13
girth of forearm	6½	6	6½	5	6	5½	5½	5
length occiput to tip	9	10	9	8	8½	8½	8½	8
girth of muzzle	9	8½	9½	7	8	8	7	6½
length of tail	12	11	11½	9	11½	12	11½	11
ears tip to tip			19	17	20	19	21	18½
height of forefeet			2½	2½	2½	3½	3	4

14

British Working Meets

THE field activities in Great Britain differ from those in the United States. The Working Meet is the equivalent of our Field Trial. Gerard Kemp, editor of the Basset Hound Club's newsletter in 1964, describes the activities as follows:

"There are only two packs of purebred Basset hounds at present being hunted in Britain. Both of them are built around the Grim's pack of Miss Peggy Keevil, one of the country's foremost breeders who lives in Inkpen, new Newbury, in Berkshire.

"Miss Keevil has loaned a bitch pack to friends in Gloucestershire and, herself, hunts with her main pack which forms the nucleus of the Basset Hound Club pack.

"Both packs hunt hares. The hunt staff in each case consists of a huntsman (responsible for the whole operation) and his 'whippers-in.' These usually number three or four and are the runners that move on the flanks of the hunt to prevent hounds straying or shooting off after distractions or causing trouble. They carry whips, more for cracking than actually striking hounds.

"The people who support the club hunts (also known as meets) travel from all over Britain, some staying overnight in hotels. Each time the hunt is held, it is in a different part of the country.

"The hounds hunt only hares. An average of about thirty people turn out each time to follow across the countryside on foot. Sometimes the followers have been known to cover as much as ten miles.

"The club has recently introduced a hunt uniform: traditional black hunting cap, white stock, with brown hunting jacket and yellow collars, white breeches, and brown knee-length stockings. Footwear is light studded boots. The huntsman carries a small copper hunting horn which he uses during the meet as a signal to hounds, 'whippers-in,' and followers.

"Miss Keevil drives her van to each meet and unloads about six or seven 'couple' of hounds, that is about twelve or fourteen dogs. These hounds are joined by those brought along by club members. The total number of hounds turning out is usually about fifteen to twenty couple. The introduction of a string of individual Bassets, to a pack trained to hunting, means that the hunt is straightaway handicapped. Over half the hounds turning out on a meet may have little idea of going in a hunting pack. The club's hunt staff realizes this only too well. The number of individual Bassets that, in fact, fall in with the Grim's hounds (all old hands at the hunting game) varies from meet to meet. Sometimes the hounds all seem to get the idea from the start; sometimes about half are left behind to hang around their owners, frolick with the other Bassets, or shoot off in other directions after odd rabbits or hares that the pack is not hunting; occasionally the situation arises where the trained Grim's hounds are going full steam after the hare, accompanied only by two or three couple of member's hounds.

"The Working Branch, as this section of the club is called, have weighed the pros and cons of all this and have come to the conclusion that more good is done by persevering with an attempt to encourage *all* the Bassets to do the job they were bred for, rather than taking out only *pack* hounds. After a few meets, the hunt's staff is rewarded by the knowledge that there are Basset Hounds (even ones who live in cities) that will hunt with the best of them.

"Our club chairman, Alex McDonald, who is also the Huntsman with the Working Branch pack, has recently written an appraisal of the practical side of hunting such a mixed bag. This is part of what he had to say, 'I am only too well aware that in trying to hunt a pack of six or seven couple of hounds that know me, and are entered to hare (put to hunt) together, with further hounds that neither know me nor a hare, I am being foolish to a degree. The chances of achieving good hunting under these conditions are minimal. I am astonished at every meet when we have a good run lasting maybe forty-five minutes. Why do I do it? The answer is not easily set out in detail but the main thing is that I believe the Basset should be kept as a working breed. To see a really happy Basset, you have to see him hunting; and I want members of the Club and Basset lovers, generally, to see this for themselves. I maintain that, until you have seen a Basset pack hunting, it is impossible for you to know and understand the Basset hound.

'There is a choice to be made between the club managing a professional pack and continuing with the quaint compromise which we now have of trying to weld together something of a regular pack plus anything else that turns up on the day. The implications of the first choice would be that we tried to stick to one part of the country and concentrated on building up a small, but regular, band of enthusiasts each with perhaps one or two couple of real workers. This would, I am sure, give much better hunting and make for far more kills. If we continue on the general lines of the past two or three seasons, we can only do so if the support we get from members takes a more helpful form.'

"Mr. McDonald's excellent account goes on to give general advice to novices turning out on hunting days. Always allow plenty of room around Miss Keevil's van when her pack hounds are unloaded. This is so that the 'whippers-in' will have a chance to move about. Members who think their hounds will go with the pack are advised to unleash their hounds to mingle with the Grims hounds. However, any signs of skittishness or nervousness and they are advised to clap the hound back on the lead straight away. Should a member's hound suddenly shoot off down the road giving tongue after a cat—and takes the pack with him—then the huntsman is quite definitely not amused.

"He goes on to give this practical advice to newcomers: 'We go into a field and I start to draw (work) with the regular hounds. If yours is a real novice, that has not hunted before, then keep him on a lead. If he is loose he won't know what it is all about and will make the job of the whippers-in far more difficult. Keep quiet and get about twenty yards behind me. Watch the hounds and when one gives tongue and the others go to him, picking up speed as I start trotting, then let yours go. With luck, we shall be away. If the hare scent is stale and we have to draw again, watch your hound carefully. He may come back to you, but, don't rate him (scold him), let him stay and run him up to the pack when they give tongue and are away again. Above all, keep him under control.'

"The worst thing, Mr. McDonald says, is for the hound to start hunting on his own hare independently of the main pack. Followers should do everything possible to avoid this: 'Make no mistake: a large field following behind the pack, particularly over plough, will put up hares very often indeed. Let me know by raising your hand above your head, by all means, but try to keep your hound quiet. At last, the pack is away, hunting fairly well. Your hound will have gone with them, in which case you should keep up as best you can so that, at the first check, you will be able to make sure your own hound is there. But, be careful, don't let him see or hear you. If he does, he may stop working and return to you. On the other hand, if this is your first meet, your hound may not have joined the pack. The only thing you can do is to keep your hound under control and try to be in position to turn him loose when the pack are near and in full cry.

'After about half an hour's run, during which time the hunt may have gone in a complete circle, the pace has dropped. Hounds are casting themselves, that is to say, they are spreading out a little, noses down, some of them feathering. This is the tricky part. I am standing still just inside the field. My whipper-in is just visible, halfway up the hedge, and, on the other side, another whipper-in can be seen streaking for the far corner on the far side of the other hedge. To the novice, it may look dull and boring. Nothing seems to be going on. The novices start to talk. Hounds lift their heads to listen and I am furious. It is, in fact, a critical moment. We all know that we are close to a tiring hare and, with patience and concentration, we shall find and kill. The novices get bored, breaking the concentration. This is the time to keep outside the field where the hounds are and quietly watch them through a gap in the hedge. Study them, see their different styles, watch Melody feather and whimper. See Gaffer go to her and try. Melody gives a funny yelp and they all go to her. Celery confirms the line and they are off again.

141

'A hunted hare plays a lot of tricks, but Bassets will work out most of them if so allowed. A hare may double back, and if the followers keep too close, the hounds' task becomes nearly impossible. Very often, when hounds are busy, followers will see a hare nearby in the next field. The best thing for them to do is to keep quiet. They should only let me know if they are absolutely certain the hare is the one being hunted.

'There are many times when it is most helpful if the followers join in and do something. For example, if hounds are heading for the road, and a follower is favourably placed, he can stop traffic. Again, if the pack splits up and a solitary hound is seen to slip off alone, a follower can tail it and send it back either by shouting 'Get to him' or slipping a lead around the hound's neck.' "

Mr. Kemp finished his article with another hunting expert's comments on overdoing the "holloaing," the term used when a hare is seen: "Recently I read about a brace of hare jumping up in the first field drawn. Hounds went away in view, but two groups of followers started to 'holloa,' then three more hares got up and more people 'holloaed,' until, each group was 'holloaing' its own particular hare and pandemonium was rife. The kindest thing to say about these particular vocalists is that they were quite inexperienced and that nobody told them anything. It does not require a very prolonged course of this sort of thing before the hounds become very flashy and wild, and, as Frostyface said of Mr. Puffington's hounds, 'always staring about for holloas and assistance.' A truly dreadful state of affairs."

The advice, offered by the authorities on Working Meets, should be carefully considered by the novices who plan to enter into the field work in countries that pattern their Working Branch after the British.

15

The Basset Hound in France

WE have already established how the Agasaeus and the Segusian spread from the Rhone district throughout the rest of France and other countries. As we study the topography of these countries, we can understand why some areas nurtured the griffons while others preferred the smooth coats.

In areas such as Ardennes, Artois, Saintonge, and Gascony, the smooth coat was a useful little hound. The terrain was grassy; much of it was fields, farmlands, and woods. The breeders in these provinces concentrated on the body structure and coloring that best suited their individual fancy and developed the characteristics that made up the distinctive strains.

The rocky land and thorny growth found in Brittany and Vendee called for a very different coat. Here the Griffon coat was necessary to protect the little dogs from the elements. Again the breeders concentrated on the points which they favored and by selective breeding developed their particular variety.

One thing all Frenchmen agree upon is that the Basset should be more agile than the dogs found in England and America. They prefer a smaller, lighter-boned hound. Throughout many writings on the subject of their use in the field, these dogs were expected to capture the hare. They often ran for hours, even days, in their pursuit, though they were also used to drive the game before the bowman's shaft in the days before gunpowder. Authors of books on sporting dogs have high praise for the work of the Basset.

Even in modern times, his work in the field is a mark of his quality. You will note that the Basset Griffon-Vendeen must pass certain tests before he is enscribed. The breeders of this variety, even now, set his price according to his hunting abilities. The Basset in France remains a useful, unspoiled-by-the-show-ring dog. Beauty, to the Frenchman, is based upon the attributes which best enable the dog to do a good day's work.

As time went on, some of the characteristics that were peculiar to certain varieties were found to be less desirable than those of others. These varieties began to die out while the others became more popular. In the mid-twentieth century, the most popular variety in France is the Basset Griffon-Vendeen. The Artesien-Normand is second in popularity. The Fauve de Bretagne and the Bleu de Gascogne have enough supporters to maintain a club to guard their purity, but they are definitely in a minority group.

16

The Basset of
Saint Hubert or
the Ardennais

THE Basset of Saint Hubert is a very old variety. It was preserved for a long time in the Ardennes but has now vanished. Its disappearance was probably largely due to its color which could be confused with the quarry in dense cover. These dogs were either shiny black-and-tan or uniformly red copper. Lacking in white, they were more difficult to see in heavy brush.

They were named in honor of the patron saint of the Abbey of St. Hubert in the province of Ardennes. It is your author's opinion that they descended from the hounds brought to the abbey when St. Hubert established it. He selected hounds from the Rhone district where the smooth-coat Agasaeus was known to have been. Undoubtedly, by selective breeding, he developed the type known as the Basset of St. Hubert, from the Agasaeus which was described as being a sorry-shaped, smooth-coated, low, slow-moving brute.

The Basset of St. Hubert was noted for its tremendous endurance.

It was able to hunt for several days without tiring. Its disposition was simple. It was used for hare hunting and was evidently first-class on roe. The Marquis de Fourdras praised the variety highly in his hunting tales.

Compared to the other very early varieties of Bassets, the St. Hubert's head was extremely large and the muzzle square. Its body was much heavier. The ear was set low, but not quite so low as the Gascogne. The voice was very strong, though the tone was slightly dull.

Description of the Basset of St. Hubert

GENERAL APPEARANCE—a strong dog very much of the Saint Hubert in miniature.

QUALITIES—straight on the track, fairly fast, very demanding, an excellent dog for hare and roe.

HEAD—well developed, large, but not wide.

SKULL—high and narrow, the occipital bone well developed.

MUZZLE—well developed, straight forehead.

EYES—brown, eyelids very loose.

NOSE—black, nostrils very open.

FLEWS—hanging and prominent.

EARS—long, soft, well set and pendant.

NECK—powerful, always with dewlaps.

SHOULDERS—sloping and dry.

BODY—strong (full), back wide, chest deep, abdomen slightly tucked up, quarters very muscular.

FORELEGS—half-crooked.

FEET—strong and closed (clenched), very sturdy.

TAIL—well set and carried with elegance.

COAT—short and dense on the body, finer on the skull.

COLOR—black-and-tan or reddish.

HEIGHT—about 14 inches.

ORIGIN—the Ardennes.

17

The Basset
Saintongeois

THIS is another of the French smooth coat varieties that has all but entirely vanished. At one time, it was popular in the province for which it was named, Saintonge, located on the eastern coast of France between Vendee and Gascony. The Saintongeois closely resembled the Bleu de Gascogne. Its smooth coat was black-and-white-mottled, though the ticking was not as profuse as that of the Gascogne, nor the black patches on the cloak as large. It was more vivid in color. The eye was brighter. The voice was loud and clear, high-pitched, rising to a howl when excited. The Saintongeois was slightly larger in size than the Gascogne.

This little hound was eager and industrious and fast on the track. In temperament, however, it was more delicate than other varieties and often lacked courage. This may be the chief reason for its disappearance.

Alain Bourbon favored these colorful hounds and bred them, as well as the Gascogne and the Artois, at his Villa of St. Hubert in Mayenne. A cross between the Saintongeois and the Gascogne proved a successful combination of the qualities of type and those of the hunt.

The present French Standard for the Artesian-Normand (formerly known as the Basset of Artois) disqualifies any ticking on the body that resembles blue-mottling. It is quite possible that this extremely impressive type of marking, seen in the American Basset, may have resulted from Bourbon's crosses between the Saintongeois, the Bleu de Gascogne, and the Artois, and was carried by imports from his bloodlines.

Description of the Basset Saintongeois

GENERAL APPEARANCE—pretty dog, a little lighter than the other varieties.
APTITUDES—powerful voice, very good on the track.
HEAD—very dry.
SKULL—narrow.
EYES—brown, dark, may sometimes be lighter.
NOSE—black, nostrils open.
FLEWS—well developed.
EARS—attached low, pendant, shorter than the Gascogne.
VOICE—high and clear, very noisy.
NECK—long and thin with less dewlap than the Gascogne.
SHOULDER—dry.
CHEST—deep but not very wide.
BACK—sufficiently long and firm.
BELLY—tucked up.
THIGH—massive and muscular.
BODY—long but not exaggerated.
FORELEGS—half-crooked.
FEET—harefoot.
COAT—fine and dense.
COLOR—black-and-tan, without cloak, will have some tan spots in undercoat.
HEIGHT—12 to 14 inches.
ORIGIN—Saintogne.

18

The Basset
Bleu de Gascogne

THESE very striking little smooth coat hounds were, like others, named for the region in which they became popular. Gascogny is a province located along the southern east coast of France. The terrain is suited to a smooth coat variety.

The Gascogne is somewhat smaller than the Artois. Though the latter is sometimes slightly mottled, the two are very different in type. The Gascogne always has a black head, black ears, and shows tan points over the eyes and on the cheeks. The body is always blue-mottled bearing large black spots. They are lighter in build than the Artois. The muzzle is snipier, a marked distinction.

The breed was almost extinct when M. Alain Bourbon, some time in the early 1900s, set to work to revive it. To accomplish this, he crossed Artois dogs with Gascogne bitches. Through many generations of selective breeding, he worked back toward the Gascogne type which has become well-fixed and very uniform.

The breed's coloring is seen in the American Basset, leading one to believe that this variety is in the background of our bloodlines. The Gascogne is noted for its particularly musical cry, and is very agile in the field.

Though the Gascogne is not the most abundant smooth coat in France, it is, in your author's opinion, the most eye-catching. It is one of the few varieties still pure in that country. The principal guardians of the variety belong to the Club du Bleu de Gascogne of which M. Boulous is the president.

Description of the Basset Bleu de Gascogne

GENERAL APPEARANCE—a strong and massive dog in relation to its size.

HEAD—rather long and well developed; skull high and narrow, peak well developed; stop slightly defined; muzzle well developed; nasal bone rather convex; lips not too pendulous.

EYES—dark brown; eye-lids not too closed.

NOSE—black, strong and long; nostrils well open.

EARS—folded, very long and nicely set on behind the line of the eye.

BODY—long; neck long and light, with dewlaps; shoulders lean and sloping; chest broad and deep; back rather long, belly drawn up.

LEGS—fore-legs half-crooked; hind-legs muscular; thighs not beefy but well-muscled.

FEET—rather long, toes rather arched; pads hard.

STERN—fine, set on low and carried upwards.

COAT—short and dense.

COLOR—tricolor, so-called trout-color, blue-mottled, white with black-and-tan spots above the eyes.

HEIGHT—at shoulder, from 13 to 15 inches.

WEIGHT—from 50 to 58 pounds.

19

The Basset
Artesien-Normand

THIRTY years ago, the Artesien-Normand was known as the Basset of Artois. It is the most popular of the smooth coats in France today. The English and American Bassets are primarily descendants of this variety.

The Artois district, for which they were named, is along the Belgian border. Its neighbor, to the west, is Ardennes, the province in which the Abbey of St. Hubert was located. Do not confuse this with Alain Bourbon's Villa of St. Hubert, built centuries later in Mayenne, to the southeast, and named for the patron saint. St. Hubert settled in the Ardennes area during the sixth century. It was here that he developed the Basset of St. Hubert.

The name of Le Couteulx will always be associated with the Basset of Artois, or Artesien-Normand, as it is now known. It was he who first set about to revive the breed when it had become almost extinct. By 1860, he had successfully built up the strain. Within the next twenty years, there were three types, previously discussed in the chapter on history. These were the Le Couteulx, the Masson, and the Lane, each named for their breeders.

These little hounds captured the hearts of those in all walks of life. Their versatility made them useful in many ways. They were held in high esteem by those who loved the sport of the chase. Peasants trained them to seek out the truffle, an edible tuber which was an important item in French cuisine. The ladies of the court found their quaintness very amusing, and the Basset became one of the few sporting dogs to be pampered in "madame's chambers." Authors filled their books with lengthy accounts of their abilities in the field. A noted French artist, Charles Olivier De Penne, abandoned the subjects of his award-winning career for the pleasure of painting portraits of animals that he admired before his death in 1897. Many pictures of Bassets are among his works.

The popularity of the Basset Artois continued to grow. M. Leon Verrier became a well-known breeder and perfected a uniformity of type which was accepted in the show ring. He produced many champions, among them Ch. Mosquetaire who was sold to Alain Bourbon. M. Ferdinand Pinel owned Meteore and Galathee. Other leading breeders, through the years, were: M. A. Cann, M. le comte de Champs, M. A. Coste, M. A. Faure, M. Gosselin, M. le vicomte de Peufeilhous, M. le baron de Segonzac who owned Ch. Troubadour, M. Villatte des Prugnes, M. Leparroux, and M. Jean Rothea.

In 1910, the Basset Artois Club was formed. The name was later changed to the Club du Basset Artesien-Normand.

The British and American breedings were directed toward large and heavy dogs. In France, the fanciers aimed for a well-built but not too heavy Basset which was capable of fulfilling its part as a running dog. The variety was used on foxes, as well as rabbits, and actually captured the rabbits.

M. Jean Rothea, current president of the Artesien-Normand Club, wrote that the breedings have been considerably reduced during the 1960s. A sickness has plagued their rabbits. As the Basset has become a specialist at this quarry, there was fear that the rabbit would become extinct unless the number of dogs was minimized. M. Rothea censures the size of American breedings. His sympathies are echoed by M. Abel Desamy, head of the Club du Griffon Vendeen, who states, "I disapprove of your dogs' excessive heaviness, which to my opinion, is a handicap for hunting."

Although earlier descriptions state that these hounds often have small black spots, or ticking, the latest Standard disqualifies any resemblance to a blue-mottled appearance. The Artesien-Normand's size varies greatly, from 10½ to 14½ inches. The depth of its muzzle is much greater than that of the Bleu de Gascogne or of the Saintongeois.

Description of the Artesien-Normand

GENERAL APPEARANCE—a long dog, longer than his size calls for; standing firm, balanced and well made; clearly indicating his great ancestry.

HEAD—domed, of medium width; the cheeks formed, · not by muscles as in the Bulldog, but only by skin which makes one or two folds on them; above all, the head must have a lean appearance.

SKULL—the stop marked, but without exaggeration; the occipital bump (la bosse de chasse) prominent.

FOREFACE—of average length; fairly wide, and slightly convex before the nose.

EYES—large, dark, and with a calm, serious expression; the red of the lower eyelid may appear.

EARS—attached low, never above the line of the eye; soft, fine in texture, narrow when coming from the skull, curling inwards, corkscrew fashion at the tips (en tire-bouchonnées), ending in a point.

NOSE—black and large, coming a little over the lip; nostrils full and wide.

NECK—fairly long, with dewlap, but not exaggerated.

SHOULDERS—round, strong, and short; well muscled.

FOREFEET—short, heavy-boned, crooked, or half-crooked, or less than half-crooked provided there is a principal of crookedness sufficiently visible, but never with the pastern displaced in front; the front of the forelegs presents several folds of skin under the articulation of the first joint.

FEET—poised upright, unless toes turn out without malformation of shape from carrying body; the feet of the Basset allow going where difficult terrain prohibits larger dogs; they leave the imprint in soft earth comparable to larger hounds.

CHEST—sternum is prominent; chest has average descent, is wide and rounded.

The Basset Artesien-Normand.

RIBS—rounded, compensating for their lack of depth by their roundness.

BACK—wide and well supported.

LOIN—slightly tucked up.

FLANK—full and descending downward.

THIGH—very muscular; should form with the rump in a spherical mass.

TAIL—well attached, long, strong at the base, tapered to the end, carried upright but never over the back. It is absolutely forbidden to support the tail of the dog while in the showring.

HINDQUARTERS—a little aslant, giving a slight dip to the rump.

HOCKS—slightly bent and strong; often has one or two folds of skin, with a slight projection of skin on the posterior part.

COAT—close, short, not too fine, and waterproof.

COLOR—tricolor, or orange-and-white; the tricolor dogs marked with tan heads, black backs, and tan extremities; white tips preferred but not essential.

SIZE—from 10½ inches to 14½ inches.

GAIT—calm but brisk.

DISQUALIFICATIONS—undershot; straight legs; though not a disqualification, the black spots are not to be encouraged; any resemblance to a blue-mottled effect is a disqualification.

FAULTS—flat head; wide forehead; flat ears, thick where attached; too high or large ears; short neck; sway-back; forefeet touching or knuckled; flat ribs; flat feet; toes separated; twisted or too-long stern; flat or close-set hocks—eyes too bright to give the proper expression.

20

The Basset
Griffon-Vendeen

THESE sturdy little hounds are the most popular
variety of Basset in France at this time. As with the other types,
they were named for the area in which they were developed. Vendee is on the east coast, midway between Brittany and Gascony.
The terrain is very rugged, rocky, covered with thorny undergrowth,
and requires a coat that can withstand such elements. The Griffon-
Vendeen is the perfect dog for hunting in this area. The dogs give
the impression of the Otterhound in miniature and are very ap-
pealing to see. Although there are none in America at this time, I
am sure if there were they would capture the fancy of many who
admire both the Basset and the Otterhound.

The Griffon-Vendeen is slightly larger than the Basset Artesien-
Normand, which is seldom over 13 inches in France, though the
Standard allows 14 inches. The Vendeen is divided into two
types: the "petite taille" (small size) ranging from 13 to 14 inches,
and the "grande taille" (large size) which are from 14 to 16 inches.
They are somewhat more short-coupled than the smooth coat
varieties, though still long in comparison to their height. In color,

they are tawny, red-and-white, tricolored, black-and-white, and solid color. They are not brilliant in these colors, as are the smooth coats. The shaggy coat often takes on a similarity to the coloring of a rabbit.

The Griffon-Vendeen's description closely resembles that of the Segusian hound of 400 A.D. which was mentioned in an earlier chapter on the History of the Breed. The Segusian, named after a Celtic tribe that inhabited the banks of the Rhone in the second century, was said to be a shaggy little dog, and the most highbred were described as being the ugliest. Though this is not very flattering to the breed, one can visualize that the shaggiest coats and the shortest legs may have seemed unsightly to certain writers. It is quite probable, as with other Griffon varieties of Bassets, that the Segusians were used to develop the variety which became known as the Basset of Vendee.

In 1881, in *The Book of the Dog,* Vero Shaw wrote of the Griffon-Vendeen: "He has straight but short legs; rough, hard coat, with a woolly undergrowth, colour iron-grey, or white with brown markings, or all white. They are powerfully built, not very long, and possess a speed which is extraordinary when one thinks of their shape. A M. d'Incourt de Metz owns a pack of these hounds that run down their hare easily in two or three hours."

Sir Everett Millais wrote of them in 1897: "Some twenty years ago, when I was at school in Paris, I used to frequently adjourn to a dog dealer's, whose shop still exists close to the Arc de Triomphe. I was there not long since, and on asking Mons. Ravry if he could find me a couple of Basset Griffons, such as he used to keep years ago, he informed me that he could not, unless I put my hand very deeply into my pocket. These hounds were like Otter-hounds in form and texture of coat, likewise of the same colour, and quite as big as the largest smooth coated Bassets over here (England). About 1874–1875, I used to see a similar type of hound in the variety class at our leading shows, owned first by Dr. Seton, and then by Mr. J. C. Macdona. This hound is registered in the Kennel Club stud book as Romano, and a very handsome specimen he was; hard coated and workmanlike, brown-grey grizzle in colour, and always admired by the hunting men who saw him either on the bench or in the ring.

"Since then I have never seen a hound like Romano in type

157

and size, except Mrs. Ellis's Rocket, which though not of exactly quite the same character, comes nearer to that mentioned above than the smaller varieties, which might pass better as rough-coated dachshounds than do duty at our show as Basset Griffons.

"In the last class of these hounds which I had the pleasure of inspecting there were no less than four types, and if he included those owned by His Royal Highness, the Prince of Wales, I may, I think, correctly state that there are five different types of Basset Griffons in this country at the present time."

Sir Everett felt that the Griffon fanciers in England had not obtained the cream of the crop, nor bred with such dedication, as did those interested in the smooth coats. The classes were very small even though M. Pussant sent entries from his kennels in France. Some beautiful specimens were seen from the Sandringham kennels of King Edward VII who always had an affection for this variety, using them for work and exhibiting them at the leading shows. His Sandringham Bobs was bred in his kennels and took many first prizes. Both King Edward and Queen Alexandria were very fond of the Bassets kept in their kennels.

At one time, it seemed likely that the Basset Griffon would equal the popularity of the smooth coat variety in England. However, they never "caught on." Special classes were provided for them, but the entries remained scant. The Sandringham entries usually appeared, plus those of Rev. W. Shield, Mr. F. Lowe, Mr. H. Jones, and George Krehl, who kept a few. The strongest kennel in Britain was Mrs. Tottie's, located in Bell Busk, near Leeds. Her Tambour, Truelove, Pervence, and Treasure were excellent specimens. Pierrot and Ringwood, owned by Mrs. E. Gerrich, Westbury-on-Tyne, Bristol, were of fine quality. Mr. Krehl's Trompette d'Erpent and Bonnbonneau were very hardy in appearance and carried the Otterhound head. As only a few people found these little hounds interesting, they never became numerous. It is believed that Mrs. Tottie eventually crossed hers with the smooth-coats in her kennel.

In France, the Griffon did not meet with this same fate. A coat such as theirs was needed, in many areas, to protect the dogs from the jagged rocks and thorny undergrowth. Here the variety began to increase. In 1895, the entry was strong at the Paris Exposition. M. Geoffrey Saint-Hilaire exhibited many fine examples. The type of Comte d'Elva commanded attention. A club was formed in 1898, with the count as president.

The Griffon was established. The Vendeen's quality of fascination for the pursuit of the hare was noted. The terrain of the region was very difficult for briquets (beagles) and impossible for the horse, so it was necessary to go by foot. M. Paul Dezamy chose a large Basset, less rapid than the briquets, but capable of catching the hare, for his breedings. These caused a sensation by their quality of beauty and hunting ability. In 1924 at the trials of Venerie, he won the Grand Prize of Honour of the Venerie Francaise.

The Club Griffon-Vendeen was founded May 30, 1907. M. Paul Dezamy became president, and the Comte d'Elva was made honorary president. A Standard was adopted. Two types were acknowledged: the large, and the small. The Standard, except for the size, was the same for both. M. Dezamy was not, at that time, a strict, uncompromising judge. His standards allowed for a beautiful subject of maximum size. They still say in the French exhibition ring, "Forty-two Dezamy." On St. Hubert Day in 1933, M. Paul Dezamy passed away. The presidency was passed on to his son-in-law, Mr. Abel Desamy (note the difference in spelling), whose young son, Hubert was also bitten by the "canine fever."

M. Hubert Desamy wrote in a recent letter to me, "My father (M. Abel Desamy) concluded very rapidly that the same standard for the large and small Basset was an anomaly. A particular standard was adopted for the small Basset. In order to permit the best selection of the race, the Club Register automatically inscribed the subjects of parents already inscribed. A dog, after one year of age, must be visited by a qualified judge of the Club Griffon-Vendeen to be enrolled on the Club Register. Also, our club preceded, by five years, the Société Centrale Canine Francaise, in the examination of conformation." In short, before a dog is certified, he is examined by delegates from all parts of France. These Bassets are in a large numerical majority, equaling the races of the fourth and fifth groups.

The Grande Basset (large) is the "type Dezamy," an ideal dog for hunting hare. He has a majestic head and a robust body. According to M. Daubigne, "The pace, accuracy, and initiative are natural qualities of the Basset Griffon-Vendeen." The Petite Basset (small)

Hardy de Vendee, owned by M. Abel Desamy in 1963, considered very good type.

Ch. Farino (1901–1909), first dog selected by M. Paul Dezamy, had been chosen as the model of the breed.

is above all a good rabbit chaser. His hair protects him and he is impervious to stone, has a good voice, leads well, and is able to keep pace with dogs of larger size.

STANDARD OF THE BASSET GRIFFON-VENDEEN

Large Size—14 to 16 inches

GENERAL ASPECTS—long structure, but not excessive; straight paw; tail nimble and gay; coat rugged, neither silky nor woolly, on all the body; head is an essential point; ears are long, covered with shorter hair; the eyes are not hidden by the long hair surrounding them.

HEAD—eyes, large, without white, and are intelligent and beautiful in expression; the red of the eyelid is not apparent; the eyebrow is bushy, but does not obscure the eye.

EARS—supple, narrow, and delicate, covered with slightly shorter hair than on the body, yet long; they end in an oval; well rounded inside, reaching under the nose, attached under the line of the eye.

SKULL—deep, long, not too large; pronounced under the eye, moderate stop; well developed occipital bone.

MUZZLE—long, deep, square to the end; slightly arched between eye and nostril; lips encircled by mustache.

NOSE—black; well developed; good openings.

NECK—long and strong; thick near shoulders; without dewlap.

SHOULDERS—flat, lean and sloping; well set to the body.

CHEST—long and deep.

RIBS—round.

FLANK—on the whole descending.

BACK—long, large and straight, beginning to arch at the junction with the loins.

LOINS—solid, full, and agile.

RUMP—very beefy and muscular.

TAIL—set high; large at base, tapering toward tip; carried erect when alert; is long.

FORELEGS—the knees do not touch; the forearm is thick; the wrist agile; the toes longish and slightly separated.

THIGH—well muscled.

HOCKS—large and well bent.

FEET—thick, compressed, and tough; claws solid.

COAT—thick, tough, not too silky and long, nor too woolly; fringe is not too abundant.

COLOR—solid color is tawny, less dark, like the fur of the rabbit in color; two-color is white and orange, white and black, white and color of rabbit fur, white and grey, or white and rust; tricolor is white, black, and tan; white, tan, and rabbit-color; or white, grey, and tan.

HIDE—thick, often marble on the tricolors, white and black, or white and grey.

SIZE—14 to 16 inches, with allowance for exceptional males; the female can be less than two centimeters as tall as the male.

GAIT—walks easily to three gaits.

SERIOUS FAULTS—flat and short head, spotted or discolored nose, light eyes, pointed muzzle, uneven jawbone, flat ears devoid of hair or attached too high, too short neck, not minimum nor maximum size indicated, sagging back, forelegs touching or bowed from supporting too much weight, flat feet, toe variations, too angular or too straight hocks, flat thigh, coat too woolly, silky, or curly.

Small Size—13 to 14 inches

GENERAL ASPECTS—a vigorous little dog with an agile, long body; inclined to haughtiness; coat long and hard without exaggeration; expressive head; ears well set under a line of the eye and furnished with long hair.

EYES—large and intelligent, showing no white, red of eyelid not apparent; hair surrounding the upper lid does not obscure the eye.

EARS—soft, narrow, covered with long hair, ending in an oval; the ear does not reach the end of the nose; it is well attached under the line of the eye.

SKULL—slightly domed, somewhat long, not too large, prominent stop, well developed occipital bone.

MUZZLE—shorter than the Grande variety but nevertheless very long; arched between the eye and nostrils; lips circled by a good mustache.

162

The Rallye Bocage, 1947: M. Desamy, master
of the hunt, and Bassets Griffon-Vendeen.

NOSE—black, well developed, with wide openings.

SHOULDERS—oblique, well moulded to the body.

CHEST—deep but not large.

RIBS—moderately round.

LOINS—well supported and muscular.

CROUP—muscular and full.

TAIL—set high; large at the base and tapering to the tip; not very long; carried erect.

MEMBERS—also strong structure but proportioned to size.

FORELEGS—straight; the forearm thick.

THIGHS—muscular and a little rounded.

HOCKS—large, well bent.

FEET—not very large, tough pad, good claw, tight paws.

COAT—hard, not too silky or woolly, less fringe than the larger variety.

COLOR—same colors accepted as larger variety, tawny color not recommended.

SIZE—13 to 14 inches, deviation of one-half inch allowed.

GAIT—very free and easy.

SERIOUS FAULTS—body too long; head too flat; poorly shaped nostrils, or discolored nostrils; light eyes; uneven jawbone; pointed muzzle; flat or high-set ears with insufficient fur; weak back; crooked forelegs; hocks too straight or crooked; flat thighs; tail too long or too curved; coat of insufficient density, frizzy, woolly, or silky.

CLUB RULES

All questions on the repertoire of the Club are to be addressed to the secretary and accompanied by:

1. pedigree of dog.
2. lawful inscription.

To be inscribed, the dogs have to earn at least the notice of very good, first or second prize in Open Class in a French exhibition recognized by the Central Canine Society.

3. The dogs are admitted by a special commission of three members, one of which must be a judge qualified by the Club. In case of false declarations, the committee will scratch the dog inscribed and remove from the Club the person who signed the sheet, if there is bad evidence. The right of inscription is ten francs ($2.04) per dog.

Inscription is limited to members of the Basset and Briquet Griffons Vendeens.

CERTIFICATE OF HUNT—B.C.

Rules: Members of the club, in order to pass for the Certificate of the Hunt, will have to present their pack for our examination. The dogs, maximum three, must enter competition assigned by the club, and be recognized for their qualities of the hunt, by three members of the jury of judges. The secretary must be notified at least one month prior to the examination.

Judges are designated by the committee and chosen from the list of the Société Centrale Canine and by the Society of Venerie for our Group.

Only dogs between the ages of twelve months and six years will be admitted to run for the B.C. They must state whether they are entered for the L.O.F., the R.D.N., or the R.-C.G.V. At each presentation, the number of candidates must be more than three. The owner must accompany them on the chase.

The land for the hunt may be supplied by the owner, if he prefers, and obtains permission. Travel expenses must be paid by the owner. Before awarding a certificate, the examiners take into consideration: age, the quality of the voice, when it is used, how it is used, scenting ability, and if they hold true to the line with few mistakes. The following is a scale of points for judging: temperament, 6; nose, 9; voice, 6; persistence and checking of the track, 9; aptitude to rally with a pack, 6; steadiness and vigor, 6; aptitude to chase and capture the rabbit, 6; what the dog does upon seeing the hare, 5; total 53. The following scale of points applies to shooting-tests: temperament, 6; nose, 8; voice, 7; disposition as a pack-dog and persistence on the track, 8; eagerness and vigor, 8; ability under fire, 8; ability to return, 8; total 53.

The dogs must obtain a minimum of 40 points, to qualify for "Excellent," with the coefficients of 20, 19, or 18. They must obtain a minimum of 35 points, with the coefficients of 17, 16, or 15, to qualify for "Very good," and 30 points, with 14, 13, or 12, to qualify for "Good."

To gain the title B.C., the dogs must have gained one of the awards as mentioned above.

The most important breeders of the Basset Griffon-Vendeen have been: M. Baillet of Rouen; M. de la Brosse of Orvault; and M. Collignon, Ch. Davy, M. Paul Dezamy, M. Gillet, M. G. Lepinay, M. F. Sellier, M. Joulia, M. Abel Desamy plus M. Hubert Desamy, all of Vendee. In the 1920's, M. Dezamy, Comte d'Elva, M. Guilli-hand, le Marquis de Maulean, and M. Leon Verrier were qualified judges.

21

The Basset
Fauve de Bretagne

O NE of the Griffons, the Basset Fauve de Bretagne, is one of the minority varieties in France. Named for the province of Brittany, where it was developed, the dog's rough coat is suitable to the rocky area along the northeast coast. In color, they are fawn or tawny-red, whichever you prefer to call it. These Bassets give one the impression of greater activity and sharpness than the other varieties. Perhaps this is due to their alert expression and short-coupled body, not usually associated with Bassets.

Their lack of popularity may be due to the fact that they are more riotous, harder to break, and do not possess the temperament usually associated with Bassets. They also lack the beautiful voice for which the breed is noted.

Nevertheless, they are useful little hounds in the particular region. A few breeders prize them highly and the strain is kept in its purity. Their interests are guarded by the Club du Basset Fauve de Bretagne, headed by M. Pambrun.

GENERAL APPEARANCE—a coarse, long dog.

HEAD—long; high and domed skull; stop slightly developed; long muzzle; lips not too pendulous.

EYES—dark in color.

NOSE—long and black; nostrils wide open.

EARS—nicely set on, rounded at the tips and slightly folded.

BODY—coarse and long; neck short and heavy; shoulders clean and sloping; chest deep and broad; back long and rather straight; belly slightly tucked up; loins long and broad.

LEGS—nearly straight, thighs beefy and round.

FEET—longish and strong; nails developed; pads hard.

STERN—of medium length, carried upwards.

COAT—wiry and broken; not too long; softer on the skull and ears.

COLOR—tawny red or fawn, white markings.

HEIGHT—at shoulder, about 12 inches.

WEIGHT—about 50 pounds.

22

The Basset Hound in Australia

THE Basset was known in Australia about 1893. The introduction of the breed in that country was influenced by Sir Everett Millais. For health reasons, Sir Everett visited that country between 1880 and 1884. Soon after, Levity was imported by Mrs. Anderson and Mr. McLoughlin.

The breed, however, became nearly extinct until 1957. Two bitches were then imported, both in whelp, and one dog. The bitches were Grims Caroline and Brockleton Country Maid. The breed was fostered by Mr. John Mackinolty and Harold Spira. According to Keith Goodwin of Wentworthville, New South Wales, Mackinolty's interest was still high in 1964. Though he did not show his dogs, he was considered a valuable judge. Mr. Spira, a distinguished veterinarian in Sydney, continued breeding his Bassets as well as contributing his services as an all-breed judge. Among others, his kennel contained Ch. Grims Vanquish, Fochno Chestnut, and Sykemoor Dauphin, all British imports, at stud. He did a great deal to popularize the breed and progeny from his famous Chevalier Kennels appear at shows throughout the area.

Ch. Chevalier Walter, owned by K. Goodwin.

Ch. Streatham Matilda (Blandville Punchinello ex Huckleberry Antoinette); breeder, Mrs. H. C. Duffell; owner, K. Goodwin.

Some of the winning show dogs in Australia are: Mr. & Mrs. R. Sharpe's male, Garrene Garabaldi; their bitch, Ch. Chevalier Davina; Capt. G. Brandis's dog, Ch. Dewburn Jasper, and his bitch, Ch. Chevalier Undine; Keith Goodwin's male, Ch. Chevalier Walter; S. Goodwin's bitch, Ch. Streatham Matilda; Miss Hamilton's bitch, Chevalier Yvonne; C. Salter's bitch, Rymrac Blanche; P. Warley's bitch, Ch. Chevalier Nicole; and R. Buchanan's male, Ch. Santana-Mendeville My Count, which was imported from the United States.

Many of the bitches had no show career. They were used only for producing litters. Two of these, Mrs. B. Hoares's Chevalier Fiona and Mr. C. Salter's Dewburn Velvet Lady, are considered fine matrons by Keith Goodwin. For many years, there were a limited number of bloodlines with which to work. Improvement was difficult. New blood was imported from the Kelperland stock by Miss Koster. Mrs. B. Walcott, of the Sepaki kennels, imported Grims Compass and some Fredwell stock.

Entries vary greatly in Sydney, ranging from 23 to 40, and even to as high as 100 at the Specialty. The Basset Club holds a point score competition annually. Dogs are judged on points won at designated all-breed shows once a month. For the 1964 season, Capt. G. Brandis's Ch. Dewburn Jasper, five-and-one-half years old and holder of over 100 Challenge Certificates, and Keith Goodwin's Ch. Chevalier Walter were high contenders in males. Miss Hamilton's tricolor, Chevalier Yvonne, led the bitch class.

By 1964, approximately 200 Bassets were being exhibited. The total population ran over 1,000. Field trials, or hunts, had not yet been attempted. The leading kennels included: Chevalier, Sepaki, Leal Ami, Rymrac, Davton, and Goodwin, in Sydney, and the Blandville kennels in Melbourne.

23

The Basset Hound
in Canada

THE first recognized Basset listed in the records of the Canadian Kennel Club was Al's Janet, 143155. Registered May 24, 1936, owned by N. E. Pegg, Janet was the product of two United States Bassets: Al's Chief of Geneseo and Woelk's Beauty. In 1903, however, there had been three Bassets entered in a show. Two types, rough and smooth, were listed in the officially recognized breeds in Canada in 1907. One of the oldest breeders in this country is still very active. Miss Dorothy Grant obtained Maytime Peg O'My Heart from the Fogelsons of Greenly Hall fame.

According to Fred Carter, president of the Basset Hound Club of Canada in 1964, Rosemary Osselton and Mr. Sees are the prominent fanciers in British Columbia. Mr. & Mrs. Stevenson of Portage le Prarie, Manitoba are very active. Many have imported dogs from the United States. Mr. & Mrs. Henderson of Peterboro have become well-known. They imported Lyn-Mar Acres Bojangles from Mr. & Mrs. M. L. Walton. Their Canadian and Bermuda Ch. Gremlyn's Aida has been a familiar entry at the shows. Mr. & Mrs. Ron Purdy of Cheltenham purchased the American and Canadian Ch. Whistle-down's Commando from Milt Stringer of Algonac, Michigan. The Purdy's had taken bitches to Commando several times before they bought him. He is the sire of many Canadian champions. The Barlindall kennel of Dick Pike, Maidstone, is known in both the United States and Canada. Mr. & Mrs. A. Digby Hunt of Ottawa based their lines on the Notrenom breedings of Richard Basset and the Santana-Mandeville line of Paul and Helen Nelson. Fred and Betty Carter purchased Ch. Schauffelein's Logy from the Purdys as a puppy. They imported Ch. Hartshead Fanfare from Emil and Effie Seitz. Their progeny, Ch. Westacre's Queen Valli and Ch. Westacre's Little Nell, as well as Valli's son Ch. Westacre Hugo the Red, have made their mark in the show ring in both Canada and the United States. Ch. Schauffelin's Logy is the top Basset at the shows in Canada to date.

The Basset Hound Club of Canada was formed by active fanciers in 1959. The first Specialty show was held in 1960. By 1964 the Basset had risen to great heights in popularity. It was third in Hound registration, preceded only by the Beagle and the Dachshund. An entry of twenty-five was not uncommon at the larger shows. Field trials and obedience work were not much in evidence though interest was being aroused in both of these fields of endeavor.

24

The Basset Hound
in New Zealand

I N September of 1960, the first Basset Hound arrived in New Zealand. She was three months old at the time, an Australian bitch named Longview Mandy, sired by Fochno Chestnut out of Calumet Camille. Mrs. E. Janee imported her and, later, two more, also from Australia. These were a male, Longview Loyalty, and a bitch in whelp, Ch. Calumet Camille, which had been bred to one of the top Australian studs, Ch. Blandville Bugler. Eight puppies were whelped in December of 1961. These, and their owners, formed the nucleus of the Basset Hound Club which was organized in 1962.

Gallic Jacobite and Lyndhaze Limerick were imported in 1960 from Australia by Mrs. Slade of Christchurch. Dr. J. Hall brought in Chrochmaid Bramble (sire, Barnspark Rakish; dam, Sungarth Bashful) from England.

Further imports were made from England and Australia. Most of them were descended from the Grims line. By 1964, there were about sixty Bassets scattered throughout the North and South Islands according to Peggy Blakeney of Auckland. To that time, all litters were sired or produced by an import.

Hubert d'Andagium (Napoleon de Bramble ex Longview Mandy), from the first litter sired by a New Zealand dog; breeder, Mrs. Joyce Beasley; owner, Peggy Blakeney.

The New Zealand Basset Hound Club was formed in October 1962 by a group of enthusiastic owners who felt that, in spite of the small number of hounds in the country, the breed should be popularized and an attempt should be made to improve the quality. This eager group tracked down imports, litters, promoted classes at shows, and kept members informed of world-wide Basset news by means of a bulletin. Twice a year they gathered together all available Bassets and held a "ribbon parade." Through the Club's publicity efforts they attracted television coverage and press writeups which brought the breed before the public.

To this time, they held no Working Meets. In 1964, Sqn. Ldr. D. A. Duthie took two hounds, one bred by Mrs. Seiffert (Grims Westward ex Lucky) and the other by Miss Keevil (Vanguard ex Welfare), from England to New Zealand. With the help of Duthie and his trained Bassets, plans were made to form a Working Branch.

The breed is judged under the English Standard. To become a New Zealand champion, eight C.Cs. (Challenge Certificates) under five judges are required. The first New Zealand-bred champion was Mr. P. Blakeney's Grantham Daveau, followed by Mrs. D. Cavanaugh's Tartarin Fleurette. Many were capable of capturing Challenge Certificates, Best Sporting Dog, Best Puppy in Show, Best Hound in Show, and Best in Show, at all-breed shows.

Some of the more prominent owners were: J. Ward of Auckland, who owned Tartarin Isadore (Chevalier Hillary ex Carillon Garland); Mrs. Andrew of Paparimu, owner of Napoleon de Bramble (Ch. Gallic Jacobite ex Chrochmaid Bramble); Mrs. Cox of Warkworth, owner of a litter by Fivefold Bounty ex Bertie of Haven; B. Norris, owner of Tartarin Honore; Mr. & Mrs. Mechaelis of Wellington; and Mr. David Fifield.

25

The Basset Hound
in Other Countries

THE first Basset in Iran was Dixie's Darrus Darling H-772297 (Ch. Bradley's Southern Rebel ex Dixie Queen Suzette), registered with the American Kennel Club. In 1957 her breeder-owners, Mr. & Mrs. William Cox, were sent to Iran by their employer, an American oil company. Their young female puppy went with them. Her dam remained in the United States. There were few dogs of any breed in Iran, no veterinarian, no dog food, no other supplies commonly taken for granted. As Abby (Dixie's Darrus Darling) advanced in years, the Cox's felt the need to add more Bassets to the household. In 1963, they imported Braun's Jolly Nicholas (Ch. Trojan Echoes Erebus ex Trojan Echoes Persephone) from your author's kennel. The Coxes undertook to raise a litter of puppies. Abby and Nicky produced three males and four females in 1964. Many of the puppies were sold to other Americans who would one day return home; some went to British owners; two remained with the breeders.

The only known Basset owner in South America is Juan Pedro Jacobsen who resides in Bogota, Colombia.

Bibliography

The American Kennel Club. *The Complete Dog Book*. Garden City Books, Garden City, New York.

Beilby, Walter. *The Dog in Australia*. Melbourne, 1897.

Blanchere, H. de la. *Les Chiens de Chasse*. Paris, 1875.

Blaze, Elzear. *Histoire du Chien*. Paris, 1846.

Bourbon, Alain. *Nos Bassets Français*. Laval, Imprimerie-Librarie, V. A. Goupil.

Bylandt, Le Comte Henri de. *Les Races De Chiens, Vol. I, Chiens de Chasse*. Deventer (Hollande) A. E. Klewer, about 1903.

Chaillou, Baron de Lage de. *Du Chien de Chasse*. Paris, 1866.

Couteulx, Comte de le. *Manuel de Venerie Française (Second Edition)*. Paris, 1902.

Dalziel, Hugh. *British Dogs (Second Editon) Vol. I*. Upcott Gill, 170 Strand, W.C., London, 1879.

Dezamy, M. Paul. *Du Basset Griffon Vendeen*. Club du Griffon Vendeen.

Jardin, Sir John Buchanan. *Hounds of the World*. Charles Scribner's Sons, New York, 1937.

Lee, Rawdon B. *Modern Dogs, Sporting Division, New Edition Vol. II, Modern Dogs of Great Britain and Ireland*. Horace Cox, Field Office: Windsor House, Beams Bldg. E. C., 1897.

Leighton, Robert. *The Complete Book of the Dog*. Cassell and Co., Ltd., London, 1952.

Masson, Edmond le. *Traite de la Chasse Souterraine di Blaireau et du Renard*. Paris, 1865.

Shaw, Vero. *The Book of the Dog*. Cassell, Petter, Galpin. & Co., New York, Paris, & London, 1881.

Shields, G. O. *The American Book of the Dog*. Rand McNally & Co., Chicago, 1891.

Smith A. Croxton. *Hounds and Dogs, The Lonsdale Library Vol. XIII*. J. B. Lippincott Co., Philadelphia, Penna., printed in Great Britain.

Stables, Gordon. *The Practical Kennel Guide*. London, 1876.

Stonehenge. *The Dog in Health and Disease (Fourth Edition)*. London, 1887.

Stonehenge. *Stonehenge on the Dog (Fourth Edition)*. Longmans & Co., 1887.

Verrier, Léon. *Les Bassets Français et Leur Utilisation*. Paris, 1921.

Watson, James. *The Dog Book Vol. II*. William Heineman, London, 1906.

Dixie's Darrus Darling.

Mrs. Cox with Nicholas, Abby, and the first litter in Iran.

Field Ch. Germann's Albertino with owner, Bill Germann.

Field Ch. Newton's Black Jackolyn and owner, Kenneth McWilliams.

Ch. Hanns Acres Piccolo Pierre, bred by June Hanns Moiseff, out of Am. and Can. Ch. Look's Dandy ex Bedelia of Pioneer.

Part II

GENERAL CARE AND TRAINING OF YOUR DOG

by

Elsworth S. Howell

Milo G. Denlinger

A. C. Merrick, D.V.M.

Introduction

THE normal care and training of dogs involve
no great mysteries. The application of common sense and good
judgment is required, however. The pages that follow distill the
combined experience and knowledge of three authorities who have
devoted most of their lives to dogs.

Milo Denlinger wrote many books out of his rich and varied
experience as a breeder, exhibitor and owner of a commercial
kennel. Elsworth Howell has been a fancier since young boyhood
and claims intimate knowledge of 25 different breeds; he is an American Kennel Club delegate and judge of the sporting breeds. Dr.
A. C. Merrick is a leading veterinarian with a wide practice.

The chapter on "Training and Simple Obedience" covers the
basic behavior and performance every dog should have to be accepted by your friends, relatives, neighbors and strangers. The good
manners and exercises described will avoid costly bills for damage
to the owner's or neighbor's property and will prevent heartbreak-
ing accidents to the dog and to the people he meets. The instructions are given in simple, clear language so that a child may easily
follow them.

"The Exhibition of Dogs" describes the kinds of dog shows, their
classes and how an owner may enter his dog and show it. If one
practices good sportsmanship, shows can be enjoyable.

The chapter on feeding offers sound advice on feeding puppies, adult dogs, the stud dog and the brood bitch. The values of proteins, carbohydrates, fats, minerals and vitamins in the dog's diet are thoroughly covered. Specific diets and quantities are not given because of the many variations among dogs, even of the same breed or size, in their individual needs, likes, dislikes, allergies, etc.

"The Breeding of Dogs" contains the fundamental precepts everyone who wishes to raise puppies should know. Suggestions for choosing a stud dog are given. The differences among outcrossing, inbreeding and line breeding are clearly explained. Care tips for the pregnant and whelping bitch will be found most helpful.

The material on "External Vermin and Parasites" gives specific treatments for removing and preventing fleas, lice, ticks and flies. With today's wonder insecticides and with proper management there is no excuse for a dog to be infested with any of these pests which often cause secondary problems.

"Intestinal Parasites and Their Control" supplies the knowledge dog owners must have of the kinds of worms that invade dogs and the symptoms they cause. While drugs used for the removal of these debilitating dog enemies are discussed, dosages are not given because it is the authors' and publisher's belief that such treatment is best left in the hands of the veterinarian. These drugs are powerful and dangerous in inexperienced hands.

The chapter on "Skin Troubles" supplies the information and treatments needed to recognize and cure these diseases. The hints appearing on coat care will do much to prevent skin problems.

One of the most valuable sections in this book is the "instant" advice on "FIRST AID" appearing on pages 95-98. The publisher strongly urges the reader to commit this section to memory. It may save a pet's life.

The information on diseases will help the dog owner to diagnose symptoms. Some dog owners rush their dogs to the veterinarian for the slightest, transitory upsets.

Finally, the chapters on "Housing for Dogs" and "Care of the Old Dog" round out this highly useful guide for all dog lovers.

Training and Simple Obedience

E VERY DOG that is mentally and physically sound can be taught good manners and simple obedience by any normal man, woman, or child over eight years old.

Certain requirements must be met by the dog, trainer and the environment if the training is to be enjoyable and effective. The dog must be rested and calm. The trainer must be rested, calm, gentle, firm, patient and persistent. The training site should be dry, comfortable and, except for certain exercises, devoid of distractions.

Proper techniques can achieve quick and sure results. Always use short, strong words for commands and always use the *same* word or words for the same command. Speak with authority; never scream or yell. Teach one command or exercise at a time and make sure the dog understands it and performs it perfectly before you proceed to the next step. Demand the dog's undivided attention; if he wavers or wanders, speak his name or pat him smartly or jerk his leash. Use pats and praise plentifully; avoid tidbit training if at all possible because tidbits may not always be available in an emergency and the dog will learn better without them. Keep lessons short; when the dog begins to show boredom, stop and do not resume in less than two hours. One or two ten-minute lessons a day should be ample, especially for a young puppy. Dogs have their good and bad days; if your well dog seems unduly lazy, tired, bored or off-color, put off the lesson until tomorrow. Try to make lessons a joy, a happy time both for you and the dog, but do demand and get the desired action. Whenever correction or punishment is needed, use ways and devices that the dog does not connect with you; some of these means are given in the following instructions. Use painful punishment only as a last resort.

"NO!"

The most useful and easily understood command is "NO!" spoken in a sharp, disapproving tone and accompanied with a shaking finger. At first, speak the dog's name following with "NO!" until the meaning of the word—your displeasure—is clear.

"COME!"

Indoors or out, let the dog go ten or more feet away from you. Speak his name following at once with "COME!" Crouch, clap your hands, pick up a stick, throw a ball up and catch it, or create any other diversion which will lure the dog to you. When he comes, praise and pat effusively. As with all commands and exercises repeat the lesson, until the dog *always* comes to you.

THE FIRST NIGHTS

Puppies left alone will bark, moan and whine. If your dog is not to have the run of the house, put him in a room where he can do the least damage. Give him a hard marrow bone and a strip of beef hide (available in supermarkets or pet shops and excellent as a teething pacifier). A very young puppy may appreciate a loud-ticking clock which, some dog trainers say, simulates the heart-beat of his former litter mates. Beyond providing these diversions, grit your teeth and steel your heart. If in pity you go to the howling puppy, he will howl every time you leave him. Suffer one night, two nights or possibly three, and you'll have it made.

The greatest boon to dog training and management is the wooden or wire crate. Any two-handed man can make a ⅜" plywood crate. It needs only four sides, a top, a bottom, a door on hinges and

6

with a strong hasp, and a fitting burlap bag stuffed with shredded newspaper, cedar shavings or 2" foam rubber. Feed dealers or seed stores should give you burlap bags; be sure to wash them thoroughly to remove any chemical or allergy-causing material. The crate should be as long, as high and three times as wide as the dog will be full grown. The crate will become as much a sanctuary to your dog as a cave was to his prehistoric ancestor; it will also help immeasurably in housebreaking.

HOUSEBREAKING

The secret to housebreaking a healthy normal dog is simple: take him out every hour if he is from two to six months old when you get him; or the first thing in the morning, immediately after every meal, and the last thing at night if he is over six months.

For very young puppies, the paper break is indicated. Lay eight or ten layers of newspapers in a room corner most remote from the puppy's bed. By four months of age or after two weeks in a new home if older, a healthy puppy should not need the paper *IF* it is exercised outdoors often and *IF* no liquid (including milk) is given after 5 P.M. and *IF* it is taken out not earlier than 10 P.M. at night and not later than 7 A.M. the next morning.

When the dog does what it should when and where it should, praise, praise and praise some more. Be patient outdoors: keep the dog out until action occurs. Take the dog to the same general area always; its own traces and those of other dogs thus drawn to the spot will help to inspire the desired action.

In extreme cases where frequent exercising outdoors fails, try to catch the dog in the act and throw a chain or a closed tin can with pebbles in it near the dog but not on him; say "NO!" loudly as the chain or can lands. In the most extreme case, a full 30-second spanking with a light strap may be indicated but be sure you catch the miscreant *in the act*. Dog memories are short.

Remember the crate discussed under "THE FIRST NIGHTS." If you give the dog a fair chance, he will NOT soil his crate.

Do not rub his nose in "it." Dogs have dignity and pride. It is permissible to lead him to his error as soon as he commits it and to remonstrate forcefully with "NO!"

7

COLLAR AND LEASH TRAINING

Put on a collar tight enough not to slip over the head. Leave it on for lengthening periods from a few minutes to a few hours over several days. A flat collar for shorthaired breeds; a round or rolled collar for longhairs. For collar breaking, do NOT use a choke collar; it may catch on a branch or other jutting object and strangle the dog.

After a few days' lessons with the collar, attach a heavy cord or rope to it without a loop or knot at the end (to avoid snagging or catching on a stump or other object). Allow the dog to run free with collar and cord attached a few moments at a time for several days. Do not allow dog to chew cord!

When the dog appears to be accustomed to the free-riding cord, pick up end of the cord, loop it around your hand and take your dog for a walk (not the other way around!). DON'T STOP WALKING if the dog pulls, balks or screams bloody murder. Keep going and make encouraging noises. If dog leaps ahead of you, turn sharply left or right whichever is *away* from dog's direction— AND KEEP MOVING! The biggest mistake in leash training is stopping when the dog stops, or going the way the dog goes when the dog goes wrong. You're the leader; make the dog aware of it. This is one lesson you should continue until the dog realizes who is boss. If the dog gets the upper leg now, you will find it difficult to resume your rightful position as master. Brutality, no; firmness, yes!

If the dog pulls ahead, jerk the cord—or by now, the leash— backward. Do not pull. Jerk or snap the leash only!

JUMPING ON PEOPLE

Nip this annoying habit at once by bumping the dog with your knee on his chest or stepping with authority on his rear feet. A sharp "NO!" at the same time helps. Don't permit this action when you're in your work clothes and ban it only when dressed in glad rags. The dog is not Beau Brummel, and it is cruel to expect him to distinguish between denim and silk.

8

THE "PROBLEM" DOG

The following corrections are indicated when softer methods fail. Remember that it's better to rehabilitate than to destroy.

Biting. For the puppy habit of mouthing or teething on the owner's hand, a sharp rap with a folded newspaper on the nose, or snapping the middle finger off the thumb against the dog's nose, will usually discourage nibbling tactics. For the biter that means it, truly drastic corrections may be preferable to destroying the dog. If your dog is approaching one year of age and is biting in earnest, take him to a professional dog trainer and don't quibble with his methods unless you would rather see the dog dead.

Chewing. For teething puppies, provide hard marrow bones and beef hide strips (see "THE FIRST NIGHTS" above). Every time the puppy attacks a chair, a rug, your hand, or any other chewable object, snap your finger or rap a newspaper on his nose, or throw the chain or a covered pebble-laden tin can near him, say "NO!" and hand him the bone or beef hide. If he persists, put him in his crate with the bone and hide. For incorrigible chewers, check diet for deficiencies first. William Koehler, trainer of many movie dogs including *The Thin Man's* Asta, recommends in his book, *The Koehler Method of Dog Training,* that the chewed object or part of it be taped crosswise in the dog's mouth until he develops a hearty distaste for it.

Digging. While he is in the act, throw the chain or noisy tin can and call out "NO!" For the real delinquent Koehler recommends filling the dug hole with water, forcing the dog's nose into it until the dog thinks he's drowning—and he'll never dig again. Drastic perhaps, but better than the bullet from an angry neighbor's gun, or a surreptitious poisoning.

The Runaway. If your dog wanders while walking with you, throw the chain or tin can and call "COME!" to him. If he persists, have a friend or neighbor cooperate in chasing him home. A very long line, perhaps 25 feet or more, can be effective if you permit the dog to run its length and then snap it sharply to remind him not to get too far from you.

Car Chasing. Your dog will certainly live longer if you make him car-wise; in fact, deathly afraid of anything on wheels. Ask a friend or neighbor to drive you in *his* car. Lie below the windows and as your dog chases the car throw the chain or tin can while your neighbor or friend says "GO HOME!" sharply. Another method is to shoot a water pistol filled with highly diluted ammonia at the dog. If your dog runs after children on bicycles, the latter device is especially effective but may turn the dog against children.

The Possessive Dog. If a dog displays overly protective habits, berate him in no uncertain terms. The chain, the noisy can, the rolled newspaper, or light strap sharply applied, may convince him that, while he loves you, there's no percentage in overdoing it.

The Cat Chaser. Again, the chain, the can, the newspaper, the strap—or the cat's claws if all else fails, but only as the last resort.

The Defiant, or Revengeful, Wetter. Some dogs seem to resent being left alone. Some are jealous when their owners play with another dog or animal. Get a friend or neighbor in this case to heave the chain or noisy tin can when the dog relieves himself in sheer spite.

For other canine delinquencies, you will find *The Koehler Method of Dog Training* effective. William Koehler's techniques have been certified as extremely successful by directors of motion pictures featuring dogs and by officers of dog obedience clubs.

OBEDIENCE EXERCISES

A well-mannered dog saves its owner money, embarrassment and possible heartbreak. The destruction of property by canine delinquents, avoidable accidents to dogs and children, and other unnecessary disadvantages to dog ownership can be eliminated by simple obedience training. The elementary exercises of heeling, sitting, staying and lying down can keep the dog out of trouble in most situations.

The only tools needed for basic obedience training are a slip collar made of chain link, leather or nylon and a strong six-foot leather leash with a good spring snap. Reviewing the requirements and basic techniques given earlier, let's proceed with the dog's schooling.

Heeling. Keep your dog on your left side, with the leash in your left hand. Start straight ahead in a brisk walk. If your dog pulls ahead, jerk (do not pull) the leash and say "Heel" firmly. If the dog persists in pulling ahead, stop, turn right or left and go on for several yards, saying "Heel" each time you change direction.

If your dog balks, fix leash *under* his throat and coax him forward by repeating his name and tapping your hip.

Whatever you do, don't stop walking! If the dog jumps up or "fights" the leash, just keep moving briskly. Sooner than later he will catch on and with the repetition of "Heel" on every correction, you will have him trotting by your side with style and respect.

Sit. Keeping your dog on leash, hold his neck up and push his rump down while repeating "Sit." If he resists, "spank" him lightly several times on his rump. Be firm, but not cruel. Repeat this lesson often until it is learned perfectly. When the dog knows the command, test him at a distance without the leash. Return to him every time he fails to sit and repeat the exercise.

Stay. If you have properly trained your dog to "Sit," the "Stay" is simple. Take his leash off and repeat "Stay" holding your hand up, palm toward dog, and move away. If dog moves toward you, you must repeat the "sit" lesson until properly learned. After your dog "stays" while you are in sight, move out of his sight and keep repeating "Stay." Once he has learned to "stay" even while you are out of his sight, you can test him under various conditions, such as when another dog is near, a child is playing close to him, or a car appears on the road. (Warning: do not tax your dog's patience on the "stay" until he has learned the performance perfectly.)

Down. For this lesson, keep your dog on leash. First tell him to "sit." When he has sat for a minute, place your shoe over his leash between the heel and sole. Slowly pull on the leash and repeat "Down" while you push his head down with your other hand. Do this exercise very quietly so that dog does not become excited and uncontrollable. In fact, this performance is best trained when the dog is rather quiet. Later, after the dog has learned the voice signal perfectly, you can command the "Down" with a hand signal, sweeping your hand from an upright position to a downward motion with your palm toward the dog. Be sure to say "Down" with the hand signal.

For more advanced obedience the following guides by Blanche Saunders are recommended:

The Complete Novice Obedience Course
The Complete Open Obedience Course
The Complete Utility Obedience Course (with Tracking)
Dog Training for Boys and Girls (includes simple tricks.)
All are published by Howell Book House at $3.00 each.

OBEDIENCE TRIALS

Booklets covering the rules and regulations of Obedience Trials may be obtained from The American Kennel Club, 221 Park Avenue South, New York 3, N.Y. In Canada, write The Canadian Kennel Club, 667 Yonge Street, Toronto, Ontario.

Both these national clubs can give you the names and locations of local and regional dog clubs that conduct training classes in obedience and run Obedience Trials in which trained dogs compete for degrees as follow: CD (Companion Dog), CDX (Companion Dog Excellent), UD (Utility Dog), TD (Tracking Dog) and UDT (Utility Dog, Tracking.)

The Exhibition
of Dogs

NOBODY should exhibit a dog in the shows unless he can win without gloating and can lose without rancor. The showing of dogs is first of all a sport, and it is to be approached in a sportsmanlike spirit. It is not always so approached. That there are so many wretched losers and so many supercilious winners among the exhibitors in dog shows is the reason for this warning.

The confidence that one's dog is of exhibition excellence is all that prompts one to enter him in the show, but, if he fails in comparison with his competitors, nobody is harmed. It is no personal disgrace to have a dog beaten. It may be due to the dog's fundamental faults, to its condition, or to inexpert handling. One way to avoid such hazards is to turn the dog over to a good professional handler. Such a man with a flourishing established business will not accept an inferior dog, one that is not worth exhibiting. He will put the dog in the best possible condition before he goes into the ring with him, and he knows all the tricks of getting out of a dog all he has to give. Good handlers come high, however. Fees for taking a dog into the ring will range from ten to twenty-five dollars, plus any cash prizes the dog may win, and plus a bonus for wins made in the group.

Handlers do not win all the prizes, despite the gossip that they do, but good handlers choose only good dogs and they usually

13

finish at or near the top of their classes. It is a mistake to assume that this is due to any favoritism or any connivance with the judges; the handlers have simply chosen the best dogs, conditioned them well, and so maneuvered them in the ring as to bring out their best points.

The services of a professional handler are not essential, however. Many an amateur shows his dogs as well, but the exhibitor without previous experience is ordinarily at something of a disadvantage. If the dog is good enough, he may be expected to win.

The premium list of the show, setting forth the prizes to be offered, giving the names of the judges, containing the entry form, and describing the conditions under which the show is to be held, are usually mailed out to prospective exhibitors about a month before the show is scheduled to be held. Any show superintendent is glad to add names of interested persons to the mailing list.

Entries for a Licensed show close at a stated date, usually about two weeks before the show opens, and under the rules no entry my be accepted after the advertised date of closing. It behooves the exhibitor to make his entries promptly. The exhibitor is responsible for all errors he may make on the entry form of his dog; such errors cannot be rectified and may result in the disqualification of the exhibit. It therefore is wise for the owner to double check all data submitted with an entry. The cost of making an entry, which is stated in the premium list, is usually from six to eight dollars. An unregistered dog may be shown at three shows, after which he must be registered or a statement must be made to the American Kennel Club that he is ineligible for registry and why, with a request for permission to continue to exhibit the dog. Such permission is seldom denied. The listing fee for an unregistered dog is twenty-five cents, which must be added to the entry fee.

Match or Sanctioned shows are excellent training and experience for regular bench shows. Entry fees are low, usually ranging from fifty cents to a dollar, and are made at the show instead of in advance. Sanctioned shows are unbenched, informal affairs where the puppy may follow his owner about on the leash and become accustomed to strange dogs, to behaving himself in the ring, and to being handled by a judge. For the novice exhibitor, too, Sanctioned shows will provide valuable experience, for ring procedure is similar to that at regular bench shows.

The classes open at most shows and usually divided by sex are as follows: Puppy Class (often Junior Puppy for dogs 6 to 9 months old, and Senior Puppy for dogs 9 to 12 months); Novice Class, for dogs that have never won first in any except the Puppy Class; Bred-by-Exhibitor Class, for dogs of which the breeder and owner are the same person or persons; the American-bred Class, for dogs whose parents were mated in America; and the Open Class, which is open to all comers. The respective first prize winners of these various classes compete in what is known as the Winners Class for points toward championship. No entry can be made in the Winners Class, which is open without additional charge to the winners of the earlier classes, all of which are obligated to compete.

A dog eligible to more than one class can be entered in each of them, but it is usually wiser to enter him in only one. A puppy should, unless unusually precocious and mature, be placed in the Puppy Class, and it is unfair to so young a dog to expect him to defeat older dogs, although an exceptional puppy may receive an award in the Winners Class. The exhibitor who is satisfied merely that his dog may win the class in which he is entered is advised to place him in the lowest class to which he is eligible, but the exhibitor with confidence in his dog and shooting for high honors should enter the dog in the Open Class, where the competition is usually the toughest. The winner of the Open Class usually (but by no means always) is also the top of the Winners Class; the runner-up to this dog is named Reserve Winners.

The winner of the Winners Class for dogs competes with the Winners Bitch for Best of Winners, which in turn competes for Best of Breed or Best of Variety with any Champions of Record which may be entered for Specials Only. In the closing hours of the show, the Best of Breed or Best of Variety is eligible to compete in the respective Variety Group to which his breed belongs. And if, perchance, he should win his Variety Group, he is obligated to compete for Best Dog in Show. This is a major honor which few inexperienced exhibitors attain and to which they seldom aspire.

Duly entered, the dog should be brought into the best possible condition for his exhibition in the show and taught to move and to pose at his best. He should be equipped with a neat, strong collar without ornaments or spikes, a show lead of the proper length, width and material for his size and coat, and a nickel bench chain of strong links with which to fasten him to his bench. Food such as the dog is used to, a bottle of the water he is accustomed to drink, and all grooming equipment should be assembled in a bag the night before departure for the show. The exhibitor's pass, on which the dog is assigned a stall number, is sent by mail by the show superintendent and should not be left behind, since it is difficult to have the pass duplicated and it enables the dog's caretaker to leave and return to the show at will.

The time of the opening of the show is stated in the premium list, and it is wise to have one's dog at the show promptly. Late arrivals are subject to disqualification if they are protested.

Sometimes examination is made by the veterinarian at the entrance of the show, and healthy dogs are quickly passed along. Once admitted to the show, if it is a "benched" show, it is wise to find one's bench, the number of which is on the exhibitor's ticket, to affix one's dog to the bench, and not to remove him from it except for exercising or until he is to be taken into the ring to be judged. A familiar blanket or cushion for the bench makes a dog feel at home there. It is contrary to the rules to remove dogs from their benches and to keep them in crates during show hours, and these rules are strictly enforced. Many outdoor shows are not "benched," and you provide your own crate or place for your dog.

At bench shows some exhibitors choose to sit by their dog's bench, but if he is securely chained he is likely to be safe in his owner's absence. Dogs have been stolen from their benches and others allegedly poisoned in the shows, but such incidents are rare indeed. The greater danger is that the dog may grow nervous and insecure, and it is best that the owner return now and again to the bench to reassure the dog of his security.

The advertised program of the show permits exhibitors to know the approximate hour of the judging of their respective breeds. Although that time may be somewhat delayed, it may be depended upon that judging will not begin before the stated hour. The dog should have been groomed and made ready for his appearance in the show ring. When his class is called the dog should be taken unhurriedly to the entrance of the ring, where the handler will receive an arm band with the dog's number.

When the class is assembled and the judge asks that the dogs be paraded before him, the handler should fall into the counter-clock-

16

wise line and walk his dog until the signal to stop is given. In moving in a circle, the dog should be kept on the inside so that he may be readily seen by the judge, who stands in the center of the ring. In stopping the line, there is no advantage to be gained in maneuvering one's dog to the premier position, since the judge will change the position of the dogs as he sees fit.

Keep the dog alert and facing toward the judge at all times. When summoned to the center of the ring for examination, go briskly but not brashly. It is unwise to enter into conversation with the judge, except briefly to reply to any questions he may ask. Do not call his attention to any excellences the dog may possess or excuse any shortcomings; the judge is presumed to evaluate the exhibit's merits as he sees them.

If asked to move the dog, he should be led directly away from the judge and again toward the judge. A brisk but not too rapid trot is the gait the judge wishes to see, unless he declares otherwise. He may ask that the movement be repeated, with which request the handler should respond with alacrity. It is best not to choke a dog in moving him, but rather to move him on a loose lead. The judge will assign or signal a dog to his position, which should be assumed without quibble.

Fig. 1

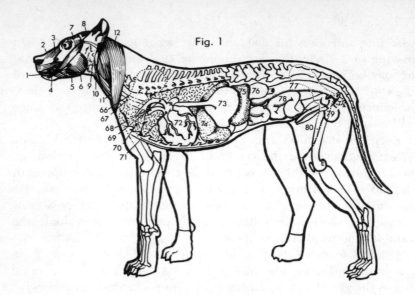

Fig. 2

Fig. 1

1 Orbicularis oris.
2 Levator nasolabialis.
3 Levator labii superioris proprius (levator of upper lip).
4 Dilator naris lateralis.
5 Zygomaticus.
6 Masseter (large and well developed in the dog).
7 Scutularis.
8 Parotid Gland.
9 Submaxillary Gland.
10 Parotido-auricularis.
11 Sterno-hyoideus.
12 Brachio-cephalicus.

(Between figures 8 and 12 on top the Elevator and Depressor muscles of the ear are to be seen.)

66 Œsophagus (gullet).
67 Trachea (wind pipe).
68 Left Carotid Artery.
69 Anterior Aorta.
70 Lungs.
71 Posterior Aorta.
72 Heart.
73 Stomach.

74 Liver. (The line in front of Liver shows the Diaphragm separating Thoracic from Abdominal cavity.)
75 Spleen.
76 Kidney (left).
77 Rectum.
77A Anal Glands (position) just inside rectum.
78 Intestine.
79 Testicle.
80 Penis.
   (Midway between 76 and 79 is the seat of the Bladder and behind this the seat of the Prostate gland in males, uterus in females.)

Fig. 2

Section of Head and Neck.

1 Nasal septum.
2 Tongue.
3 Cerebrum.
4 Cerebellum.
5 Medulla oblongata.
6 Spinal Cord.
7 Œsophagus (gullet).
8 Trachea (wind pipe).
9 Hard palate.
10 Soft palate.
11 Larynx, containing vocal cords.

18

The Feeding of Dogs, Constitutional Vigor

IN selecting a new dog, it is quite as essential that he shall be of sound constitution as that he shall be of the correct type of his own particular breed. The animal that is thoroughly typical of his breed is likely to be vigorous, with a will and a body to surmount diseases and ill treatment, but the converse of this statement is not always true. A dog may have constitutional vigor without breed type. We want both.

Half of the care and effort of rearing a dog is saved by choosing at the outset a puppy of sound constitution, one with a will and an ability to survive and flourish in spite of such adversity and neglect as he may encounter in life. This does not mean that the reader has any intention of obtaining a healthy dog and ill treating it, trusting its good constitution to bring it through whatever crises may beset it. It only means that he will save himself work, expense, and disappointment if only he will exercise care in the first place to obtain a healthy dog, one bred from sound and vigorous parents and one which has received adequate care and good food.

The first warning is not to economize too much in buying a dog. Never accept a cull of the litter at any price. The difference in first cost between a fragile, ill nourished, weedy, and unhealthy puppy and a sound, vigorous one, with adequate substance and the will to survive, may be ten dollars or it may be fifty dollars. But whatever it may be, it is worthwhile. A dog is an investment and it is not the cost but the upkeep that makes the difference. We may save fifty dollars on the first price of a dog, only to lay out twice or five times that sum for veterinary fees over and above what it would cost to rear a dog of sound fundamental constitution and structure.

The vital, desirable dog, the one that is easy to rear and worth the care bestowed upon him, is active, inquisitive, and happy. He is sleek, his eyes free from pus or tears, his coat shining and alive, his flesh adequate and firm. He is not necessarily fat, but a small amount of surplus flesh, especially in puppyhood, is not undesirable. He is free from rachitic knobs on his joints or from crooked bones resultant from rickets. His teeth are firm and white and even. His breath is sweet to the smell. Above all, he is playful and responsive. Puppies, like babies, are much given to sleep, but when they are awake the sturdy ones do not mope lethargically around.

An adult dog that is too thin may often be fattened; if he is too fat he may be reduced. But it is essential that he shall be sound and healthy with a good normal appetite and that he be active and full of the joy of being alive. He must have had the benefit of a good heredity and a good start in life.

A dog without a fundamental inheritance of good vitality, or one that has been neglected throughout his growing period is seldom worth his feed. We must face these facts at the very beginning. Buy only from an owner who is willing to guarantee the soundness of his stock, and before consummating the purchase, have the dog, whether puppy or adult, examined by a veterinarian in order to determine the state of the dog's health.

If the dog to be cared for has been already acquired, there is nothing to do but to make the best of whatever weaknesses or frailties he may possess. But, when it is decided to replace him with another, let us make sure that he has constitutional vigor.

THE FEEDING AND NUTRITION OF
THE ADULT DOG

The dog is a carnivore, an eater of meat. This is a truism that cannot be repeated too often. Dog keepers know it but are prone to disregard it, although they do so at their peril and the peril of their dogs. Despite all the old-wives' tales to the contrary, meat does not cause a dog to be vicious, it does not give him worms nor cause him to have fits. It is his food. This is by no means all that is needed to know about food for the dog, but it is the essential knowledge. Give a dog enough sound meat and he will not be ill fed.

The dog is believed to have been the first of the animals that was brought under domestication. In his feral state he was almost exclusively an eater of meat. In his long association with man, however, his metabolism has adjusted itself somewhat to the consumption of human diet until he now can eat, even if he cannot flourish upon, whatever his master chooses to share with him, be it caviar or corn pone. It is not to be denied that a mature dog can survive without ill effects upon an exclusive diet of rice for a considerable period, but it is not to be recommended that he should be forced to do so.

Even if we had no empirical evidence that dogs thrive best upon foods of animal origin, and we possess conclusive proof of that fact, the anatomy and physiology of the dog would convince us of it. An observation of the structure of the dog's alimentary canal, superimposed upon many trial and error methods of feeding, leads us to the conclusion that a diet with meat predominating is the best food we can give a dog.

To begin with, the dental formation of the dog is typical of the carnivores. His teeth are designed for tearing rather than for mastication. He bolts his food and swallows it with a minimum of chewing. It is harmless that he should do this. No digestion takes place in the dog's mouth.

The capacity of the dog's stomach is great in comparison with the size of his body and with the capacity of his intestines. The amounts of carbohydrates and of fats digested in the stomach are minimal. The chief function of the dog's stomach is the digestion of proteins. In the dog as in the other carnivores, carbohydrates

21

and fats are digested for the most part in the small intestine, and absorption of food materials is largely from the small intestine. The enzymes necessary for the completion of the digestion of proteins which have not been fully digested in the stomach and for the digestion of sugars, starches, and fats are present in the pancreatic and intestinal juices. The capacity of the small intestine in the dog is not great and for that reason digestion that takes place there must be rapid.

The so-called large intestine (although in the dog it is really not "large" at all) is short and of small capacity in comparison with that of animals adapted by nature to subsist wholly or largely upon plant foods. In the dog, the large gut is designed to serve chiefly for storage of a limited and compact bulk of waste materials, which are later to be discharged as feces. Some absorption of water occurs there, but there is little if any absorption there of the products of digestion.

It will be readily seen that the short digestive tract of the dog is best adapted to a concentrated diet, which can be quickly digested and which leaves a small residue. Foods of animal origin (flesh, fish, milk, and eggs) are therefore suited to the digestive physiology of the dog because of the ease and completeness with which they are digested as compared with plant foods, which contain considerable amounts of indigestible structural material. The dog is best fed with a concentrated diet with a minimum of roughage.

This means meat. Flesh, milk, and eggs are, in effect, vegetation partly predigested. The steer or horse eats grain and herbage, from which its long digestive tract enables it to extract the food value and eliminate the indigestible material. The carnivore eats the flesh of the herbivore, thus obtaining his grain and grass in a concentrated form suitable for digestion in his short alimentary tract. Thus it is seen that meat is the ideal as a chief ingredient of the dog's ration.

Like that of all other animals, the dog's diet must be made up of proteins, carbohydrates, fats, minerals, vitamins, and water. None of these substances may be excluded if the dog is to survive. If he fails to obtain any of them from one source, it must come from another. It may be argued that before minerals were artificially supplied in the dog's diet and before we were aware of the existence of the various vitamins, we had dogs and they (some of them) appeared to thrive. However, they obtained such substances in their foods, although we were not aware of it. It is very likely that few dogs obtained much more than their very minimum of requirements of the minerals and vitamins. It is known that rickets were more prevalent before we learned to supply our dogs with ample calcium, and black tongue, now almost unknown, was a common canine disease before we supplied in the dog's diet that fraction of the vitamin B complex known as nicotinic acid. There is no way for us to know how large a portion of our dogs died for want of some particular food element before we learned to supply all the necessary ones. The dogs that survived received somewhere in their diet some of all of these compounds.

PROTEIN

The various proteins are the nitrogenous part of the food. They are composed of the amino acids, singly or in combination. There are at least twenty-two of these amino acids known to the nutritional scientists, ten of which are regarded as dietary essentials, the others of which, if not supplied in the diet, can be compounded in the body, which requires an adequate supply of all twenty-two. When any one of the essential ten amino acids is withdrawn from the diet of any animal, growth ceases or is greatly retarded. Thus, a high protein content in any food is not an assurance of its food value if taken alone; it may be lacking in one or more of the essential ten amino acids. When the absent essential amino acids are added to it in sufficient quantities or included separately in the diet, the protein may be complete and fully assimilated.

Proteins, as such, are ingested and in the digestive tract are broken down into the separate amino acids of which they are composed. These amino acids have been likened to building stones, since they are taken up by the blood stream and conveyed to the various parts of the animal as they may be required, where they are deposited and re-united with other complementary amino acids again to form bone and muscles in the resumed form of protein.

To correct amino acid deficiencies in the diet, it is not necessary to add the required units in pure form. The same object may be accomplished more efficiently by employing proteins which contain the required amino acids.

Foods of animal origin—meat, fish, eggs, and milk—supply proteins of high nutritive value, both from the standpoint of digestibility and amino acid content. Gelatin is an exception to that statement, since gelatin is very incomplete.

Even foods of animal origin vary among themselves in their protein content and amino acid balance. The protein of muscle meat does not rank quite as high as that of eggs or milk. The glandular tissues—such as liver, kidneys, sweetbreads or pancreas—contain proteins of exceptionally high nutritive value, and these organs should be added to the dog's diet whenever it is possible to do so. Each pint of milk contains two-thirds of an ounce (dry weight) of particularly high class protein, in addition to minerals, vitamins, carbohydrates, and fats. (The only dietary necessity absent

24

from milk is iron.) Animal proteins have a high content of dietary-essential amino acids, which makes them very effective in supplementing many proteins of vegetable origin. The whites of eggs, while somewhat inferior to the yolks, contain excellent proteins. The lysine of milk can be destroyed by excessive heat and the growth promoting value of its protein so destroyed. Evaporated tinned milk has not been subjected to enough heat to injure its proteins.

Thus we can readily see why meat with its concentrated, balanced, and easily assimilated proteins should form the major part of dry weight of a dog's ration.

It has never been determined how much protein the dog requires in his diet. It may be assumed to vary as to the size, age, and breed of the dog under consideration; as to the individual dog, some assimilating protein better, or utilizing more of it than others; as to the activity or inactivity of the subject; and as to the amino acid content of the protein employed. When wheat protein gliadin is fed as the sole protein, three times as much of it is required as of the milk protein, lactalbumin. It has been estimated that approximately twenty to twenty-five percent of animal protein (dry weight) in a dog's diet is adequate for maintenance in good health, although no final conclusion has been reached and probably never can be.

Our purpose, however, is not to feed the dog the minimum ration with which he can survive or even the minimum ration with which he can flourish. It is rather to give him the maximum food in quantity and balance which he can digest and enjoy without developing a paunch. Who wants to live on the minimum diet necessary for adequate sustenance? We all enjoy a full belly of good food, and so do our dogs.

Roy G. Daggs found from experimentation that milk production in the dog was influenced by the different kinds of proteins fed to it. He has pointed out that relatively high protein diets stimulate lactation and that, in the bitch, animal proteins are better suited to the synthesis of milk than plant proteins. He concluded that liver was a better source of protein for lactation than eggs or round steak.

THE CARBOHYDRATES

The carbohydrates include all the starches, the sugars, and the cellulose and hemicellulose, which last two, known as fiber, are the chief constituents of wood, of the stalks and leaves of plants, and of the coverings of seeds. There remains considerable controversy as to the amount of carbohydrates required or desirable in canine nutrition. It has been shown experimentally that the dog is able to digest large quantities of cornstarch, either raw or cooked. Rice fed to mature dogs in amounts sufficient to satisfy total energy requirements has been found to be 95 percent digested. We know that the various commercial biscuits and meals which are marketed as food for dogs are well tolerated, especially if they are supplemented by the addition of fresh meat. There seems to be no reason why they should not be included in the dog's ration.

Carbohydrates are a cheap source of energy for the dog, both in their initial cost and in the work required of the organism for their metabolism. Since there exists ample evidence that the dog has no difficulty in digesting and utilizing considerable amounts of starches and sugars for the production of energy, there is no reason why they should be excluded from his diet. Some carbohydrate is necessary for the metabolism of fats. The only danger from the employment of carbohydrates is that, being cheap, they may be employed to the exclusion of proteins and other essential elements of the dog's diet. It should be noted that meat and milk contain a measure of carbohydrates as well as of proteins.

Thoroughly cooked rice or oatmeal in moderate quantities may well be used to supplement and cheapen a meat diet for a dog without harm to him, as may crushed dog biscuit or shredded wheat waste or the waste from manufacture of other cereal foods. They are not required but may be used without harm.

Sugar and candy, of which dogs are inordinately fond, used also to be *verboten*. They are an excellent source of energy—and harmless. They should be fed in only moderate quantities.

FATS

In the dog as in man, body fat is found in largest amounts under the skin, between the muscles and around the internal organs. The fat so stored serves as a reserve source of heat and energy when the caloric value of the food is insufficient, or for temporary periods when no food is eaten. The accumulation of a certain amount of fat around vital organs provides considerable protection against cold and injury.

Before fats can be carried to the body cells by means of the circulating blood, it is necessary for them to be digested in the intestines with the aid of enzymes. Fats require a longer time for digestion than carbohydrates or proteins. For this reason, they are of special importance in delaying the sensations of hunger. This property of fats is frequently referred to as "staying power."

It is easily possible for some dogs to accumulate too much fat, making them unattractive, ungainly, and vaguely uncomfortable. This should be avoided by withholding an excess of fats and carbohydrates from the diets of such dogs whenever obesity threatens them. There is greater danger, however, that dogs may through inadequacy of their diets be permitted to become too thin.

Carbohydrates can in part be transformed to fats within the animal body. The ratio between fats and carbohydrates can therefore be varied within wide limits in the dog's ration so long as the requirements for proteins, vitamins, and minerals are adequately met. Some dogs have been known to tolerate as much as forty percent of fat in their diets over prolonged periods, but so much is not to be recommended as a general practice. Perhaps fifteen to twenty percent of fat is adequate without being too much.

Fat is a heat producing food, and the amount given a dog should be stepped up in the colder parts of the year and reduced in the summer months. In a ration low in fat it is particularly important that a good source of the fat-soluble vitamins be included or that such vitamins be artificially supplied. Weight for weight, fat has more than twice the food value of the other organic food groups—carbohydrates and proteins. The use of fat tends to decrease the amount of food required to supply caloric needs. The fats offer a means of increasing or decreasing the total sum of energy in the diet with the least change in the volume of food intake.

It is far less important that the dog receive more than a minimum amount of fats, however, than that his ration contain an adequate amount and quality balance of proteins. Lean meat in adequate quantities will provide him with such proteins, and fats may be added to it in the form of fat meat, suet, or lard. Small quantities of dog biscuits, cooked rice, or other cereals in the diet will supply the needed carbohydrates. However, cellulose or other roughage is not required in the diet of the carnivore. It serves only to engorge the dog's colon, which is not capacious, and to increase the volume of feces, which is supererogatory.

MINERALS

At least eleven minerals are present in the normal dog, and there are probably others occurring in quantities so minute that they have not as yet been discovered. The eleven are as follows: Calcium (lime), sodium chloride (table salt), copper, iron, magnesium, manganese, phosphorus, zinc, potassium, and iodine.

Of many of these only a trace in the daily ration is required and that trace is adequately found in meat or in almost any other normal diet. There are a few that we should be at pains to add to the diet. The others we shall ignore.

Sodium chloride (salt) is present in sufficient quantities in most meats, although, more to improve the flavor of the food than to contribute to the animal's nutrition, a small amount of salt may be added to the ration. The exact amount makes no material difference, since the unutilized portions are eliminated, largely in the urine. If the brand of salt used is iodized, it will meet the iodine requirements, which are very small. Iodine deficiency in dogs is rare, but food crops and meats grown in certain areas contain little or no iodine, and it is well to be safe by using iodized salt.

Sufficient iron is usually found in meat and milk, but if the dog appears anemic or listless the trace of iron needed can be supplied with one of the iron salts—ferric sulphate, or oxide, or ferrous gluconate. Iron is utilized in the bone marrow in the synthesis of hemoglobin in the blood corpuscles. It is used over and over; when a corpuscle is worn out and is to be replaced, it surrenders its iron before being eliminated.

When more iron is ingested than can be utilized, some is stored in the liver, after which further surplus is excreted. The liver of the newborn puppy contains enough iron to supply the organism up until weaning time. No iron is present in milk, which otherwise provides a completely balanced ration.

A diet with a reasonable content of red meat, especially of liver or kidney, is likely to be adequate in respect to its iron. However, bitches in whelp require more iron than a dog on mere maintenance. It is recommended that the liver content of bitches' diets be increased for the duration of pregnancy.

Iron requires the presence of a minute trace of copper for its utilization, but there is enough copper in well nigh any diet to supply the requirements.

Calcium and phosphorous are the only minerals of which an insufficiency is a warranted source of anxiety. This statement may not be true of adult dogs not employed for breeding purposes, but it does apply to brood bitches and to growing puppies. The entire skeleton and teeth are made largely from calcium and phosphorus, and it is essential that the organism have enough of those minerals.

If additional calcium is not supplied to a bitch in her diet, her own bone structure is depleted to provide her puppies with their share of calcium. Moreover, in giving birth to her puppies or shortly afterward she is likely to go into eclampsia as a result of calcium depletion.

The situation, however, is easily avoided. The addition of a small amount of calcium phosphate diabasic to the ration precludes any possible calcium deficiency. Calcium phosphate diabasic is an inexpensive substance and quite tasteless. It may be sprinkled in or over the food, especially that given to brood bitches and puppies. It is the source of strong bones and vigorous teeth of ivory whiteness.

But it must be mentioned that calcium cannot be assimilated into the bone structure, no matter how much of it is fed or otherwise administered, except in the presence of vitamin D. That is D's function, to facilitate the absorption of calcium and phosphorus. This will be elaborated upon in the following discussion of the vitamins and their functions.

VITAMINS

Vitamins have in the past been largely described by diseases resulting from their absence. It is recognized more and more that many of the subacute symptoms of general unfitness of dogs may be attributable to an inadequate supply in the diet of one or more of these essential food factors. It is to be emphasized that vitamins are to be considered a part of the dog's food, essential to his health and well being. They are not to be considered as medication. Often the morbid conditions resultant from their absence in the diet may be remedied by the addition of the particular needed vitamin.

The requirements of vitamins, as food, not as medication, in the diet cannot be too strongly emphasized. These vitamins may be in the food itself, or they may better be added to it as a supplement to insure an adequate supply. Except for vitamin D, of which it is remotely possible (though unlikely) to supply too much, a surplus of the vitamin substances in the ration is harmless. They are somewhat expensive and we have no disposition to waste them, but if too much of them are fed they are simply eliminated with no subsequent ill effect.

It must be realized that vitamins are various substances, each of which has a separate function. It is definitely not safe to add to a dog's (or a child's) diet something out of a bottle or box indefinitely labeled "Vitamins," as is the practice of so many persons. We must know which vitamins we are giving, what purpose each is designed to serve, and the potency of the preparation of the brand of each one we are using.

Any one of the "shotgun" vitamin preparations is probably adequate if administered in large enough dosages. Such a method may be wasteful, however; to be sure of enough of one substance, the surplus of the others is wasted. It is much better to buy a product that contains an adequate amount of each of the needed vitamins and a wasteful surplus of none. Such a procedure is cheaper in the long run.

There follows a brief description of each of the various vitamins so far discovered and a statement of what purpose in the diet they are respectively intended to serve:

Vitamin A—This vitamin in some form is an absolute requisite for good health, even for enduring life itself. Symptoms of ad-

31

vanced deficiency of vitamin A in dogs are an eye disease with resulting impaired vision, inflammation of the conjunctiva or mucous membranes which line the eyelid, and injury to the mucous membranes of the body. Less easily recognized symptoms are an apparent lowered resistance to bacterial infection, especially of the upper respiratory tract, retarded growth, and loss of weight. Diseases due to vitamin A deficiency may be well established while the dog is still gaining in weight. Lack of muscular coordination and paralysis have been observed in dogs and degeneration of the nervous system. Some young dogs deprived of vitamin A become wholly or partially deaf.

The potency of vitamin A is usually calculated in International Units, of which it has been estimated that the dog requires about 35 per day for each pound of his body weight. Such parts as are not utilized are not lost, but are stored in the liver for future use in time of shortage. A dog well fortified with this particular vitamin can well go a month or more without harm with none of it in his diet. At such times he draws upon his liver for its surplus.

It is for its content of vitamins A and D that cod-liver oil (and the oils from the livers of other fish) is fed to puppies and growing children. Fish liver oils are an excellent source of vitamin A, and if a small amount of them is included in the diet no anxiety about deficiency of vitamin A need be entertained. In buying cod-liver oil, it pays to obtain the best grade. The number of International Units it contains per teaspoonful is stated on most labels. The vitamin content of cod-liver oil is impaired by exposure to heat, light, and air. It should be kept in a dark, cool place and the bottle should be firmly stopped.

Another source of vitamin A is found in carrots but it is almost impossible to get enough carrots in a dog to do him any good. It is better and easier to use a preparation known as carotene, three drops of which contains almost the vitamin A in a bushel of carrots.

Other natural sources of vitamin A are liver, kidney, heart, cheese, egg yolks, butter and milk. If these foods, or any one of them, are generously included in the adult dog's maintenance ration, all other sources of vitamin A may be dispensed with. The ration for all puppies, however, and for pregnant and lactating bitches should be copiously fortified either with fish liver oil or with tablets containing vitamin A.

Vitamin B. What was formerly known as a single vitamin B has now been found to be a complex of many different factors. Some of them are, in minute quantities, very important parts of the diets of any kind of animals. The various factors of this complex, each a separate vitamin, are designated by the letter B followed by an inferior number, as B_1, B_2, or B_6.

The absence or insufficiency in the diet of Vitamin B_1, otherwise known as thiamin, has been blamed for retarded growth, loss of weight, decreased fertility, loss of appetite, and impaired digestion. A prolonged shortage of B_1 may result in paralysis, the accumulation of fluid in the tissues, and finally in death, apparently from heart failure.

It is not easy to estimate just how much B_1 a dog requires per pound of body weight, since dogs as individuals vary in their needs, and the activity of an animal rapidly depletes the thiamin in his body. The feeding of 50 International Units per day per pound of body weight is probably wasteful but harmless. That is at least enough.

Thiamin is not stored in the system for any length of time and requires a daily dosage. It is destroyed in part by heat above the boiling point. It is found in yeast (especially in brewer's yeast), liver, wheat germ, milk, eggs, and in the coloring matter of vegetables. However, few dogs or persons obtain an optimum supply of B_1 from their daily diet, and it is recommended that it be supplied to the dog daily.

Brewer's yeast, either in powdered or tablet form affords a cheap and rather efficient way to supply the average daily requirements. An overdose of yeast is likely to cause gas in the dog's stomach.

Another factor of the vitamin B complex, riboflavin, affects particularly the skin and hair. Animals fed a diet in which it is deficient are prone to develop a scruffy dryness of the skin, especially about the eyes and mouth, and the hair becomes dull and dry, finally falling out, leaving the skin rough and dry. In experiments with rats deprived of riboflavin the toes have fallen off.

Riboflavin is present in minute quantities in so many foods that a serious shortage in any well balanced diet is unlikely. It is especially to be found in whey, which is the explanation of the smooth skin and lively hair of so many dogs whose ration contains cottage cheese.

While few dogs manifest any positive shortage of riboflavin, experiments on various animals have shown that successively more liberal amounts of it in their diets, up to about four times as much as is needed to prevent the first signs of deficiency, result in increased positive health.

Riboflavin deteriorates with exposure to heat and light. Most vitamin products contain it in ample measure.

Dogs were immediately responsible for the discovery of the existence of vitamin B_2, or nicotinic acid, formerly known as vitamin G. The canine disease of black tongue is analogous with the human disease called pellagra, both of which are prevented and cured by sufficient amounts of nicotinic acid in the diet. Black tongue is not a threat for any dog that eats a diet which contains even a reasonable quantity of lean meat, but it used to be prevalent among dogs fed exclusively upon corn bread or corn-meal mush, as many were.

No definite optimum dosage has been established. However, many cases of vaguely irritated skin, deadness of coat, and soft, spongy, or bleeding gums have been reported to be remedied by administration of nicotinic acid.

It has been demonstrated that niacin is essential if a good sound healthy appetite is to be maintained. Pantothenic acid is essential to good nerve health. Pyridoxin influences proper gastro-intestinal functions. Vitamin B_{12}, the "animal protein factor," is essential for proper growth and health in early life. And the water soluble B factor affects the production of milk.

Vitamin C, the so-called anti-scorbutic vitamin, is presumed to be synthesized by the dog in his own body. The dog is believed not to be subject to true scurvy. Vitamin C, then, can well be ignored as pertains to the dog. It is the most expensive of the vitamins, and, its presence in the vitamin mixture for the dog will probably do no good.

Vitamin D, the anti-rachitic vitamin, is necessary to promote the assimilation of calcium and phosphorus into the skeletal structure. One may feed all of those minerals one will, but without vitamin D they will pass out of the system unused. It is impossible to develop sound bones and teeth without its presence. Exposure to sunshine unimpeded by glass enables the animal to manufacture vitamin D in his system, but sunshine is not to be depended upon for an entire supply.

34

Vitamin D is abundant in cod-liver oil and in the liver oils of some other fish, or it may be obtained in a dry form in combination with other vitamins. One International Unit per pound of body weight per day is sufficient to protect a dog from rickets. From a teaspoonful to a tablespoonful of cod-liver oil a day will serve well instead for any dog.

This is the only one of the vitamins with which overdosage is possible and harmful. While a dog will not suffer from several times the amount stated and an excess dosage is unlikely, it is only fair to warn the reader that it is at least theoretically possible.

Vitamin E is the so-called fertility vitamin. Whether it is required for dogs has not as yet been determined. Rats fed upon a ration from which vitamin E was wholly excluded became permanently sterile, but the finding is not believed to pertain to all animals. Some dog keepers, however, declare that the feeding of wheat germ oil, the most abundant source of vitamin E, has prevented early abortions of their bitches, has resulted in larger and more vigorous litters of puppies, has increased the fertility of stud dogs, has improved the coats of their dogs and furthered the betterment of their general health. Whether vitamin E or some other factor or factors in the wheat germ oil is responsible for these alleged benefits is impossible to say.

Vitamin E is so widely found in small quantities in well nigh all foods that the hazard of its omission from any normal diet is small.

Numerous other vitamins have been discovered and isolated in recent years, and there are suspected to be still others as yet unknown. The ones here discussed are the only ones that warrant the use of care to include them in the dog's daily ration. It is well to reiterate that vitamins are not medicine, but are food, a required part of the diet. Any person interested in the complete nutrition of his dog will not neglect them.

It should go without saying that a dog should have access to clean, fresh, pure drinking water at all times, of which he should be permitted to drink as much or as little as he chooses. The demands of his system for drinking water will depend in part upon the moisture content of his food. Fed upon dry dog biscuits, he will probably drink considerable water to moisten it; with a diet which contains much milk or soup, he will need little additional water.

That he chooses to drink water immediately after a meal is harmless. The only times his water should be limited (but not entirely withheld from him) is after violent exercise or excitement, at which times his thirst should be satisfied only gradually.

The quantities of food required daily by dogs are influenced and determined by a number of factors: the age, size, individuality, and physical condition of the animal; the kind, quality, character, and proportions of the various foods in the ration; the climate, environment and methods of management; and the type and amount of work done, or the degree of exercise. Of these considerations, the age and size of the dog and the kind and amount of work are particularly important in determining food requirements. During early puppyhood a dog may require two or three (or even more) times as much food per pound of body weight as the same dog will require at maturity.

Any statement we should make here about the food requirements of a dog as to weight or volume would be subject to modification. Dogs vary in their metabolism. One dog might stay fat and sleek on a given amount of a given ration, whereas his litter brother in an adjoining kennel might require twice or only half as much of the same ration to maintain him in the same state of flesh.

The only sound determiners of how much to feed a dog are his appetite and his condition. As a general rule, a dog should have as much food for maintenance as he will readily clean up in five or ten minutes, unless he tends to lay on unwanted fat, in which case his intake of food should be reduced, especially its content of fats and carbohydrates. A thin dog should have his ration increased and be urged to eat it. The fats in his ration should be increased, and he may be fattened with a dessert of candy, sugar, or sweet cake following his main meal. These should never be used before a meal, lest they impair the appetite, and they should not be given to a fat dog at all. Rightly employed, they are useful and harmless, contrary to the prevalent belief.

Growing puppies require frequent meals, as will be discussed later. Pregnant and lactating bitches and frequently used stud dogs should have at least two meals, and better three, each day. For the mere maintenance of healthy adult dogs, one large meal a day appears to suffice as well as more smaller ones. Many tenderhearted dog keepers choose to divide the ration into two parts and to feed their dogs twice each day. There can be no objection offered to such a program except that it involves additional work for the keeper. Whether one meal or two, they should be given at regular hours, to which dogs soon adjust and expect their dinner at a given time.

It is better to determine upon an adequate ration, with plenty of meat in it, and feed it day after day, than to vary the diet in the assumption that a dog tires of eating the same thing. There is no evidence that he does, and it is a burden upon his carnivorous digestion to be making constant adjustments and readjustments to a new diet.

Today there are available for dogs many brands of canned foods, some good and others not so good. But it is safe to feed your dog exclusively—if you do not object to the cost—a canned dog food which has been produced by a reliable concern. Many of the producers of canned dog foods are subject to Federal inspection because they also process meat and meat products for human consumption. The Federal regulations prohibit the use of diseased or unsuitable by-products in the preparation of dog food. Some of the canned dog foods on the market are mostly cereal. A glance at the analysis chart on the label will tell you whether a particular product is a good food for your dog.

If fish is fed, it should be boned—thoroughly. The same is true of fowl and rabbit meats. Small bones may be caught in the dog's throat or may puncture the stomach or intestines. Large, raw shank bones of beef may be given to the dog with impunity, but they should be renewed at frequent intervals before they spoil. A dog obtains much amusement from gnawing a raw bone, and some nutrition. Harm does not accrue from his swallowing of bone fragments, which are dissolved by the hydrochloric acid in his stomach. If the dog is fed an excessive amount of bones, constipation may result. When this occurs, the best way to relieve the condition is by the use of the enema bag. Medicinal purges of laxatives given at this time may cause irreparable damage.

Meat for dogs may be fed raw, or may be roasted, broiled, or boiled. It is not advisable to feed fried foods to dogs. All soups, gravies and juices from cooked meat must be conserved and included in the food, since they contain some of the minerals and vitamins extracted from the meat.

A well-known German physician selected a medium sized, strong, healthy bitch, and after she had been mated, he fed her on chopped horse meat from which the salts were to a large extent extracted by boiling for two hours in distilled water. In addition to this she was given each day a certain quantity of fried fat. As drink she had only distilled water. She gave birth to six healthy puppies, one of which was killed immediately, and its bones found to be strong and well built and free from abnormalities. The other puppies did not thrive, but remained weak, and could scarcely walk at the end of a month, when four died from excessive feebleness. And the sixth was killed two weeks later. The mother in the meantime had become very lean but was tolerably lively and had a fair appetite. She was killed one hundred and twenty-six days after the beginning of the experiment, and it was then found that the bones of her spine and pelvis were softened—a condition known to physicians as osteomalacia.

The results of this experiment are highly interesting and instructive, showing clearly as they do that the nursing mother sends out to her young, in her milk, a part of her store of lime, which is absolutely essential to their welfare. They show also that if proper food is denied her, when in whelp and when nursing, not only her puppies but she as well must suffer greatly in consequence. And in the light of these facts is uncovered one of the most potential causes of rickets, so common among large breeds.

It may therefore be accepted that bitches in whelp must have goodly quantities of meat; moreover, that while cooking may be the rule if the broth is utilized, it is a wise plan to give the food occasionally in the raw state.

There is little choice among the varieties of meat, except that pork is seldom relished by dogs, usually contains too much fat, and should be cooked to improve its digestibility when it is used at all. Beef, mutton, lamb, goat, and horse flesh are equally valuable. The choice should be made upon the basis of their comparative cost and their availability in the particular community. A dog suddenly changed from another diet to horse flesh may develop a harmless and temporary diarrhea, which can be ignored. Horse flesh is likely to be deficient in fats, which may be added in the form of suet, lard or pure corn oil.

The particular cuts of whatever meat is used is of little consequence. Liver and kidney are especially valuable and when it is possible they should be included as part of the meat used. As the only meat in the ration, liver and kidney tend to loosen the bowels. It is better to include them as a part of each day's ration than to permit them to serve as the sole meat content one or two days a week.

It makes no difference whether meat is ground or is fed to the dog in large or medium sized pieces. He is able to digest pieces of meat as large as he can swallow. The advantage of grinding meat is that it can be better mixed with whatever else it is wished to include in the ration, the dog being unable to pick out the meat and reject the rest. There is little harm in his doing so, except for the waste, since it is the meat upon which we must depend for the most part for his nutrition.

Fresh ground meat can be kept four or five days under ordinary refrigeration without spoiling. It may be kept indefinitely if solidly frozen. Frozen ground horse meat for dogs is available in many markets, is low in price, and is entirely satisfactory for the purpose intended.

A suggested ration is made as follows: Two-thirds to three-quarters by weight of ground meat including ten to twenty percent of fat and a portion of liver or kidney, with the remainder thoroughly cooked rice or oatmeal, or shredded wheat, or dog biscuit, or wheat germ, with a sprinkling of calcium phosphate diabasic. Vitamins may be added, or given separately.

If it is desired to offer the dog a second meal, it may be of shredded wheat or other breakfast cereal with plenty of milk, with or without one or more soft boiled eggs. Evaporated canned milk or powdered milk is just as good food for the dog as fresh milk. Cottage cheese is excellent for this second meal.

These are not the only possible rations for the dog, but they will prove adequate. Leavings from the owner's table can be added to either ration, but can hardly be depended upon for the entire nourishment of the dog.

The dog's food should be at approximately body heat, tepid but never hot.

Little consideration is here given to the costs of the various foods. Economies in rations and feeding practices are admittedly desirable, but not if they are made at the expense of the dog's health.

SOME BRIEF PRECEPTS ABOUT FEEDING

Many dogs are overfed. Others do not receive adequate rations. Both extremes should be avoided, but particularly overfeeding of grown dogs. Coupled with lack of exercise, overfeeding usually produces excessive body weight and laziness, and it may result in illness and sterility. Prolonged undernourishment causes loss of weight, listlessness, dull coats, sickness, and death.

An adequate ration will keep most mature dogs at a uniform body weight and in a thrifty, moderately lean condition. Observation of condition is the best guide in determining the correct amount of food.

The axiom, "One man's meat is another man's poison," is applicable to dogs also. Foods that are not tolerated by the dog or those that cause digestive and other disturbances should be discontinued. The use of moldy, spoiled, or rotten food is never good practice. Food should be protected from fouling by rats or mice, especially because rats are vectors of leptospirosis. The excessive use of food of low energy content and low biological values will often result in poor condition and may cause loss of weight and paunchiness.

All feeding and drinking utensils must be kept scrupulously clean. They should be washed after each using.

It is usually desirable to reduce the food allotment somewhat during hot weather. Dogs should be fed at regular intervals, and the best results may be expected when regular feeding is accompanied by regular, but not exhausting, exercise.

Most dogs do not thrive on a ration containing large amounts of sloppy foods, and excessive bulk is to be avoided especially for hardworking dogs, puppies, and pregnant or lactating bitches. If the ration is known to be adequate and the dog is losing weight or is not in good condition, the presence of intestinal parasites is to be suspected. However, dogs sometimes go "off feed" for a day or two. This is cause for no immediate anxiety, but if it lasts more than two or three days, a veterinarian should be consulted.

FOOD FOR THE STUD DOG

The stud dog that is used for breeding only at infrequent intervals requires only the food needed for his maintenance in good health, as set forth in the foregoing pages. He should be well fed with ample meat in his diet, moderately exercised to keep his flesh firm and hard, and not permitted to become too thin or too fat.

More care is required for the adequate nutrition of the dog offered at public stud and frequently employed for breeding. A vigorous stud dog may very handily serve two bitches a week over a long period without a serious tax upon his health and strength if he is fully nourished and adequately but not excessively exercised. Such a dog should have at least two meals a day, and they should consist of even more meat, milk (canned is as good as fresh), eggs, cottage cheese, and other foods of animal origin than is used in most maintenance rations. Liver and some fat should be included, and the vitamins especially are not to be forgotten. In volume this will be only a little more than the basic maintenance diet, the difference being in its richness and concentration.

An interval of an hour or two should intervene between a dog's meal and his employment for breeding. He may be fed, but only lightly, immediately after he has been used for breeding.

The immediate reason that a stud dog should be adequately fed and exercised is the maintenance of his strength and virility. The secondary reason is that a popular stud dog is on exhibition at all times, between the shows as well as at the shows. Clients with bitches to be bred appear without notice to examine a dog at public stud, and the dog should be presented to them in the best possible condition—clean, hard, in exactly the most becoming state of flesh, and with a gleaming, lively coat. These all depend largely upon the highly nutritious diet the dog receives.

FOOD FOR THE BROOD BITCH

Often a well fed bitch comes through the ordeal of rearing a large litter of puppies without any impairment of her vitality and flesh. In such case she may be returned to a good maintenance ration until she is ready to be bred again. About the time she weans her puppies her coat will be dead and ready to drop out, but if she is healthy and well fed a new and vigorous coat will grow in, and she will be no worse off for her maternal ordeal. Some bitches, either from a deficient nutrition or a constitutional disposition to contribute too much of their own strength and substance to the nutrition of the puppies, are thin and exhausted at the time of weaning. Such a bitch needs the continuance of at least two good and especially nutritious meals a day for a month or more until her flesh and strength are restored before she is returned to her routine maintenance ration, upon which she may be kept until time comes to breed her again.

At breeding time a bitch's flesh should be hard, and she should be on the lean side rather than too fat. No change in her regular maintenance diet need be made until about the fourth or fifth week of her pregnancy. The growth of the fetus is small up until the middle of the pregnancy, after which it becomes rapid.

The bitch usually begins to "show in whelp" in four to six weeks after breeding, and her food consumption should be then gradually stepped up. If she has been having only one meal a day, she should be given two; if she has had two, both should be larger. Henceforth until her puppies are weaned, she must eat not merely for two, as is said of the pregnant woman, but for four or five, possibly for ten or twelve. She is not to be encouraged to grow fat. Especial emphasis should be laid upon her ration's content of meat, including liver, milk, calcium phosphate, and vitamins A and D, both of which are found in cod-liver oil.

Some breeders destroy all but a limited number of puppies in a litter in the belief that a bitch will be unable adequately to nourish all the puppies she has whelped. In some extreme cases it may be necessary to do this or to obtain a foster mother or wet nurse to share the burden of rearing the puppies. However, the healthy bitch with normal metabolism can usually generate enough milk to feed adequately all the puppies she has produced, provided she is well enough fed and provided the puppies are fed additionally as soon as they are able to eat.

After whelping until the puppies are weaned, throughout the lactating period, the bitch should have all the nourishing food she can be induced to eat—up to four or five meals a day. These should consist largely of meat and liver, some fat, a small amount of cereals, milk, eggs, cottage cheese, calcium phosphate, and vitamins, with especial reference to vitamins A and D. At that time it is hardly possible to feed a bitch too much or to keep her too fat. The growth of the puppies is much more rapid after they are born than was their growth in the dam's uterus, and the large amount of food needed to maintain that rapid growth must pass through the bitch and be transformed to milk, while at the same time she must maintain her own body.

THE FEEDING OF PUPPIES

If the number of puppies in a litter is small, if the mother is vigorous, healthy, and a good milker, the youngsters up until their weaning time may require no additional food over and above the milk they suck from their dam's breasts. If the puppies are numerous or if the dam's milk is deficient in quality or quantity, it is wise to begin feeding the puppies artificially as soon as they are able and willing to accept food. This is earlier than used to be realized.

It is for the sake of the puppies' vigor rather than for the sake of their ultimate size that their growth is to be promoted as rapidly as possible. Vigorous and healthy puppies attain early maturity if they are given the right amounts of the right quality of food. The ultimate size of the dog at maturity is laid down in his germ plasm, and he can be stunted or dwarfed, if at all, only at the expense of his type. If one tries to prevent the full growth of a dog by withholding from him the food he needs, one will wind up with a rachitic, cowhocked dog, one with a delicate digestive apparatus, a sterile one, one with all of these shortcomings combined, or even a dead dog.

Growth may be slowed with improper food, sometimes without serious harm, but the dog is in all ways better off if he is forced along with the best food and encouraged to attain his full size at an early age. Dogs of the smaller breeds usually reach their full maturity several months earlier than those of the larger breeds. A well grown dog reaches his sexual maturity and can be safely used for limited breeding at one year of age.

As soon as teeth can be felt with the finger in a puppy's mouth, which is usually at about seventeen or eighteen days of age, it is safe to begin to feed him. His first food (except for his mother's milk) should be of scraped raw beef at body temperature. The first day he may have ¼ to 2 teaspoonfuls, according to size. He will not need to learn to eat this meat; he will seize upon it avidly and lick his chops for more. The second day he may have ⅓ to 3 teaspoonfuls, according to size, with two feedings 12 hours apart. Thereafter, the amount and frequency of this feeding may be rapidly increased. By the twenty-fifth day the meat need not be scraped, but only finely ground. This process of the early feeding of raw meat to puppies not only gives them a good start in life, but it also relieves their mother of a part of her burden of providing milk for them.

At about the fourth week, some cereal (thoroughly cooked oatmeal, shredded wheat, or dried bread) may be either moistened and mixed with the meat or be served to the puppies with milk, fresh or canned. It may be necessary to immerse their noses into such a mixture to teach them to eat it. Calcium phosphate and a small amount of cod-liver oil should be added to such a mixture, both of which substances the puppies should have every day until their maturity. At the fourth week, while they are still at the dam's breast, they may be fed three or four times a day upon this extra ration, or something similar, such as cottage cheese or soft boiled egg. By the sixth week their dam will be trying to wean them, and they may have four or five meals daily. One of these may be finely broken dog biscuit thoroughly soaked in milk. One or two of the meals should consist largely or entirely of meat with liver.

The old advice about feeding puppies "little and often" should be altered to "much and often." Each puppy at each meal should have all the food he will readily clean up. Food should not be left in front of the puppies. They should be fed and after two or three minutes the receptacle should be taken away. Young puppies should be roly-poly fat, and kept so up to at least five or six months of age. Thereafter they should be slightly on the fat side, but not pudgy, until maturity.

The varied diet of six-week-old puppies may be continued, but at eight or nine weeks the number of meals may be reduced to four, and at three months, to three large rations per day. After six months the meals may be safely reduced again to two a day, but they must be generous meals with meat, liver, milk, cod-liver oil, and calcium phosphate. At full maturity, one meal a day suffices, or two may be continued.

The secret of turning good puppies into fine, vigorous dogs is to keep them growing through the entire period of their maturation. The most important item in the rearing of puppies is adequate and frequent meals of highly nourishing foods. Growth requires two or three times as much food as maintenance. Time between meals should be allowed for digestion, but puppies should never be permitted to become really hungry. Water in a shallow dish should be available to puppies at all times after they are able to walk.

45

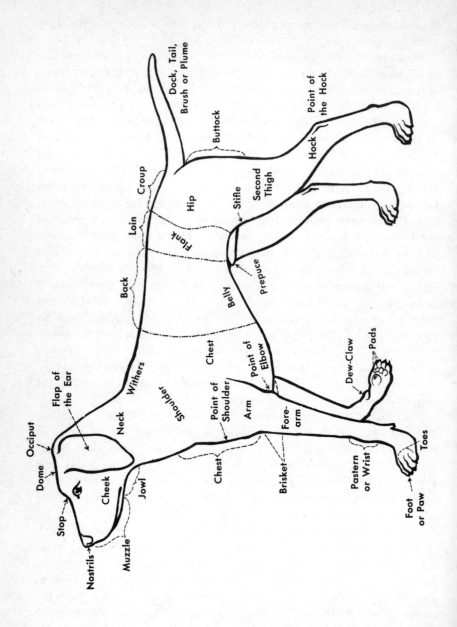

46

The Breeding
of Dogs

HERE, if anywhere in the entire process of the care
and management of dogs, the exercise of good judgment is involved.
Upon the choice of the two dogs, male and female, to be mated
together depends the future success or failure of one's dogs. If the
two to be mated are ill chosen, either individually or as pertains
to their fitness as mates, one to the other, all the painstaking care
to feed and rear the resultant puppies correctly is wasted. The
mating together of two dogs is the drafting of the blueprints and
the writing of the specifications of what the puppies are to be
like. The plans, it is true, require to be executed; the puppies,
when they arrive, must be adequately fed and cared for in order
to develop them into the kinds of dogs they are in their germ plasm
designed to become. However, if the plans as determined in the
mating are defective, just so will the puppies that result from them
be defective, in spite of all the good raising one can give them.

The element of luck in the breeding of dogs cannot be discounted,
for it exists. The mating which on paper appears to be the best
possible may result in puppies that are poor and untypical of
their breed. Even less frequently, a good puppy may result from
a chance mating together of two ill chosen parents. These results
are fortuitous and unusual, however. The best dogs as a lot come
from parents carefully chosen as to their individual excellences and
as to their suitability as mates for each other. It is as unwise as

47

it is unnecessary to trust to luck in the breeding of dogs. Careful planning pays off in the long run, and few truly excellent dogs are produced without it.

Some breeders without any knowledge of genetics have been successful, without knowing exactly why they succeeded. Some of them have adhered to beliefs in old wives' tales and to traditional concepts that science has long since exploded and abandoned. Such as have succeeded have done so in spite of their lack of knowledge and not because of it.

There is insufficient space at our disposal in this book to discuss in detail the science of genetics and the application of that science to the breeding of dogs. Whole books have been written about the subject. One of the best, clearest, and easiest for the layman to understand is *The New Art of Breeding Better Dogs,* by Philip Onstott, which may be obtained from Howell Book House, the publisher. In it and in other books upon the subject of genetics will be found more data about the practical application of science to the breeding of livestock than can be included here.

The most that can be done here is to offer some advice soundly based upon the genetic laws. Every feature a dog may or can possess is determined by the genes carried in the two reproductive cells, one from each parent, from the union of which he was developed. There are thousands of pairs of these determiners in the life plan of every puppy, and often a complex of many genes is required to produce a single recognizable attribute of the dog.

These genes function in pairs, one member of each pair being contributed by the father and the other member of the pair coming from the mother. The parents obtained these genes they hand on from their parents, and it is merely fortuitous which half of any pair of genes present in a dog's or a bitch's germ plasm may be passed on to any one of the progeny. Of any pair of its own genes, a dog or a bitch may contribute one member to one puppy and the other member to another puppy in the same litter or in different litters. The unknown number of pairs of genes is so great that there is an infinite number of combinations of them, which accounts for the differences we find between two full brothers or two full sisters. In fact, it depends upon the genes received whether a dog be a male or a female.

We know that the male dog contributes one and the bitch the

other of every pair of genes that unite to determine what the puppy will be like and what he will grow into. Thus, the parents make exactly equal contributions to the germ plasm or zygote from which every puppy is developed. It was long believed that the male dog was so much more important than the bitch in any mating that the excellence or shortcomings of the bitch might be disregarded. This theory was subsequently reversed and breeders considered the bitch to be more important than the dog. We now know that their contribution in every mating and in every individual puppy is exactly equal, and neither is to be considered more than the other.

There are two kinds of genes—the recessive genes and the dominant. And there are three kinds of pairs of genes: a recessive from the sire plus a recessive from the dam; a dominant from the sire plus a dominant from the dam; and a dominant from one parent plus a recessive from the other. It is the last combination that is the source of our trouble in breeding. When both members of a pair of genes are recessive, the result is a recessive attribute in the animal that carries them; when both members of the pair are dominant, the result is a pure dominant attribute; but when one member of the pair is recessive and the other member dominant, the result will be a wholly or only partially dominant attribute, which will breed true only half of the time. This explains why a dog or a bitch may fail to produce progeny that looks at all like itself.

If all the pairs of a dog's genes were purely dominant, we could expect him to produce puppies that resembled himself in all particulars, no matter what kind of mate he was bred to. Or if all his genes were recessive and he were mated to a bitch with all recessive genes, the puppies might be expected to look quite like the parents. However, a dog with mixed pairs of genes bred to a bitch with mixed pairs of genes may produce anything at all, puppies that bear no resemblance to either parent.

Long before the Mendelian laws were discovered, some dogs were known to be "prepotent" to produce certain characters, that is the characters would show up in their puppies irrespective of what their mates might be like. For instance, some dogs, themselves with dark eyes, might be depended upon never to produce a puppy with light eyes, no matter how light eyed the mate to which he was bred. This was true despite the fact that the dog's litter brother which had equally dark eyes, when bred to a light eyed bitch might produce a large percentage of puppies with light eyes.

Before it is decided to breed a bitch, it is well to consider whether she is worth breeding, whether she is good enough as an individual and whether she came from a good enough family to warrant the expectations that she will produce puppies worth the expense and trouble of raising. It is to be remembered that the bitch contributes exactly half the genes to each of her puppies; if she has not good genes to contribute, the time and money involved in breeding her and rearing her puppies will be wasted.

It is conceded that a bad or mediocre bitch when bred to an excellent dog will probably produce puppies better than herself. But while one is "grading up" from mediocre stock, other breeders are also grading upward from better stock and they will keep just so far ahead of one's efforts that one can never catch up with them. A merely pretty good bitch is no good at all for breeding. It is better to dispose of a mediocre bitch or to relegate her to the position of a family pet than to breed from her. It is difficult enough, with all the care and judgment one is able to muster, to obtain superlative puppies even from a fine bitch, without cluttering the earth with inferior puppies from just any old bitch.

If one will go into the market and buy the best possible bitch from the best possible family one's purse can afford and breed her sensibly to the best and most suitable stud dog one can find, success is reasonably sure. Even if for economy's sake, the bitch is but a promising puppy backed up by the best possible pedigree, it will require only a few months until she is old enough to be bred. From such a bitch, one may expect first-rate puppies at the first try, whereas in starting with an inferior bitch one is merely lucky if in two or three generations he obtains a semblance of the kind of dog he is trying to produce.

Assuming it is decided that the bitch is adequate to serve as a brood bitch, it becomes necessary to choose for her a mate in collaboration with which she may realize the ultimate of her possibilities. It is never wise to utilize for stud the family pet or the neighbor's pet just because he happens to be registered in the studbook or because his service costs nothing. Any dog short of the best and most suitable (wherever he may be and whoever may own him) is an extravagance. If the bitch is worth breeding at all, she is worth shipping clear across the continent, if need be, to obtain for her a mate to enable her to realize her possibilities. Stud fees may range from fifty to one hundred dollars or even more. The average value of each puppy, if well reared, should at the time of weaning approximate the legitimate stud fee of its sire. With a good bitch it is therefore profitable to lay out as much as may be required to obtain the services of the best and most suitable stud dog—always assuming that he is worth the price asked. However, it is never wise to choose an inferior or unsuitable dog just because he is well ballyhooed and commands an exorbitant stud fee.

There are three considerations by which to evaluate the merits of a stud dog—his outstanding excellence as an individual, his pedigree and the family from which he derived, and the excellence or inferiority of the progeny he is known to have produced.

As an individual a good stud dog may be expected to be bold and aggressive (not vicious) and structurally typical of his breed, but without any freakish exaggerations of type. He must be sound, a free and true mover, possess fineness and quality, and be a gentleman of his own breed. Accidentally acquired scars or injuries such as broken legs should not be held against him, because he can transmit only his genes to his puppies and no such accidents impair his genes.

A dog's pedigree may mean much or little. One of two litter brothers, with pedigrees exactly alike, may prove to be a superlative show and stud dog, and the other worth exactly nothing for either purpose. The pedigree especially is not to be judged on its length, since three generations is at most all that is required, although further extension of the pedigree may prove interesting to a curious owner. No matter how well-bred his pedigree may show a dog to be, if he is not a good dog the ink required to write the pedigree was wasted.

The chief value of a pedigree is to enable us to know from which of a dog's parents, grandparents, or great-grandparents, he derived his merits, and from which his faults. In choosing a mate for him (or for her, as the case may be) one seeks to reinforce the one and to avoid the other. Let us assume that one of the grandmothers was upright in shoulder, whereas the shoulder should be well laid back; we can avoid as a mate for such a dog one with any

51

tendency to straight shoulders or one from straight shouldered ancestry. The same principle would apply to an uneven mouth, a light eye, a soft back, splayed feet, cowhocks, or to any other inherited fault. Suppose, on the other hand, that the dog himself, the parents, and all the grandparents are particularly nice in regard to their fronts; in a mate for such a dog, one desires as good a front as is obtainable, but if she, or some of her ancestors are not too good in respect to their fronts, one may take a chance anyway and trust to the good fronted dog with his good fronted ancestry to correct the fault. That then is the purpose of the pedigree as a guide to breeding.

A stud dog can best be judged, however, by the excellence of the progeny he is known to have produced, if it is possible to obtain all the data to enable the breeder to evaluate that record. A complete comparative evaluation is perhaps impossible to make, but one close enough to justify conclusions is available. Not only the number but the quality of the bitches to which the dog has been bred must enter into the consideration. A young dog may not have had the opportunity to prove his prowess in the stud. He may have been bred to few bitches and those few of indifferent merits, or his get may not be old enough as yet to hit the shows and establish a record for themselves or for their sire. Allowance may be made for such a dog.

On the other hand, a dog may have proved himself to be phenomenal in the show ring, or may have been made to seem phenomenal by means of the owner's ballyhoo and exploitation. Half of the top bitches in the entire country may have been bred to him upon the strength of his winning record. Merely from the laws of probability such a dog, if he is not too bad, will produce some creditable progeny. It is necessary to take into consideration the opportunities a dog has had in relation to the fine progeny he has produced.

That, however, is the chief criterion by which a good stud dog may be recognized. A dog which can sire two or three excellent puppies in every litter from a reasonably good bitch may be considered as an acceptable stud. If he has in his lifetime sired one or two champions each year, and especially if one or two of the lot are superlative champions, top members of their breed, he is a great stud dog. Ordinarily and without other considerations, such a dog is to be preferred to one of his unproved sons, even though the son be as good or better an individual. In this way one employs genes one knows to produce what one wants. The son may be only hybrid dominant for his excellent qualities.

In the choice of a stud dog no attention whatever need be paid to claims that he sires numerically big litters. Unless the sire is deficient in sperm, the number of puppies in the litter, provided there are any puppies at all, depends entirely upon the bitch. At one service, a dog deposits enough spermatozoa to produce a million puppies, if there were so many ova to be fertilized. In any event, the major purpose should be to obtain good puppies, not large numbers of them.

There are three methods of breeding employed by experienced breeders—outcrossing, inbreeding, and line breeding. By outcrossing is meant the breeding together of mates of which no blood relationship can be traced. It is much favored by novice breeders, who feel that the breeding together of blood relatives is likely to result in imbecility, constitutional weakness, or some other kind of degeneration. Inbreeding is the mating together of closely related animals—father to daughter, mother to son, brother to sister, half brother to half sister. Some of the best animals ever produced have been bred from some such incestuous mating, and the danger from such practices, if they are carried out by persons who know what they are about, is minimal. Line breeding is the mating together of animals related one to another, but less closely—such as first cousins, grandsire to granddaughter, granddam to grandson, uncle to niece, or aunt to nephew.

Absolute outcrossing is usually impossible, since all the good dogs in any breed are more or less related—descended from some common ancestor in the fifth or sixth or seventh generation of their pedigrees. In any event, it is seldom to be recommended, since the results from it in the first generation of progeny are usually not satisfactory. It may be undertaken by some far-sighted and experienced breeder for the purpose of bringing into his strain some particular merit lacking in it and present in the strain of the unrelated dog. While dogs so bred may obtain an added vigor from what is known in genetics as *heterosis,* they are likely to manifest a coarseness and a lack of uniformity in the litter which is not to be found in more closely bred puppies. Good breeders never outcross if it is possible to obtain the virtues they want by sticking to their own strain. And when they do outcross, it is for the purpose of utilizing the outcrossed product for further breeding. It is not an end in itself.

Inbreeding (or incest breeding, as it is· sometimes called) involves no such hazards as are and in the past have been attributed to it. It produces some very excellent dogs when correctly employed, some very bad ones even when correctly employed, and all bad ones when carelessly used. All the standard breeds of dogs were established as uniform breeds through intense inbreeding and culling over many generations. Inbreeding brings into manifestation undesirable recessive genes, the bearers of which can be discarded and the strain can thus be purged of its bad recessives.

Dogs of great soundness and excellence, from excellent parents and grandparents, all of them much alike, may be safely mated together, no matter how closely they may be related, with reasonable hope that most of the progeny will be sound and typical with a close resemblance to all the members of their ancestry. However, two such superlative and well-bred dogs are seldom to be found. It is the way to make progress rapidly and to establish a strain of dogs much alike and which breeds true. The amateur with the boldness and courage to try such a mating in the belief that his dogs are good enough for it is not to be discouraged. But if his judgment is not justified by the results, let him not complain that he has not been warned.

Line breeding is the safest course between the Scylla of outcrossing and the Charybdis of inbreeding for the inexperienced navigator in the sea of breeding. It, too, is to be used with care, because when it succeeds it partakes much of the nature of inbreeding. At any rate, its purpose is the pairing of like genes.

Here the pedigrees come into use. We examine the pedigree of the bitch to be bred. We hope that all the dogs named in it are magnificent dogs, but we look them over and choose the best of the four grandparents. We check this grandparent's breeding and find it good, as it probably is if it is itself a dog or bitch of great excellence. We shall assume that this best dog in the bitch's pedigree is the maternal grandsire. Then our bitch may be bred back to this particular grandsire, to his full brother if he has one of equal excellence, to his best son or best grandson. In such a fashion we compound the genes of this grandsire, and hope to obtain some puppies with his excellences intensified.

The best name in the pedigree may be some other dog or bitch, in which case it is his or her germ plasm that is to be doubled to serve for the foundation of the pedigrees of the puppies of the projected litter.

In making a mating, it is never wise to employ two dogs with the same positive fault. It is wise to use two dogs with as many of the same positive virtues as it is possible to obtain. Neither should faults balance each other, as one with a front too wide, the other with a front too narrow; one with a sway back, the other roach backed. Rather, one member of the mating should be right where the other is wrong. We cannot trust to obtain the intermediate, if we overcompensate the fault of one mate with a fault of the other.

NEGOTIATIONS TO USE THE STUD DOG

Plans to use a stud dog should be laid far enough in advance to enable one to make sure that the services of the dog will be available when they are required. Most men with a dog at public stud publish "stud cards," on which are printed the dog's pedigree and pertinent data pertaining to its record. These should be requested for all the dogs one contemplates using. Most such owners reserve the right to refuse to breed their dogs to bitches they deem unsuitable for them; they wish to safeguard their dog's reputation as a producer of superior puppies, by choosing the bitches to which he shall be bred. Therefore, it is advisable to submit a description of the bitch, with or without a picture of her, and her pedigree to the stud dog's owner at the time the application to use him is made.

Notification should be sent to the owner of the dog as soon as the bitch begins to show in heat, and she should be taken or sent by air or by railway express to the dog's owner about the time she is first recognized to be in full heat and ready to breed. The stud dog's owner should be advised by telegram or telephone just how she has been sent and just when she may be expected, and instruction should be given about how she is to be returned.

Extreme care should be used in securely crating a bitch for shipment when she is in heat. Such bitches are prone to chew their way out of insecure boxes and escape to be bred by some vagrant mongrel. A card containing a statement of the bitch's condition should be attached to the crate as a warning to the carrier to assure her greater security.

MATING

The only time the bitch may become pregnant is during her period of oestruation, a time also variously referred to as the "oestrus," "the season," and as being in "heat." A bitch's first season usually occurs when she is between six and nine months of age, with the average age being eight months. In rare instances it may occur as early as five months or as late as thirteen months of age. After the first season, oestrus usually recurs at intervals of approximately six months, though this too is subject to variation. Also, the bitch's cycle may be influenced by factors such as a change of environment or a change of climate, and her cycle will, of course, be changed if it is interrupted by pregnancy. Most bitches again come in season four to six months after whelping.

There is a decided controversy among breeders as to the wisdom of breeding a bitch during her first season. Some believe a really fine bitch should be bred during her first season in order that she may produce as many puppies as possible during the fertile years of her life span. Others feel that definite physical harm results from breeding a bitch at her first season. Since a normal healthy bitch can safely produce puppies until she is about nine years old, she can comfortably yield eight to ten litters with rests between them in her life. Any breeder should be satisfied with this production from one animal. It seems wiser, therefore, to avoid the risk of any harm and pass her first season. Bitches vary in temperament and in the ages at which they reach sufficient maturity for motherhood and its responsibilities. As with the human animal, stability comes with age and a dam is much more likely to be a good mother if she is out of the puppy phase herself. If the bitch is of show quality, she might become a champion between her first and second heats if not bred.

Usually, oestruation continues for a period of approximately three weeks, but this too is subject to variation. Prior to the beginning of the oestrus, there may be changes in the bitch's actions and demeanor; she may appear restless, or she may become increasingly affectionate. Often there is increased frequency of urination and the bitch may be inclined to lick her external parts. The breeder should be alert for any signs of the approach of oestrus since the bitch must be confined and protected at this time in order to preclude the possibility of the occurrence of a mating with any but the selected stud.

The first physical sign of oestrus is a bloody discharge of watery consistency. The mucous membrane lining the vulva becomes congested, enlarged, and reddened, and the external parts become puffy and swollen. The color of the discharge gradually deepens during the first day or two until it is a rich red color; then it gradually becomes lighter until by the tenth to twelfth day it has only a slightly reddish, or straw-colored, tinge. During the next day or so it becomes almost clear. During this same period, the swelling and hardness of the external parts gradually subside, and by the time the discharge has lost most of its color, the parts are softened and spongy. It is at this time that ovulation, the production of ripened ova (or eggs), takes place, although physical manifestations of oestrus may continue for another week.

A normal bitch has two ovaries which contain her ova. All the eggs she will produce during her lifetime are present in the ovaries at birth. Ordinarily, some of the ova ripen each time the bitch comes in season. Should a bitch fail to ovulate (produce ripened ova), she cannot, of course, become pregnant. Actually, only one ovary is necessary for ovulation, and loss of or damage to one ovary without impairment of the other will not prevent the bitch from producing puppies.

If fertilization does not occur, the ova (and this is also true of the sperm of the male) live only a short time—probably a couple of days at the most. Therefore, if mating takes place too long before or after ovulation, a bitch will not conceive, and the unfertilized ova will pass through the uterus into the vagina. Eventually they will either be absorbed or will pass out through the vulva by the same opening through which urination takes place. If fertilization does occur, the fertilized eggs become implanted on the inner surface of the uterus and grow to maturity.

Obviously, the breeder must exercise great care in determining when the dog and the bitch should be put together. Because the length of time between the beginning of the oestrus and the time of ovulation varies in different bitches, no hard and fast rule can be established, although the twelfth to fourteenth day is in most cases the correct time. The wise breeder will keep a daily record of the changes in the bitch's condition and will arrange to put the bitch and dog together when the discharge has become almost clear and the external parts are softened and spongy. If the bitch refuses the advances of the dog, it is preferable to separate the two, wait a day, then again permit the dog to approach the bitch.

Ordinarily, if the bitch is willing to accept the dog, fertilization of the ovum will take place. Usually one good service is sufficient, although two at intervals of twenty-four to forty-eight hours are often allowed.

Male dogs have glands on the penis which swell after passing the sphincter muscle of the vagina and "tie" the two animals together. The time may last for a period of a few minutes, a half hour, or occasionally up to an hour or more, but will end naturally when the locking glands have deflated the needful amount. While tying may increase the probability of success, in many cases no tie occurs, yet the bitches become pregnant.

Sperm are produced in the dog's testicles and are stored in the epididymis, a twisting tube at the side of the testicle. The occasional male dog whose testicles are not descended (a cryptorchid) is generally conceded to be sterile, although in a few instances it has been asserted that cryptorchids were capable of begetting progeny. The sterility in cryptorchids is believed to be due to the fact that the sperm are destroyed if the testicle remains within the abdominal cavity because the temperature is much higher there than in the normally descended testicle. Thus all sperm produced by the dog may be destroyed if both testicles are undescended. A monorchid (a dog with one testicle descended, the other undescended) may be fertile. Nevertheless, it is unwise to use a monorchid for stud purposes, because monorchidism is believed to be a heritable trait, and the monorchid, as well as the cryptorchid, is ineligible for the show ring.

After breeding, a bitch should be confined for a week to ten days to avoid mismating with another dog.

WHELPING CALENDAR

Find the month and date on which your bitch was bred in one of the left-hand columns. Directly opposite that date, in the right-hand column, is her expected date of whelping, bearing in mind that 61 days is as common as 63.

Date bred	Date due to whelp	Date bred	Date due to whelp	Date bred	Date due to whelp	Date bred	Date due to whelp	Date bred	Date due to whelp	Date bred	Date due to whelp	Date bred	Date due to whelp	Date bred	Date due to whelp	Date bred	Date due to whelp	Date bred	Date due to whelp	Date bred	Date due to whelp	Date bred
January	March	February	April	March	May	April	June	May	July	June	August	July	September	August	October	September	November	October	December	November	January	December
1	5	1	5	1	3	1	3	1	3	1	3	1	2	1	3	1	3	1	3	1	3	1
2	6	2	6	2	4	2	4	2	4	2	4	2	3	2	4	2	4	2	4	2	4	2
3	7	3	7	3	5	3	5	3	5	3	5	3	4	3	5	3	5	3	5	3	5	3
4	8	4	8	4	6	4	6	4	6	4	6	4	5	4	6	4	6	4	6	4	6	4
5	9	5	9	5	7	5	7	5	7	5	7	5	6	5	7	5	7	5	7	5	7	5
6	10	6	10	6	8	6	8	6	8	6	8	6	7	6	8	6	8	6	8	6	8	6
7	11	7	11	7	9	7	9	7	9	7	9	7	8	7	9	7	9	7	9	7	9	7
8	12	8	12	8	10	8	10	8	10	8	10	8	9	8	10	8	10	8	10	8	10	8
9	13	9	13	9	11	9	11	9	11	9	11	9	10	9	11	9	11	9	11	9	11	9
10	14	10	14	10	12	10	12	10	12	10	12	10	11	10	12	10	12	10	12	10	12	10
11	15	11	15	11	13	11	13	11	13	11	13	11	12	11	13	11	13	11	13	11	13	11
12	16	12	16	12	14	12	14	12	14	12	14	12	13	12	14	12	14	12	14	12	14	12
13	17	13	17	13	15	13	15	13	15	13	15	13	14	13	15	13	15	13	15	13	15	13
14	18	14	18	14	16	14	16	14	16	14	16	14	15	14	16	14	16	14	16	14	16	14
15	19	15	19	15	17	15	17	15	17	15	17	15	16	15	17	15	17	15	17	15	17	15
16	20	16	20	16	18	16	18	16	18	16	18	16	17	16	18	16	18	16	18	16	18	16
17	21	17	21	17	19	17	19	17	19	17	19	17	18	17	19	17	19	17	19	17	19	17
18	22	18	22	18	20	18	20	18	20	18	20	18	19	18	20	18	20	18	20	18	20	18
19	23	19	23	19	21	19	21	19	21	19	21	19	20	19	21	19	21	19	21	19	21	19
20	24	20	24	20	22	20	22	20	22	20	22	20	21	20	22	20	22	20	22	20	22	20
21	25	21	25	21	23	21	23	21	23	21	23	21	22	21	23	21	23	21	23	21	23	21
22	26	22	26	22	24	22	24	22	24	22	24	22	23	22	24	22	24	22	24	22	24	22
23	27	23	27	23	25	23	25	23	25	23	25	23	24	23	25	23	25	23	25	23	25	23
24	28	24	28	24	26	24	26	24	26	24	26	24	25	24	26	24	26	24	26	24	26	24
25	29	25	29	25	27	25	27	25	27	25	27	25	26	25	27	25	27	25	27	25	27	25
26	30	26	30	26	28	26	28	26	28	26	28	26	27	26	28	26	28	26	28	26	28	26
27	31	27	May 1	27	29	27	29	27	29	27	29	27	28	27	29	27	29	27	29	27	29	27
28	Apr. 1	28	2	28	30	28	30	28	30	28	30	28	29	28	30	28	30	28	30	28	30	28
29	2			29	31	29	July 1	29	31	29	31	29	30	29	31	29	Dec. 1	29	31	29	31	29
30	3			30	June 1	30	2	30	Aug. 1	30	Sep. 1	30	Oct. 1	30	Nov. 1	30	2	30	Jan. 1	30	Feb. 1	30
31	4			31	2			31	2			31	2	31	2			31	2			31

THE PREGNANCY AND WHELPING
OF THE BITCH

The "period of gestation" of the bitch, by which is meant the duration of her pregnancy, is usually estimated at sixty-three days. Many bitches, especially young ones, have their puppies as early as sixty days after they are bred. Cases have occurred in which strong puppies were born after only fifty-seven days, and there have been cases that required as many as sixty-six days. However, if puppies do not arrive by the sixty-fourth day, it is time to consult a veterinarian.

For the first five to six weeks of her pregnancy, the bitch requires no more than normal good care and unrestricted exercise. For that period, she needs no additional quantity of food, although her diet must contain sufficient amounts of all the food factors, as is stated in the division of this book that pertains to food. After the fifth to sixth week, the ration must be increased and the violence of exercise restricted. Normal running and walking are likely to be better for the pregnant bitch than a sedentary existence but she should not be permitted to jump, hunt, or fight during the latter half of her gestation. Violent activity may cause her to abort her puppies.

About a week before she is due to whelp, a bed should be prepared for her and she be persuaded to use it for sleeping. This bed may be a box of generous size, big enough to accommodate her with room for activity. It should be high enough to permit her to stand upright, and is better for having a hinged cover. An opening in one side will afford her ingress and egress. This box should be placed in a secluded location, away from any possible molestation by other dogs, animals, or children. The bitch must be made confident of her security in her box.

A few hours, or perhaps a day or two, before her whelping, the bitch will probably begin arranging the bedding of the box to suit herself, tearing blankets or cushions and nosing the parts into the corners. Before the whelping actually starts, however, it is best to substitute burlap sacking, securely tacked to the floor of the box. This is to provide traction for the puppies to reach the dam's breast.

The whelping may take place at night without any assistance from the owner. The box may be opened in the morning to reveal the happy bitch nursing a litter of complacent puppies. But she may need some assistance in her parturition. If whelping is recognized to be in process, it is best to help the bitch.

As the puppies arrive, one by one, the enveloping membranes should be removed as quickly as possible, lest the puppies suffocate. Having removed the membrane, the umbilical cord should be severed with clean scissors some three or four inches from the puppy's belly. (The part of the cord attached to the belly will dry up and drop off in a few days.) There is no need for any medicament or dressing of the cord after it is cut.

The bitch should be permitted to eat the afterbirth if she so desires, and she normally does. If she has no assistance, she will probably remove the membrane and sever the cord with her teeth. The only dangers are that she may delay too long or may bite the cord too short. Some bitches, few of them, eat their newborn puppies (especially bitches not adequately fed during pregnancy). This unlikelihood should be guarded against.

As they arrive, it is wise to remove all the puppies except one, placing them in a box or basket lined and covered by a woolen cloth, somewhere aside or away from the whelping bed, until all have come and the bitch's activity has ceased. The purpose of this is to prevent her from walking or lying on the whelps, and to keep her from being disturbed by the puppies' whining. A single puppy should be left with the bitch to ease her anxiety.

It is best that the "midwife" be somebody with whom the bitch is on intimate terms and in whom she has confidence. Some bitches exhibit a jealous fear and even viciousness while they are whelping. Such animals are few, and most appear grateful for gentle assistance through their ordeal.

The puppies arrive at intervals of a few minutes to an hour until all are delivered. It is wise to call a veterinarian if the interval is greater than one hour. Though such service is seldom needed, an experienced veterinarian can usually be depended upon to withdraw with obstetrical forceps an abnormally presented puppy. It is possible, but unlikely, that the veterinarian will recommend a Caesarian section. This surgery in the dog is not very grave, but it should be performed only by an expert veterinarian. It is unnecessary to describe the process here, or the subsequent management of the patient, since, if a Caesarian section should be necessary, the veterinarian will provide all the needed instructions.

Some bitches, at or immediately after their whelping period, go into a convulsive paralysis, which is called *eclampsia*. This is unlikely if the bitch throughout her pregnancy has had an adequate measure of calcium in her rations. The remedy for eclampsia is the intravenous or intramuscular administration of parenteral calcium. The bitch suspected of having eclampsia should be attended by a veterinarian.

Assuming that the whelping has been normal and without untoward incident, all of the puppies are returned to the bitch, and put, one by one, to the breast, which strong puppies will accept with alacrity. The less handling of puppies for the first four or five hours of their lives, the better. However, the litter should be looked over carefully for possible defectives and discards, which should be destroyed as soon as possible. There is no virtue in rearing hare-lipped, crippled, or mismarked puppies.

It is usually unwise to destroy sound, healthy puppies just to reduce the number in the litter, since it is impossible to sort young puppies for excellence and one may be destroying the best member of the litter, a future champion. Unless a litter is extraordinarily numerous, the dam, if well fed, can probably suckle them all. If it is found that her milk is insufficient, the litter may be artificially fed or may be divided, and the surplus placed on a foster mother if it is possible to obtain one. The foster mother need not be of the same breed as the puppies, a mongrel being as good as any. She should be approximately the same size as the actual mother of the puppies, clean, healthy, and her other puppies should be of as nearly the same age as the ones she is to take over as possible. She should be removed from her own puppies (which may well be destroyed) and her breasts be permitted to fill with milk until she is somewhat uncomfortable, at which time her foster puppies can be put to her breasts and will usually be accepted without difficulty. Unless the services of the foster mother are really required, it is better not to use her.

The whelping bitch may be grateful for a warm meal even between the arrivals of her puppies. As soon as her chore is over, she should be offered food in her box. This should be of cereal and milk or of meat and broth, something sloppy. She will probably not leave her puppies to eat and her meals must be brought to her.

It is wise to give a mild laxative for her bowels, also milk of magnesia. She will be reluctant to get out of her box even to relieve herself for about two days, but she should be urged, even forced, to do so regularly. A sensible bitch will soon settle down to care for her brood and will seldom give further trouble. She should be fed often and well, all that she can be induced to eat during her entire lactation.

As a preventive for infections sometimes occurring after whelping, some experienced breeders and veterinarians recommend injecting the bitch with penicillin or another antibiotic immediately following the birth of the last puppy. Oral doses of the same drug may be given daily thereafter for the first week. It is best to consult your veterinarian about this treatment.

ACID MILK

Occasionally a bitch produces early milk (colostrum) so acid that it disagrees with, sometimes kills, her puppies. The symptoms of the puppies are whining, disquiet, frequently refusal to nurse, frailty, and death. It is true that all milk is slightly acid, and it should be, turning blue litmus paper immersed in it a very light pink. However, milk harmfully on the acid side will readily turn litmus paper a vivid red. It seems that only the first two or three days milk is so affected. Milk problems come also from mastitis and other infections in the bitch.

This is not likely to occur with a bitch that throughout her pregnancy has received an adequate supply of calcium phosphate regularly in her daily ration. That is the best way to deal with the situation—to see to the bitch's correct nutrition in advance of her whelping. The owner has only himself to blame for the bitch's too acid milk, since adequate calcium in advance would have neutralized the acid.

If it is found too late that her milk is too acid, the puppies must be taken from her breast and either given to a foster mother or artificially fed from bottle or by medicine dropper. Artificial feeding of very young puppies seldom is successful. Sometimes the acidity of the dam's milk can be neutralized by giving her large doses of bicarbonate of soda (baking soda), but the puppies should not be restored to her breasts until her milk ceases to turn litmus paper red.

If it is necessary to feed the puppies artificially, "Esbilac," a commercial product, or the following orphan puppy formula, may be used.

7 oz. whole milk
1 oz. cream (top milk)
1 egg yolk
2 tbsp. corn syrup
2 tbsp. lime water

REARING THE PUPPIES

Puppies are born blind and open their eyes at approximately the ninth day thereafter. If they were whelped earlier than the full sixty-three days after the breeding from which they resulted, the difference should be added to the nine days of anticipated blindness. The early eye color of young puppies is no criterion of the color to which the eyes are likely to change, and the breeder's anxiety about his puppies' having light eyes is premature.

In breeds that require the docking of the tail, this should be done on the third day and is a surgical job for the veterinarian. Many a dog has had his tail cut off by an inexperienced person, ruining his good looks and his possibility for a win in the show ring. Dew claws should be removed at the same time. There is little else to do with normal puppies except to let them alone and permit them to grow. The most important thing about their management is their nutrition, which is discussed in another chapter. The first two or three weeks, they will thrive and grow rapidly on their mother's milk, after which they should have additional food as described.

Puppies sleep much of the time, as do other babies, and they should not be frequently awakened to be played with. They grow more and more playful as they mature.

After the second week their nails begin to grow long and sharp. The mother will be grateful if the puppies' nails are blunted with scissors from time to time so that in their pawing of the breast they do not lacerate it. Sharp nails tend to prompt the mother to wean the whelps early, and she should be encouraged to keep them with her as long as she will tolerate them. Even the small amount of milk they can drain from her after the weaning process is begun is the

65

best food they can obtain. It supplements and makes digestible the remainder of their ration.

Many bitches, after their puppies are about four weeks of age, eat and regurgitate food, which is eaten by the puppies. This food is warmed and partly digested in the bitch's stomach. This practice, while it may appear digusting to the novice keeper of dogs, is perfectly normal and should not be discouraged. However, it renders it all the more necessary that the food of the bitch be sound, clean, and nutritious.

It is all but impossible to rear a litter of puppies without their becoming infested with roundworms. Of course, the bitch should be wormed, if she harbors such parasites, before she is bred, and her teats should be thoroughly washed with mild soap just before she whelps to free them from the eggs of roundworms. Every precaution must be taken to reduce the infestation of the puppies to a minimum. But, in spite of all it is possible to do, puppies will have roundworms. These pests hamper growth, reduce the puppies' normal resistance to disease, and may kill them outright unless the worms are eliminated. The worming of puppies is discussed in the chapter entitled "Intestinal Parasites and Their Control."

External Vermin
and Parasites

U NDER this heading the most common external parasites will be given consideration. Fleas, lice, ticks, and flies are those most commonly encountered and causing the most concern. The external parasite does not pose the problem that it used to before we had the new "miracle" insecticides. Today, with DDT, lindane, and chlordane, the course of extermination and prevention is much easier to follow. Many of the insecticide sprays have a four to six weeks residual effect. Thus the premises can be sprayed and the insect pests can be quite readily controlled.

FLEAS

Neglected dogs are too often beset by hundreds of blood-thirsty fleas, which do not always confine their attacks to the dogs but also sometimes feast upon their masters. Unchecked, they overrun kennels, homes, and playgrounds. Moreover, they are the intermediate hosts for the development of the kind of tapeworm most frequently found in dogs, as will be more fully discussed under the subject of *Intestinal Parasites*. Fleas are all-round bad actors and nuisances. Although it need hardly concern us in America, where the disease is not known to exist, fleas are the recognized and only vectors of bubonic plague.

There are numerous kinds and varieties of fleas, of which we shall discuss here only the three species often found on dogs. These are the human flea (*Pulex irritans*), the dog flea (*Ctenocephalides canis*), and the so-called chicken flea or sticktight flea (*Echidnophaga gallinacea*).

Of these the human flea prefers the blood of man to that of the dog, and unless humans are also bothered, are not likely to be found on the dog. They are small, nearly black insects, and occur mostly in the Mississippi Valley and in California. Their control is the same as for the dog flea.

The dog flea is much larger than his human counterpart, is dark brown in color and seldom bites mankind. On an infested dog these dog fleas may be found buried in the coat of any part of the anatomy, but their choicest habitat is the area of the back just forward from the tail and over the loins. On that part of a badly neglected dog, especially in summer, fleas by the hundreds will be found intermixed with their dung and with dried blood. They may cause the dog some discomfort or none. It must not be credited that because a dog is not kept in a constant or frequent agitation of scratching that he harbors no fleas. The coats of pet animals are soiled and roughened by the fleas and torn by the scratching that they sometimes induce. Fleas also appear to be connected with summer eczema of dogs; at least the diseased condition of the skin often clears up after fleas are eradicated.

Although the adults seldom remain long away from the dog's body, fleas do not reproduce themselves on the dog. Rather, their breeding haunts are the debris, dust, and sand of the kennel floor, and especially the accumulations of dropped hair, sand, and loose soil of unclean sleeping boxes. Nooks and cracks and crannies of the kennel may harbor the eggs or maggot-like larvae of immature fleas.

This debris and accumulation must be eliminated—preferably by incineration—after which all possible breeding areas should be thoroughly sprayed with a residual effect spray.

The adult dog may be combed well, then bathed in a detergent solution, rinsed thoroughly in warm water, and allowed to drip fairly dry. A solution of Pine Oil (1 oz. to a quart of water) is then used as a final rinse. This method of ridding the dog of its fleas is ideal in warm weather. The Pine Oil imparts a pleasant odor to the dog's coat and the animal will enjoy being bathed and groomed.

The same procedure may be followed for young puppies except that the Pine Oil solution should be rinsed off. When bathing is not feasible, then a good flea powder—one containing lindane—should be used.

Sticktight fleas are minute, but are to be found, if at all, in patches on the dog's head and especially on the ears. They remain quiescent and do not jump, as the dog fleas and human fleas do. Their tiny heads are buried in the dog's flesh. To force them loose from the area decapitates them and the heads remain in the skin which is prone to fester from the irritation. They may be dislodged by placing a cotton pad or thick cloth well soaked in ether or alcohol over the flea patch, which causes them immediately to relinquish their hold, after which they can be easily combed loose and destroyed.

These sticktights abound in neglected, dirty, and abandoned chicken houses, which, if the dogs have access to them, should be cleaned out thoroughly and sprayed with DDT.

Fleas, while a nuisance, are only a minor problem. They should be eliminated not only from the dog but from all the premises he inhabits. Dogs frequently are reinfested with fleas from other dogs with which they play or come in contact. Every dog should be occasionally inspected for the presence of fleas, and, if any are found, immediate means should be taken to eradicate them.

LICE

There are even more kinds of lice than of fleas, although as they pertain to dogs there is no reason to differentiate them. They do not infest dogs, except in the events of gross neglect or of unforeseen accident. Lice reproduce themselves on the body of the dog. To rid him of the adult lice is easy. The standard Pine Oil solution used to kill fleas will also kill lice. However, the eggs or "nits" are harder to remove. Weather permitting, it is sometimes best to have the dog clipped of all its hair. In heavily infested dogs this is the only sure way to cope with the situation. When the hair is clipped, most of the "nits" are removed automatically. A good commercial flea and louse powder applied to the skin will then keep the situation under control.

69

Rare as the occurrence of lice upon dogs may be, they must be promptly treated and eradicated. Having a dog with lice can prove to be embarrassing, for people just do not like to be around anything lousy. Furthermore, the louse may serve as the intermediate host of the tapeworm in dogs.

The dog's quarters should be thoroughly sprayed with a residual spray of the same type recommended for use in the control of fleas. The problem of disinfecting kennel and quarters is not as great as it is in the case of fleas, for the louse tends to stay on its host, not leaving the dog as the flea does.

TICKS

The terms "wood ticks" and "dog ticks," as usually employed, refer to at least eight different species, whose appearances and habits are so similar that none but entomologists are likely to know them apart. It is useless to attempt to differentiate between these various species here, except to warn the reader that the Rocky Mountain spotted fever tick (*Dermacentor andersoni*) is a vector of the human disease for which it is named, as well as of rabbit fever (tularemia), and care must be employed in removing it from dogs lest the hands be infected. Some one or more of these numerous species are to be found in well nigh every state in the Union, although there exist wide areas where wood ticks are seldom seen and are not a menace to dogs.

All the ticks must feed on blood in order to reproduce themselves. The eggs are always deposited on the ground or elsewhere after the female, engorged with blood, has dropped from the dog or other animal upon which she has fed. The eggs are laid in masses in protected places on the ground, particularly in thick clumps of grass. Each female lays only one such mass, which contains 2500 to 5000 eggs. The development of the American dog tick embraces four stages: the egg, the larva or seed tick, the nymph, and the adult. The two intermediate stages in the growth of the tick are spent on rodents, and only in the adult stage does it attach itself to the dog. Both sexes affix themselves to dogs and to other animals and feed on their blood; the males do not increase in size, although the female is tremendously enlarged as she gorges. Mating occurs while the female is feeding. After some five to thirteen days, she drops

70

from her host, lays her eggs and dies. At no time do ticks feed on anything except the blood of animals.

The longevity and hardihood of the tick are amazing. The larvae and nymphs may live for a full year without feeding, and the adults survive for more than two years if they fail to encounter a host to which they may attach. In the Northern United States the adults are most active in the spring and summer, few being found after July. But in the warmer Southern states they may be active the year around.

Although most of the tick species require a vegetative cover and wild animal hosts to complete their development, at least one species, the brown tick (*Rhipicephalus sanguinius*), is adapted to life in the dryer environment of kennels, sheds, and houses, with the dog as its only necessary host. This tick is the vector of canine piroplasmosis, although this disease is at this time almot negligible in the United States.

This brown dog tick often infests houses in large numbers, both immature and adult ticks lurking around baseboards, window casings, furniture, the folds of curtains, and elsewhere. Thus, even dogs kept in houses are sometimes infested with hundreds of larvae, nymphs, and adults of this tick. Because of its ability to live in heated buildings, the species has become established in many Northern areas. Unlike the other tick species, the adult of the brown dog tick does not bite human beings. However, also unlike the other ticks, it is necessary not only to rid the dogs of this particular tick but also to eliminate the pests from their habitat, especially the dogs' beds and sleeping boxes. A spray with a 10% solution of DDT suffices for this purpose. Fumigation of premises seldom suffices, since not only are brown dog ticks very resistant to mere fumigation, but the ticks are prone to lurk around entry ways, porches and outbuildings, where they cannot be reached with a fumigant. The spraying with DDT may not penetrate to spots where some ticks are in hiding, and it must be repeated at intervals until all the pests are believed to be completely eradicated.

Dogs should not be permitted to run in brushy areas known to be infested with ticks, and upon their return from exercise in a place believed to harbor ticks, dogs should be carefully inspected for their presence.

If a dog's infestation is light, the ticks may be picked individually from his skin. To make tick release its grip, dab with alcohol or a drop of ammonia. If the infestation is heavy, it is easier and quicker to saturate his coat with a derris solution (one ounce of soap and two ounces of derris powder dissolved in one gallon of water). The derris should be of an excellent grade containing at least 3% of rotenone. The mixture may be used and reused, since it retains its strength for about three weeks if it is kept in a dark place.

If possible, the dip should be permitted to dry on the dog's coat. It should not get into a dog's eyes. The dip will not only kill the ticks that are attached to the dog, but the powder drying in the hair will repel further infestation for two or three days and kill most if not all the boarders. These materials act slowly, requiring sometimes as much as twenty-four hours to complete the kill.

If the weather is cold or the use of the dip should be otherwise inconvenient, derris powder may be applied as a dust, care being taken that it penetrates the hair and reaches the skin. Breathing or swallowing derris may cause a dog to vomit, but he will not be harmed by it. The dust and liquid should be kept from his eyes.

Since the dog is the principal host on which the adult tick feeds and since each female lays several thousand eggs after feeding, treating the dog regularly will not only bring him immediate relief but will limit the reproduction of the ticks. Keeping underbrush, weeds, and grass closely cut tends to remove protection favorable to the ticks. Burning vegetation accomplishes the same results.

Many of the ticks in an infested area may be killed by the thorough application of a spray made as follows: Four tablespoonfuls of nicotine sulphate (40% nicotine) in three gallons of water. More permanent results may be obtained by adding to this solution four ounces of sodium fluorides, but this will injure the vegetation.

Besides the ticks that attach themselves to all parts of the dog, there is another species that infests the ear specifically. This pest, the spinose ear tick, penetrates deep into the convolutions of the ear and often causes irritation and pain, as evidenced by the dog's scratching its ears, shaking its head or holding it on one side. One part derris powder (5% rotenone) mixed with ten parts medicinal mineral oil and dropped into the ear will kill spinose ear ticks. Only a few drops of the material is required, but it is best to massage the base of the ear to make sure the remedy penetrates to the deepest part of the ear to reach all the ticks.

FLIES

Flies can play havoc with dogs in outdoor kennels, stinging them and biting the ears until they are raw. Until recently the only protection against them was the screening of the entire kennel. The breeding places of flies, which are damp filth and stagnant garbage, are in most areas now happily abated, but the chief agent for control of the pest is DDT.

A spray of a 10% solution of DDT over all surfaces of the kennel property may be trusted to destroy all the flies that light on those surfaces for from two weeks to one month. It must, of course, be repeated from time to time when it is seen that the efficacy of the former treatment begins to diminish.

Intestinal Parasites and Their Control

THE varieties of worms that may inhabit the alimentary tract of the dog are numerous. Much misapprehension exists, even among experienced dog keepers, about the harm these parasites may cause and about the methods of getting rid of them. Some dog keepers live in terror of these worms and continually treat their dogs for them whether they are known to be present or not; others ignore the presence of worms and do nothing about them. Neither policy is justified.

Promiscuous dosing, without the certainty that the dog harbors worms or what kind he may have, is a practice fraught with danger for the well-being of the animal. All drugs for the expulsion or destruction of parasites are poisonous or irritant to a certain degree and should be administered only when it is known that the dog is infested by parasites and what kind. It is hardly necessary to say that when a dog is known to harbor worms he should be cleared of them, but in most instances there is no such urgency as is sometimes manifested.

It may be assumed that puppies at weaning time are more or less infested with intestinal roundworms or ascarids (*Toxocara canis*) and that such puppies need to be treated for worms. It is all but impossible to rear a litter of puppies to weaning age free from those parasites. Once the puppies are purged of them, it is amazing to see the spurt of their growth and the renewal of their thriftiness.

Many neglected puppies surmount the handicap of their worms and at least some of them survive. This, however, is no reason that good puppies—puppies that are worth saving—should go unwormed and neglected.

The ways to find out that a dog actually has worms are to see some of the worms themselves in the dog's droppings or to submit a sample of his feces to a veterinarian or to a biological laboratory for microscopic examination. From a report of such an examination, it is possible to know whether or not a dog is a host to intestinal parasites at all and intelligently to undertake the treatment and control of the specific kind he may harbor.

All of the vermifuges, vermicides, and anthelmintic remedies tend to expel other worms besides the kind for which they are specifically intended, but it is better to employ the remedy particularly effective against the individual kind of parasite the dog is known to have, and to refrain from worm treatment unless or until it is known to be needed.

ROUNDWORMS

The ascarids, or large intestinal roundworms, are the largest of the worm parasites occurring in the digestive tract of the dog, varying in length from 1 to 8 inches, the females being larger than the males. The name "spool worms," which is sometimes applied to them, is derived from their tendency to coil in a springlike spiral when they are expelled, either from the bowel or vomited, by their hosts. There are at least two species of them which frequently parasitize dogs: *Toxocara canis* and *Toxascaris leonina,* but they are so much alike except for some minor details in the life histories of their development that it is not practically necessary for the dog keeper to seek to distinguish between them.

Neither specie requires an intermediate host for its development. Numerous eggs are deposited in the intestinal tract of the host animal; these eggs are passed out by the dog in his feces and are swallowed by the same or another animal, and hatching takes place in its small intestine. Their development requires from twelve to sixteen days under favorable circumstances.

It has been shown that puppies before their birth may be infested by roundworms from their mother. This accounts for the occasional finding of mature or nearly mature worms in very young puppies. It cannot occur if the mother is entirely free from worms, as she should be.

These roundworms are particularly injurious to young puppies. The commonest symptoms of roundworm infestation are general unthriftiness, digestive disturbances, and bloat after feeding. The hair grows dead and lusterless, and the breath may have a peculiar sweetish odor. Large numbers of roundworms may obstruct the intestine, and many have been known to penetrate the intestinal wall. In heavy infestations the worms may wander into the bile ducts, stomach, and even into the lungs and upper respiratory passages where they may cause pneumonia, especially in very young animals.

The control of intestinal roundworms depends primarily upon prompt disposal of feces, keeping the animals in clean quarters and on clean ground, and using only clean utensils for feed and water. Dampness of the ground favors the survival of worm eggs and larvae. There is no known chemical treatment feasible for the destruction of eggs in contaminated soil, but prolonged exposure to sunlight and drying has proved effective.

Numerous remedies have been in successful use for roundworms, including turpentine, which has a recognized deleterious effect upon the kidneys; santonin, an old standby; freshly powdered betel nut and its derivative, arecoline, both of which tend to purge and sicken the patient; oil of chenopodium, made from American wormseed; carbon tetrachloride, widely used as a cleaning agent; tetrachlorethylene, closely related chemically to the former, but less toxic; and numerous other medicaments. While all of them are effective as vermifuges or vermicides, if rightly employed, to each of them some valid objection can be interposed.

In addition to the foregoing, there are other vermifuges available for treatment of roundworms. Some may be purchased without a prescription, whereas others may be procured only when prescribed by a veterinarian.

HOOKWORMS

Hookworms are the most destructive of all the parasites of dogs. There are three species of them—*Ancylostoma caninum, A. braziliense,* and *Uncinaria stenocephalia*—all to be found in dogs in some parts of the United States. The first named is the most widespread; the second found only in the warmer parts of the South and Southwest; the last named, in the North and in Canada. All are similar one to another and to the hookworm that infests mankind (*Ancylostoma uncinariasis*). For purposes of their eradication, no distinction need be made between them.

It is possible to keep dogs for many years in a dry and well drained area without an infestation with hookworms, which are contracted only on infested soils. However, unthrifty dogs shipped from infested areas are suspect until it is proved that hookworm is not the cause of their unthriftiness.

Hookworm males seldom are longer than half an inch, the females somewhat larger. The head end is curved upward, and is equipped with cutting implements, which may be called teeth, by which they attach themselves to the lining of the dog's intestine and suck his blood.

The females produce numerous eggs which pass out in the dog's feces. In two weeks or a little more these eggs hatch, the worms pass through various larval stages, and reach their infective stage. Infection of the dog may take place through his swallowing the organism, or by its penetration of his skin through some lesion. In the latter case the worms enter the circulation, reach the lungs, are coughed up, swallowed, and reach the intestine where their final development occurs. Eggs appear in the dog's feces from three to six weeks after infestation.

Puppies are sometimes born with hookworms already well developed in their intestines, the infection taking place before their birth. Eggs of the hookworm are sometimes found in the feces of puppies only thirteen days old. Assumption is not to be made that all puppies are born with hookworms or even that they are likely to become infested, but in hookworm areas the possibility of either justifies precautions that neither shall happen.

Hookworm infestation in puppies and young dogs brings about a condition often called kennel anemia. There may be digestive disturbances and blood streaked diarrhea. In severe cases the feces may be almost pure blood. Infested puppies fail to grow, often lose weight, and the eyes are sunken and dull. The loss of blood results in an anemia with pale mucous membranes of the mouth and eyes. This anemia is caused by the consumption of the dog's blood by the worms and the bleeding that follows the bites. The worms are not believed to secrete a poison or to cause damage to the dog except loss of blood.

There is an admitted risk in worming young puppies before weaning time, but it is risk that must be run if the puppies are known to harbor hookworms. The worms, if permitted to persist, will ruin the puppies and likely kill them. No such immediacy is needful for the treatment of older puppies and adult dogs, although hookworm infestation will grow steadily worse until it is curbed. It should not be delayed and neglected in the belief or hope that the dog can cure himself.

If treatment is attempted at home, there are available three fairly efficacious and safe drugs that may be used: normal butyl chloride, hexaresorcinal, and methyl benzine.

If a dog is visibly sick and a diagnosis of hookworm infestation has been made, treatment had best be under professional guidance.

Brine made by stirring common salt (sodium chloride) into boiling water, a pound and a half of salt to the gallon of water, will destroy hookworm infestation in the soil. A gallon of brine should be sufficient to treat eight square feet of soil surface. One treatment of the soil is sufficient unless it is reinfested.

TAPEWORMS

The numerous species of tapeworm which infest the dog may, for practical purposes, be divided into two general groups, the armed forms and the unarmed forms. Species of both groups resemble each other in their possession of a head and neck and a chain of segments. They are, however, different in their life histories, and the best manner to deal with each type varies. This is unfortunately not well understood, since to most persons a tapeworm is a tapeworm.

The armed varieties are again divided into the single pored forms of the genera *Taenia, Multiceps,* and *Echinococcus,* and the double pored tapeworm, of which the most widespread and prevalent among dogs in the United States is the so-called dog tapeworm, *Dipylidium caninum.* This is the variety with segments shaped like cucumber-seeds. The adult rarely exceeds a foot in length, and the head is armed with four or five tiny hooks. For the person with well cared for and protected dogs, this is the only tapeworm of which it is necessary to take particular cognizance.

The dog tapeworm requires but a single intermediate host for its development, which in most cases is the dog flea or the biting louse. Thus, by keeping dogs free from fleas and lice the major danger of tapeworm infestation is obviated.

The tapeworm is bi-sexual and requires the intermediate host in order to complete its life cycle. Segments containing the eggs of the tapeworm pass out with the stool, or the detached proglottid may emerge by its own motile power and attach itself to the contiguous hair. The flea then lays its eggs on this segment, thus affording sustenance for the larva. The head of the tapeworm develops in the lung chamber of the baby flea. Thus, such a flea, when it develops and finds its way back to a dog, is the potential carrier of tapeworm. Of course, the cycle is complete when the flea bites the dog and the dog, in biting the area to relieve the itching sensation, swallows the flea.

Since the egg of the tapeworm is secreted in the segment that breaks off and passes with the stool, microscopic examination of the feces is of no avail in attempting to determine whether tapeworms infest a dog. It is well to be suspicious of a finicky eater— a dog that refuses all but the choicest meat and shows very little appetite. The injury produced by this armed tapeworm to the dog that harbors it is not well understood. Frequently it produces no symptoms at all, and it is likely that it is not the actual cause of many of the symptoms attributed to it. At least, it is known that a dog may have one or many of these worms over a long period of time and apparently be no worse for their presence. Nervous symptoms or skin eruptions, or both, are often charged to the presence of tapeworm, which may or may not be the cause of the morbid condition.

Tapeworm-infested dogs sometimes involuntarily pass segments of worms and so soil floors, rugs, furniture, or bedding. The passage by dogs of a segment or a chain of segments via the anus is a frequent cause of the dog's itching, which he seeks to allay by sitting and dragging himself on the floor by his haunches. The segments or chains are sometimes mistakenly called pinworms, but pinworms are a kind of roundworm to which dogs are not subject.

Despite that they may do no harm, few dogs owners care to tolerate tapeworms in their dogs. These worms, it has been definitely established, are not transmissible from dog to dog or to man. Without the flea or the louse, it is impossible for the adult dog tapeworm to reproduce itself, and by keeping dogs free from fleas and lice it is possible to keep them also free from dog tapeworm.

The various unarmed species of tapeworm find their intermediate hosts in the flesh and other parts of various animals, fish, crustacians and crayfish. Dogs not permitted to eat raw meats which have not been officially inspected, never have these worms, and it is needless here to discuss them at length. Hares and rabbits are the intermediate hosts to some of these worms and dogs should not be encouraged to feed upon those animals.

Little is known of the effects upon dogs of infestations of the unarmed tapeworms, but they are believed to be similar to the effects (if any) of the armed species.

The prevention of tapeworm infestation may be epitomized by saying: Do not permit dogs to swallow fleas or lice nor to feed upon uninspected raw meats. It is difficult to protect dogs from such contacts if they are permitted to run at large, but it is to be presumed that persons interested enough in caring for dogs to read this book will keep their dogs at home and protect them.

The several species of tapeworm occurring in dogs are not all removable by the same treatment. The most effective treatment for the removal of the armed species, which is the one most frequently found in the dogs, is arecoline hydrobromide. This drug is a drastic purgative and acts from fifteen to forty-five minutes after its administration. The treatment should be given in the morning after the dog has fasted overnight, and food should be withheld for some three hours after dosing.

Arecoline is not so effective against the double-pored tapeworm as against the other armed species, and it may be necessary to repeat the dose after a few days waiting, since some of the tapeworm heads may not be removed by the first treatment and regeneration of the tapeworm may occur in a few weeks. The estimatedly correct dosage is not stated here, since the drug is so toxic that the dosage should be estimated for the individual dog by a competent veterinarian, and it is better that he should be permitted to administer the remedy and control the treatment.

WHIPWORMS

The dog whipworm (*Trichuris vulpis*) is so called from its fancied resemblance to a tiny blacksnake whip, the front part being slender and hairlike and the hinder part relatively thick. It rarely exceeds three inches in its total length. Whipworms in dogs exist more or less generally throughout the world, but few dogs in the United States are known to harbor them. They are for the most part confined to the caecum, from which they are hard to dislodge, but sometimes spill over into the colon, whence they are easy to dislodge.

The complete life history of the whipworm is not well established, but it is known that no intermediate host is required for its development. The eggs appear to develop in much the same way as the eggs of the large roundworm, but slower, requiring from two weeks to several months for the organisms to reach maturity.

It has not as yet been definitely established that whipworms are the true causes of all the ills of which they are accused. In many instances they appear to cause little damage, even in heavy infestations. A great variety of symptoms of an indefinite sort have been ascribed to whipworms, including digestive disturbances, diarrhea, loss of weight, nervousness, convulsions, and general unthriftiness, but it remains to be proved that whipworms were responsible.

To be effective in its removal of whipworms, a drug must enter the caecum and come into direct contact with them; but the entry of the drug into this organ is somewhat fortuitous, and to increase the chances of its happening, large doses of a drug essentially harmless to the dog must be used. Normal butyl chloride meets this requirement, but it must be given in large doses. Even then, complete clearance of whipworms from the caecum may not be expected; the best to be hoped is that their numbers will be reduced and the morbid symptoms will subside.

Before treatment the dog should be fasted for some eighteen hours, although he may be fed two hours after being treated. It is wise to follow the normal butyl chloride in one hour with a purgative dose of castor oil. This treatment, since it is not expected to be wholly effective, may be repeated at monthly intervals.

The only known means of the complete clearance of whipworms from the dog is the surgical removal of the caecum, which of course should be undertaken only by a veterinary surgeon.

HEART WORMS

Heart worms (*Dirofilaria immitis*) in dogs are rare. They occur largely in the South and Southeast, but their incidence appears to be increasing and cases have been reported along the Atlantic Seaboard as far north as New York. The various species of mosquitoes are known to be vectors of heart worms, although the flea is also accused of spreading them.

The symptoms of heart worm infestation are somewhat vague, and include coughing, shortness of breath and collapse. In advanced cases, dropsy may develop. Nervous symptoms, fixity of vision, fear of light, and convulsions may develop. However, all such symptoms may occur from other causes and it must not be assumed because a dog manifests some of these conditions that he has heart worms. The only way to be sure is a microscopic examination of the blood and the presence or absence of the larvae. Even in some cases where larvae have been found in the blood, post mortem examinations have failed to reveal heart worms in the heart.

Both the diagnosis and treatment of heart worm are functions of the veterinarian. They are beyond the province of the amateur. The drug used is a derivative from antimony known as fuadin, and many dogs are peculiarly susceptible to antimony poisoning. If proper treatment is used by a trained veterinarian, a large preponderance of cases make a complete recovery. But even the most expert of veterinarians may be expected to fail in the successful treatment of a percentage of heart worm infestations. The death of some of the victims is to be anticipated.

LESS FREQUENTLY FOUND WORMS

Besides the intestinal worms that have been enumerated, there exist in some dogs numerous other varieties and species of worms which are of so infrequent occurrence that they require no discussion in a book for the general dog keeper. These include, esophageal worms, lungworms, kidney worms, and eye worms. They are in North America, indeed, so rare as to be negligible.

COCCIDIA

Coccidia are protozoic, microscopic organisms. The forms to which the dog is a host are *Isospora rivolta, I. bigeminia* and *I. felis.* Coccidia eggs, called *oocysts,* can be carried by flies and are picked up by dogs as they lick themselves or eat their stools.

These parasides attack the intestinal wall and cause diarrhea. They are particularly harmful to younger puppies that have been weaned, bringing on fever, running eyes, poor appetite and debilitation as well as the loose stools.

The best prevention is scrupulous cleanliness of the puppy or dog, its surroundings and its playmates whether canine or human. Flies should be eliminated as described in the preceding chapter and stools removed promptly where the dog cannot touch it.

Infection can be confirmed by microscopic examination of the stool. Treatment consists of providing nourishing food, which should be force-fed if necessary, and whatever drug the veterinarian recommends. Puppies usually recover, though occasionally their teeth may be pitted as in distemper.

A dog infected once by one form develops immunity to that form but may be infected by another form.

Skin Troubles

THERE is a tendency on the part of the amateur dog keeper to consider any lesion of the dog's skin to be mange. Mange is an unusual condition in clean, well fed, and well cared for dogs. Eczema occurs much more frequently and is often more difficult to control.

MANGE OR SCABIES

There are at least two kinds of mange that effect dogs—sarcoptic mange and demodectic or red mange, the latter rare indeed and difficult to cure.

Sarcoptic mange is caused by a tiny spider-like mite (*Sarcoptes scabiei canis*) which is similar to the mite that causes human scabies or "itch." Indeed, the mange is almost identical with scabies and is transmissible from dog to man. The mite is approximately 1/100th of an inch in length and without magnification is just visible to acute human sight.

Only the female mites are the cause of the skin irritation. They burrow into the upper layers of the skin, where each lays twenty to forty eggs, which in three to seven days hatch into larvae. These larvae in turn develop into nymphs which later grow into adults. The entire life cycle requires from fourteen to twenty-one days for completion. The larvae, nymphs, and males do not burrow into the skin, but live under crusts and scabs on the surface.

The disease may make its first appearance on any part of the dog's body, although it is usually first seen on the head and muzzle, around the eyes, or at the base of the ears. Sometimes it is first noticed in the armpits, the inner parts of the thighs, the lower abdomen or on the front of the chest. If not promptly treated it may cover the whole body and an extremely bad infestation may cause the death of the dog after a few months.

Red points which soon develop into small blisters are the first signs of the disease. These are most easily seen on the unpigmented parts of the skin, such as the abdomen. As the female mites burrow into the skin, there is an exudation of serum which dries and scabs. The affected parts soon are covered with bran-like scales followed with grayish crusts. The itching is intense, especially in hot weather or after exercise. The rubbing and scratching favor secondary bacterial infections and the formation of sores. The hair may grow matted and fall out, leaving bare spots. The exuded serum decomposes and gives rise to a peculiar mousy odor which increases as the disease develops and which is especially characteristic.

Sarcoptic mange is often confused with demodectic (red) mange, ringworm, or with simple eczema. If there is any doubt about the diagnosis, a microscopic examination of the scrapings of the lesions will reveal the true facts.

It is easy to control sarcoptic mange if it is recognized in its earlier stages and treatment is begun immediately. Neglected, it may be very difficult to eradicate. If it is considered how rapidly the causative mites reproduce themselves, the necessity for early treatment becomes apparent. That treatment consists not only of medication of the dog but also of sterilization of his bedding, all tools and implements used on him, and the whole premises upon which he has been confined. Sarcoptic mange is easily and quickly transmissible from dog to dog, from area to area on the same dog, and even from dog to human.

In some manner which is not entirely understood, an inadequate or unbalanced diet appears to predispose a dog to sarcoptic mange, and few dogs adequately fed and cared for ever contract it. Once a dog has contracted mange, however, improvement in the amount of quality of his food seems not to hasten his recovery.

There are various medications recommended for sarcoptic mange, sulphur ointment being the old standby. However, it is messy, difficult to use, and not always effective. For the treatment of sarcoptic mange, there are available today such insecticides as lindane, chlordane, and DDT. The use of these chemicals greatly facilitates treatment and cure of the dogs affected with mange and those exposed to it.

A bath made by dissolving four ounces of derris powder (containing at least 5% rotenone) and one ounce of soap in one gallon of water has proved effective, especially if large areas of the surface of the dog's skin are involved. All crusts and scabs should be removed before its application. The solution must be well scrubbed into the skin with a moderately stiff brush and the whole animal thoroughly soaked. Only the surplus liquid should be taken off with a towel and the remainder must be permitted to dry on the dog. This bath should be repeated at intervals of five days until all signs of mange have disappeared. Three such baths will usually suffice.

The advantage of such all over treatment is that it protects uninfected areas from infection. It is also a precautionary measure to bathe in this solution uninfected dogs which have been in contact with the infected one.

Isolated mange spots may be treated with oil of lavender. Roll a woolen cloth into a swab with which the oil of lavender can be applied and rubbed in thoroughly for about five minutes. This destroys all mites with which the oil of lavender comes into contact.

Even after a cure is believed to be accomplished, vigilance must be maintained to prevent fresh infestations and to treat new spots immediately if they appear.

DEMODECTIC OR RED MANGE

Demodectic mange, caused by the wormlike mite *Demodex canis*, which lives in the hair follicles and the sebaceous glands of the skin, is difficult to cure. It is a baffling malady of which the prognosis is not favorable. The life cycle of the causative organism is not well understood, the time required from the egg to maturity being so far unknown. The female lays eggs which hatch into young of appearance similar to that of the adult, except that they are smaller and have but three pairs of legs instead of four.

One peculiar feature about demodectic mange is that some dogs appear to be genetically predisposed to it while others do not contract it whatever their contact with infected animals may be. Young animals seem to be especially prone to it, particularly those with short hair. The first evidence of its presence is the falling out of the hair on certain areas of the dog. The spots may be somewhat reddened, and they commonly occur near the eyes, on the hocks, elbows, or toes, although they may be on any part of the dog's body. No itching occurs at the malady's inception, and it never grows so intense as in sarcoptic mange.

In the course of time, the hairless areas enlarge, and the skin attains a copper hue; in severe cases it may appear blue or leadish gray. During this period the mites multiply and small pustules develop. Secondary invasions may occur to complicate the situation. Poisons are formed by the bacteria in the pustules, and the absorption of toxic materials deranges the body functions and eventually affects the whole general health of the dog, leading to emaciation, weakness, and the development of an acrid, unpleasant odor.

This disease is slow and subtle in its development, runs a casual course, and frequently extends over a period of two or even three years. Unless it is treated, it usually terminates in death, although spontaneous recovery occasionally occurs, especially if the dog has been kept on a nourishing diet. As in other skin diseases, correct nutrition plays a major part in recovery from demodectic mange, as it plays an even larger part in its prevention.

It is possible to confuse demodectic mange with sarcoptic mange, fungus infection, acne, or eczema. A definite diagnosis is possible only from microscopic examination of skin scrapings and of material from the pustules. The possibility of demodectic mange, particularly in its earlier stages, is not negated by the failure to find the mites under the microscope, and several examinations may be necessary to arrive at a definite diagnosis.

The prognosis is not entirely favorable. It may appear that the mange is cured and a new and healthy coat may be re-established only to have the disease manifest itself in a new area, and the whole process of treatment must be undertaken afresh.

In the treatment of demodectic mange, the best results have been obtained by the persistent use of benzine hexachloride, chlordane, rotenone, and 2-mercapto benzothiazole. Perseverance is necessary, but even then failure is possible.

EAR MITES OR EAR MANGE

The mites responsible for ear mange (*Ododectes cynotis*) are considerably larger than the ones which cause sarcoptic mange. They inhabit the external auditory canal and are visible to the unaided eye as minute, slowly moving, white objects. Their life history is not known, but is probably similar to that of the mite that causes sarcoptic mange.

These mites do not burrow into the skin, but are found deep in the ear canal, near the eardrum. Considerable irritation results from their presence, and the normal secretions of the ear are interfered with. The ear canal is filled with inflammatory products, modified ear wax, and mites, causing the dog to scratch and rub its ears and to shake its head. While ear mange is not caused by incomplete washing or inefficient drying of the ears, it is encouraged by such negligence.

The ear mange infestation is purely local and is no cause for anxiety. An ointment containing benzine hexachloride is very effective in correcting this condition. The ear should be treated every third or fourth day.

ECZEMA

Eczema is probably the most common of all ailments seen in the dog. Oftentimes it is mistaken for mange or ringworm, although there is no actual relationship between the conditions. Eczema is variously referred to by such names as "hot spots," "fungitch," and "kennel itch."

Some years ago there was near-unanimity of opinion among dog people that the food of the animal was the major contributing factor of eczema. Needless to say, the manufacturers of commercial dog foods were besieged with complaints. Some research on the cause of eczema placed most of the blame on outside environmental factors, and with some help from other sources it was found that a vegetative organism was the causative agent in a great majority of the cases.

Some dogs do show an allergic skin reaction to certain types of protein given to them as food, but this is generally referred to as the "foreign protein" type of dermatitis. It manifests itself by raising numerous welts on the skin, and occasionally the head, face, and ears will become alarmingly swollen. This condition can be controlled by the injection of antihistamine products and subsequent dosage with antihistaminic tablets or capsules such as chlortrimenton or benedryl. Whether "foreign protein" dermatitis is due to an allergy or whether it is due to some toxin manufactured and elaborated by the individual dog is a disputed point.

Most cases of eczema start with reddening of the skin in certain parts. The areas most affected seem to be the region along the spine and at the base of the tail. In house dogs this may have its inception from enlarged and plugged anal glands. The glands when full and not naturally expressed are a source of irritation. The dog will rub his hind parts on the grass in order to alleviate the itching sensation. Fleas, lice, and ticks may be inciting factors, causing the dog to rub and roll in the grass in an attempt to scratch the itchy parts.

In hunting dogs, it is believed that the vegetative cover through which the dogs hunt causes the dermatitis. In this class of dogs the skin becomes irritated and inflamed in the armpits, the inner surfaces of the thighs, and along the belly. Some hunting dogs are bedded down in straw or hay, and such dogs invariably show a general reddening of the skin and a tendency to scratch.

As a general rule, the difference between moist and dry eczema lies in the degree to which the dog scratches the skin with his feet or chews it with his teeth. The inflammation ranges from a simple reddening of the skin to the development of papules, vesicles, and pustules with a discharge. Crusts and scabs like dandruff may form, and if the condition is not treated, it will become chronic and then next to impossible to treat with any success. In such cases the skin becomes thickened and may be pigmented. The hair follicles become infected, and the lesions are constantly inflamed and exuding pus.

When inflammation occurs between the toes and on the pads of the feet, it closely resembles "athletes foot" in the human. Such inflammation generally causes the hair in the region to turn a reddish brown. The ears, when they are affected, emit a peculiar moldy odor and exude a brownish black substance. It is thought that most cases of canker of the ear are due to a primary invasion of the ear canal by a vegetative fungus. If there is a pustular discharge, it is due to the secondary pus-forming bacteria that gain a foothold after the resistance of the parts is lowered by the fungi.

Some breeds of dogs are more susceptible to skin ailments than are others. However, all breeds of dogs are likely to show some degree of dermatitis if they are exposed to causative factors.

Most cases of dermatitis are seen in the summer time, which probably accounts for their being referred to as "summer itch" or "hot spots." The warm moist days of summer seem to promote the growth and development of both fleas and fungi. When the fleas bite the dog, the resulting irritation causes the dog to scratch or bite to alleviate the itch. The area thus becomes moist and makes a perfect place for fungi spores to propagate. That the fungi are the cause of the trouble seems evident, because most cases respond when treated externally with a good fungicide. Moreover, the use of a powder containing both an insecticide and a fungicide tends to prevent skin irritation. Simply dusting the dog once or twice a week with a good powder of the type mentioned is sound procedure in the practice of preventive medicine.

(Editor's note: I have had some success with hydrogen peroxide in treating mild skin troubles. Saturate a cotton pad with a mixture of 2 parts 3% hydrogen peroxide to 1 part boiled water. Apply, but do NOT rub, to affected skin. Let dry naturally and when *completely* dry apply an antiseptic talcum powder like Johnson & Johnson's Medicated Powder. When this treatment was suggested to my veterinarian, he confirmed that he had had success with it. If the skin irritation is not noticeably better after two of these treatments, once daily, the case should be referred to a veterinarian.)

RINGWORM

Ringworm is a communicable disease of the skin of dogs, readily transmissible to man and to other dogs and animals. The disease is caused by specific fungi, which are somewhat similar to ordinary molds. The lesions caused by ringworm usually first appear on the face, head, or legs of the dog, but they may occur on any part of the surface of his body.

The disease in dogs is characterized by small, circular areas of dirty gray or brownish-yellow crusts or scabs partially devoid of hair, the size of a dime. As the disease progresses, the lesions increase both in size and in number and merge to form larger patches covered with crusts containing broken off hair. A raw, bleeding surface may appear when crusts are broken or removed by scratching or rubbing to relieve itching. In some cases, however, little or no itching is manifested. Microscopic examination and culture tests are necessary for accurate diagnosis.

If treatment of affected dogs is started early, the progress of the disease can be immediately arrested. Treatment consists of clipping the hair from around the infected spots, removing the scabs and painting the spots with tincture of iodine, five percent salicylic acid solution, or other fungicide two or three times weekly until recovery takes place. In applying these remedies it is well to cover the periphery of the circular lesion as well as its center, since the spots tend to expand outward from their centers. Scabs, hair, and debris removed from the dog during his treatments should be burned to destroy the causative organisms and to prevent reinfection. Precautions in the handling of animals affected with ringworm should be observed to preclude transmission to man and other animals. Isolation of affected dogs is not necessary if the treatment is thorough.

COAT CARE

Skin troubles can often be checked and materially alleviated by proper grooming. Every dog is entitled to the minimum of weekly attention to coat, skin and ears; ideally, a daily stint with brush and comb is highly recommended. Frequent examination may catch skin disease in its early stages and provide a better chance for a quick cure.

The outer or "guard" hairs of a dog's coat should glint in the sunlight. There should be no mats or dead hair in the coat. Wax in the outer ear should be kept at a minimum.

It is helpful to stand the dog on a flat, rigid surface off the floor at a height convenient to the groomer. Start at the head and ears brushing briskly *with* the lay of short hair, *against* the lay of long hair at first then with it. After brushing, use a fine comb with short teeth on fine, short hair and a coarse comb with long teeth on coarse or long hair. If mats cannot be readily removed with brush or comb, use barber's thinning shears and cut into the matted area several times until mat pulls free easily. Some mats can be removed with the fingers if one has the patience to separate the hair a bit at a time.

After brushing and combing, run your palms over the dog's coat from head to tail. Natural oils in your skin will impart sheen to your dog's coat.

The ears of some dogs secrete and exude great amounts of wax. Frequent examination will determine when your dog's ears need cleaning. A thin coating of clean, clear wax is not harmful. But a heavy accumulation of dirty, dark wax needs removal by cotton pads soaked in diluted hydrogen peroxide (3% cut in half with boiled water), or alcohol or plain boiled water if wax is not too thick.

There are sprays, "dry" bath preparations and other commercial products for maintaining your dog's coat health. Test them first, and if they are successful, you may find them beneficial time-savers in managing your dog's coat.

First Aid

JOHN STEINBECK, the Nobel Prize winning author, in *Travels with Charley in Search of America* bemoans the lack of a good, comprehensive book of home dog medicine. Charley is the aged Poodle that accompanies his illustrious author-owner on a motor tour of the U.S.A.

As in human medicine, most treatment and dosing of dogs are better left in the experienced, trained hands and mind of a professional—in this case, the veterinarian. However, there are times and situations when professional aid is not immediately available and an owner's prompt action may save a life or avoid permanent injury. To this purpose, the following suggestions are given.

The First Aid Kit

For instruments keep on hand a pair of tweezers, a pair of pliers, straight scissors, a rectal thermometer, a teaspoon, a tablespoon, and swabs for cotton.

For dressings, buy a container of cotton balls, a roll of cotton and a roll of 2″ gauze. Strips of clean, old sheets may come in handy.

For medicines, stock ammonia, aspirin, brandy, 3% hydrogen peroxide, bicarbonate of soda, milk of bismuth, mineral oil, salt, tea, vaseline, kaopectate, baby oil and baby talcum powder.

Handling the Dog for Treatment

Approach any injured or sick dog calmly with reassuring voice and gentle, steady hands. If the dog is in pain, slip a gauze or sheet strip noose over its muzzle tying the ends first under the throat and then back of the neck. Make sure the dog's lips are not caught between his teeth, but make noose around muzzle *tight*.

If the dog needs to be moved, grasp the loose skin on the back of the neck with one hand and support chest with the other hand. If the dog is too large to move in this manner, slide him on a large towel, blanket or folded sheet which may serve as a stretcher for two to carry.

If a pill or liquid is to be administered, back the dog in a corner in a sitting position. For a pill, pry back of jaws apart with thumb and forefinger of one hand and with the same fingers of your other hand place pill as far back in dog's throat as possible; close and hold jaws, rubbing throat to cause swallowing. If dog does not gulp, hold one hand over nostrils briefly; he will gulp for air and swallow pill. For liquids, lift the back of the upper lip and tip spoon into the natural pocket formed in the rear of the lower lip; it may be necessary to pull this pocket out with forefinger. Do not give liquids by pouring directly down the dog's throat; this might choke him or make the fluid go down the wrong way.

After treatment keep dog quiet, preferably in his bed or a room where he cannot injure himself or objects.

Bites and Wounds

Clip hair from area. Wash gently with pure soap and water or hydrogen peroxide. If profuse bleeding continues, apply sheet strip or gauze tourniquet between wound and heart but nearest the wound. Release tourniquet briefly at ten-minute intervals. Cold water compresses may stop milder bleeding.

For insect bites and stings, try to remove stinger with tweezers or a dab of cotton, and apply a few drops of ammonia. If dog is in pain, give aspirin at one grain per 10 pounds. (An aspirin tablet is usually 5 grains.)

Burns

Clip hair from area. Apply strong, lukewarm tea (for its tannic acid content) on a sheet strip compress. Vaseline may be used for slight burns. Give aspirin as recommended if dog is in pain. Keep him warm if he seems to be in shock.

Constipation

Give mineral oil: one-quarter teaspoon up to 10 pounds; half teaspoon from 10 to 25 pounds; full teaspoon from 25 to 75 pounds; three-quarters tablespoon over 75 pounds.

Diarrhea

Give kaopectate in same doses by size as indicated for mineral oil above, but repeat within four and eight hours.

Fighting

Do not try forcibly to separate dogs. If available throw a pail of cold water on them. A sharp rap on the rump of each combatant with a strap or stick may help. A heavy towel or blanket dropped over the head of the aggressor, or a newspaper twisted into a torch, lighted and held near them, may discourage the fighters. If a lighted newspaper is used, be careful that sparks do not fall or blow on dogs.

Fits

Try to get the dog into a room where he cannot injure himself. If possible, cover him with a towel or blanket. When the fit ends, give aspirin one grain for every 10 pounds.

Nervousness

Remove cause or remove the dog from the site of the cause. Give the recommended dose of aspirin. Aspirin acts as a tranquilizer.

Poisoning

If container of the poison is handy, use recommended antidote printed thereon. Otherwise, make a strong solution of household salt in water and force as much as possible into the dog's throat using the lip pocket method. Minutes count with several poisons; if veterinarian cannot be reached immediately, try to get dog to an MD or registered nurse.

Shock

If dog has chewed electric cord, protect hand with rubber glove or thick dry towel and pull cord from socket. If dog has collapsed, hold ammonia under its nose or apply artificial respiration as follows: place dog on side with its head low, press on abdomen and rib cage, releasing pressure at one- or two-second intervals. Keep dog warm.

Stomach Upsets

For mild stomach disorders, milk of bismuth in same doses as recommended for mineral oil under *Constipation* will be effective. For more severe cases brandy in the same doses but diluted with an equal volume of water may be helpful.

Swallowing Foreign Objects

If object is still in mouth or throat, reach in and remove it. If swallowed, give strong salt solution as for *Poisoning*. Some objects that are small, smooth or soft may not give trouble.

Porcupines and Skunks

Using tweezers or pliers, twist quills one full turn and pull out. Apply hydrogen peroxide to bleeding wounds. For skunk spray, wash dog in tomato juice.

WARNING! Get your dog to a veterinarian *soonest* for severe bites, wounds, burns, poisoning, fits and shock.

98

Internal Canine Diseases
and Their Management

THE word *management* is employed in this chapter heading rather than *treatment,* since the treatment of disease in the dog is the function of the veterinarian, and the best counsel it is possible to give the solicitous owner of a sick dog is to submit the case to the best veterinarian available and to follow his instructions implicitly. In general, it may be said, the earlier in any disease the veterinarian is consulted, the more rapid is the sick animal's recovery and the lower the outlay of money for the services of the veterinarian and for the medicine he prescribes.

Herein are presented some hints for the prevention of the various canine maladies and for their recognition when they occur. In kennel husbandry, disease is a minor problem, and, if preventive methods are employed, it is one that need not be anticipated.

DISTEMPER

Distemper, the traditional bugbear of keeping dogs, the veritable scourge of dog-kind, has at long last been well conquered. Compared with some years ago when "over distemper" was one of the best recommendations for the purchase of a dog, the incidence of distemper in well-bred and adequately cared for dogs is now minimal.

The difference between then and now is that we now have available preventive sera, vaccines, and viruses, which may be employed to forestall distemper before it ever appears. There are valid differences of opinion about which of these measures is best to use and at what age of the dog they are variously indicated. About the choice of preventive measures and the technique of administering them, the reader is advised to consult his veterinarian and to accept his advice. There can be no doubt, however, that any person with a valued or loved young dog should have him immunized.

For many years most veterinarians used the so-called "three-shot" method of serum, vaccine and virus, spaced two weeks apart after the puppy was three or four months old, for permanent immunization. For temporary immunization lasting up to a year, some veterinarians used only vaccine; this was repeated annually if the owner wished, though since a dog was considered most susceptible to distemper in the first year of his life, the annual injection was often discontinued. Under both these methods, serum was used at two-week intervals from weaning to the age when permanent or annual immunization was given.

Until 1950 living virus, produced by the methods then known to and used by laboratories, was considered too dangerous to inject without the preparation of the dog for it by prior use of serum or vaccine (killed virus). Then, researchers in distemper developed an attenuated or weakened live virus by injecting strong virus into egg embryos and other intermediate hosts. The weakened virus is now often used for permanent, one-shot distemper immunization of puppies as young as eight weeks.

Today certain researchers believe that the temporary immunity given by the bitch to her young depends on her own degree of immunity. If she has none, her puppies have none; if she has maximum immunity, her puppies may be immune up to the age of 12 weeks or more. By testing the degree of the bitch's immunity early in her pregnancy, these researchers believe they can determine the proper age at which her puppies should receive their shots.

The veterinarian is best qualified to determine the method of distemper immunization and the age to give it.

Canine distemper is an acute, highly contagious, febrile disease caused by a filterable virus. It is characterized by a catarrhal inflammation of all the mucous membranes of the body, frequently

100

accompanied by nervous symptoms and pustular eruptions of the skin. Its human counterpart is influenza, which, though not identical with distemper, is very similar to it in many respects. Distemper is so serious and complicated a disease as to require expert attention; when a dog is suspected of having it, a veterinarian should be consulted immediately. It is the purpose of this discussion of the malady rather to describe it that its recognition may be possible than to suggest medication for it or means of treating it.

Distemper is known in all countries and all parts of the United States in all seasons of the year, but it is most prevalent during the winter months and in the cold, damp weather of early spring and late autumn. No breed of dogs is immune. Puppies of low constitutional vigor, pampered, overfed, unexercised dogs, and those kept in overheated, unventilated quarters contract the infection more readily and suffer more from it than hardy animals, properly fed and living in a more natural environment. Devitalizing influences which decrease the resistance of the dog, such as rickets, parasitic infestations, unsanitary quarters, and especially an insufficient or unbalanced diet, are factors predisposing to distemper.

While puppies as young as ten days or two weeks have been known to have true cases of distemper, and very old dogs in rare instances, the usual subjects of distemper are between two months (after weaning) and full maturity at about eighteen months. The teething period of four to six months is highly critical. It is believed that some degree of temporary protection from distemper is passed on to a nursing litter through the milk of the mother.

As was first demonstrated by Carré in 1905 and finally established by Laidlaw and Duncan in their work for the Field Distemper Fund in 1926 to 1928, the primary causative agent of distemper is a filterable virus. The clinical course of the disease may be divided into two parts, produced respectively by the primary Carré filterable virus and by a secondary invasion of bacterial organisms which produce serious complicating conditions usually associated with the disease. It is seldom true that uncomplicated Carré distemper would cause more than a fever with malaise and indisposition if the secondary bacterial invasion could be avoided. The primary disease but prepares the ground for the secondary invasion which produces the havoc and all too often kills the patient.

Although it is often impossible to ascertain the source of infection in outbreaks of distemper, it is known that the infection may spread from affected to susceptible dogs by either direct or indirect contact. The disease, while highly infectious throughout its course, is especially easy to communicate in its earliest stages, even before clinical symptoms are manifested. The virus is readily destroyed by heat and by most of the common disinfectants in a few hours, but it resists drying and low temperatures for several days, and has been known to survive freezing for months.

The period of incubation (the time between exposure to infection and the development of the first symptoms) is variable. It has been reported to be as short as three days and as long as two weeks. The usual period is approximately one week. The usual course of the disease is about four weeks, but seriously complicated cases may prolong themselves to twelve weeks.

The early symptoms of distemper, as a rule, are so mild and subtle as to escape the notice of any but the most acute observer. These first symptoms may be a rise in temperature, a watery discharge from the eyes and nose, an impaired appetite, a throat-clearing cough, and a general sluggishness. In about a week's time the symptoms become well marked, with a discharge of mucus or pus from the eyes and nose, and complications of a more or less serious nature, such as broncho-pneumonia, hemorrhagic inflammation of the gastro-intestinal tract, and disturbances of the brain and spinal cord, which may cause convulsions. In the early stages of distemper the body temperature may suddenly rise from the normal 101°F. to 103°. Shivering, dryness of the nostrils, a slight dry cough, increased thirst, a drowsy look, reluctance to eat, and a desire to sleep may follow. Later, diarrhea (frequently streaked with blood or wholly of blood), pneumonia, convulsions, paralysis, or chorea (a persistent twitching condition) may develop. An inflammation of the membranes of the eye may ensue; this may impair or destroy the sight through ulceration or opacity of the cornea. Extreme weakness and great loss of body weight occur in advanced stages.

All, any, or none of these symptoms may be noticeable. It is believed that many dogs experience distemper in so mild a form as to escape the owner's observation. Because of its protean and obscure nature and its strong similarity to other catarrhal affections, the diagnosis of distemper, especially in its early stages, is difficult. In young dogs that are known to have been exposed to the disease, a rise of body temperature, together with shivering, sneezing, loss of appetite, eye and nasal discharge, sluggishness, and diarrhea (all or any of these symptoms), are indicative of trouble.

There is little specific that can be done for a dog with primary distemper. The treatment is largely concerned with alleviating the symptoms. No drug or combination of drugs is known at this time that has any specific action on the disease. Distemper runs a definite course, no matter what is done to try to cure it.

Homologous anti-distemper serum, administered subcutaneously or intravenously by the veterinarian, is of value in lessening the severity of the attack. The veterinarian may see fit to treat the secondary pneumonia with penicillin or one of the sulpha drugs, or to allay the secondary intestinal infection with medication. It is best to permit him to manage the case in his own way. The dog is more prone to respond to care in his own home and with his own people, if suitable quarters and adequate nursing are available to him. Otherwise, he is best off in a veterinary hospital.

The dog affected with distemper should be provided with clean, dry, warm but not hot, well ventilated quarters. It should be given moderate quantities of nourishing, easily digested food—milk, soft boiled eggs, cottage cheese, and scraped lean beef. The sick dog should not be disturbed by children or other dogs. Discharges from eyes and nose should be wiped away. The eyes may be bathed with boric acid solution, and irritation of the nose allayed with greasy substances such as petrolatum. The dog should not be permitted to get wet or chilled, and he should have such medication as the veterinarian prescribes and no other.

When signs of improvement are apparent, the dog must not be given an undue amount of food at one meal, although he may be fed at frequent intervals. The convalescing dog should be permitted to exercise only very moderately until complete recovery is assured.

In the control of distemper, affected animals should be promptly isolated from susceptible dogs. After the disease has run its course, whether it end in recovery or death, the premises where the patient has been kept during the illness should be thoroughly cleaned and disinfected, as should all combs, brushes, or other utensils used on the dog, before other susceptible dogs are brought in. After an apparent recovery has been made in the patient, the germs are present for about four weeks and can be transmitted to susceptible dogs.

CHOREA OR ST. VITUS DANCE

A frequent sequela of distemper is chorea, which is characterized by a more or less pronounced and frequent twitching of a muscle or muscles. There is no known remedy for the condition. It does not impair the usefulness of a good dog for breeding, and having a litter of puppies often betters or cures chorea in the bitch. Chorea is considered a form of unsoundness and is penalized in the show ring. The condition generally becomes worse.

ECLAMPSIA OR WHELPING TETANY

Convulsions of bitches before, during, or shortly after their whelping are called eclampsia. It seldom occurs to a bitch receiving a sufficient amount of calcium and vitamin D in her diet during her pregnancy. The symptoms vary in their severity for nervousness and mild convulsions to severe attacks which may terminate in coma and death. The demands of the nursing litter for calcium frequently depletes the supply in the bitch's system.

Eclampsia can be controlled by the hypodermic administration of calcium gluconate. Its recurrence is prevented by the addition to the bitch's ration of readily utilized calcium and vitamin D.

RICKETS, OR RACHITIS

The failure of the bones of puppies to calcify normally is termed rickets, or more technically rachitis. Perhaps more otherwise excellent puppies are killed or ruined by rickets than by any other disease. It is essentially a disease of puppies, but the malformation of the skeleton produced by rickets persists through the life of the dog.

The symptoms of rickets include lethargy, arched neck, crouched stance, knobby and deformed joints, bowed legs, and flabby muscles. The changes characteristic of defective calcification in the puppy are most marked in the growth of the long bones of the leg, and at the cartilaginous junction of the ribs. In the more advanced stages of rickets the entire bone becomes soft and easily deformed or broken. The development of the teeth is also retarded.

Rickets results from a deficiency in the diet of calcium, phosphorus, or vitamin D. It may be prevented by the inclusion of sufficient amounts of those substances in the puppy's diet. It may also be cured, if not too far advanced, by the same means, although distortions in the skeleton that have already occurred are seldom rectified. The requirements of vitamin D to be artificially supplied are greater for puppies raised indoors and with limited exposure to sunlight or to sunlight filtered through window glass.

(It is possible to give a dog too much vitamin D, but very unlikely without deliberate intent.)

Adult dogs that have had rickets in puppyhood and whose recovery is complete may be bred from without fear of their transmission to their puppies of the malformations of their skeletons produced by the disease. The same imbalance or absence from their diet that produced rickets in the parent may produce it in the progeny, but the disease in such case is reproduced and not inherited.

The requirements of adult dogs for calcium, phosphorus, and vitamin D are much less than for puppies and young dogs, but a condition called osteomalacia, or late rickets, is sometimes seen in grown dogs as the result of the same kind of nutritional deficiency that causes rickets in puppies. In such cases a softening of the bones leads to lameness and deformity. The remedy is the same as in the rickets of puppyhood, namely the addition of calcium, phosphorus, and vitamin D to the diet. It is especially essential that bitches during pregnancy and lactation have included in their diets ample amounts of these elements, both for their own nutrition and for the adequate skeletal formations of their fetuses and the development of their puppies.

BLACKTONGUE

Blacktongue (the canine analogue of pellagra in the human) is no longer to be feared in dogs fed upon an adequate diet. For many years, it was a recognized scourge among dogs, and its cause and treatment were unknown. It is now known to be caused solely by the insufficiency in the ration of vitamin B complex and specifically by an insufficiency of nicotinic acid. (Nicotinic acid is vitamin B_2, formerly known as vitamin G.)

Blacktongue may require a considerable time for its full development. It usually begins with a degree of lethargy, a lack of appetite for the kind of food the dog has been receiving, constipation, often with spells of vomiting, and particularly with a foul odor from the mouth. As the disease develops, the mucous membranes of the mouth, gums, and tongue grow red and become inflamed, with purple splotches of greater or lesser extent, especially upon the front part of the tongue, and with ulcers and pustules on the lips and the lining of the cheeks. Constipation may give way to diarrhea as the disease develops. Blacktongue is an insidious malady, since its development is so gradual.

This disease is unlikely to occur except among dogs whose owners are so unenlightened, careless, or stingy as to feed their dogs exclusively on a diet of cornmeal mush, salt pork, cowpeas, sweet potatoes, or other foodstuffs that are known to be responsible for the development of pellagra in mankind. Blacktongue is not infectious or contagious, although the same deficiency in the diet of dogs may produce the malady in all the inmates throughout a kennel.

Correct treatment involves no medication as such, but consists wholly in the alteration of the diet to include foods which are good sources of the vitamin B complex, including nicotinic acid; such food as the muscles of beef, mutton, or horse, dried yeast, wheat germ, milk, eggs, and especially fresh liver. As an emergency treatment, the hypodermic injection of nicotinic acid may be indicated. Local treatments of the mouth, its cleansing and disinfection, are usually included, although they will avail nothing without the alteration in the diet.

LEPTOSPIROSIS OR CANINE TYPHUS

Leptospirosis, often referred to as canine typhus, is believed to be identical with Weil's disease (infectious jaundice) in the human species. It is not to be confused with non-infectious jaundice in the dog, which is a mere obstruction in the bile duct which occurs in some liver and gastric disorders. Leptospirosis is a comparatively rare disease as yet, but its incidence is growing and it is becoming more widespread.

It is caused by either of two spirocheates, *Leptospira canicola* or *Leptospira icterohenorrhagiae*. These causative organisms are found in the feces or urine of infected rats, and the disease is transmitted to dogs by their ingestion of food fouled by those rodents. It is therefore wise in rat infested houses to keep all dog food in covered metal containers to which it is impossible for rats to gain access. It is also possible for an ill dog to transmit the infection to a well one, and, it is believed, to man. Such cases, however, are rare.

Symptoms of leptospirosis include a variable temperature, vomiting, loss of appetite, gastroenteritis, diarrhea, jaundice and depression. Analysis of blood and urine may be helpful toward diagnosis. The disease is one for immediate reference to the veterinarian whenever suspected.

Prognosis is not entirely favorable, especially if the disease is neglected in its earlier stages. Taken in its incipience, treatment with penicillin has produced excellent results, as has antileptospiral serum and vaccine.

Control measures include the extermination of rats in areas where the disease is known to exist, and the cleaning and disinfection of premises where infected dogs have been kept.

INFECTIOUS HEPATITIS

This is a virus disease attacking the liver. Apparently it is not the same virus that causes hepatitis in humans. Symptoms include an unusual thirst, loss of appetite, vomiting, diarrhea, pain causing the dog to moan, anemia and fever. The afflicted dog may try to hide.

The disease runs a fast course and is often fatal. A dog recovering from it may carry the virus in his urine for a long period, thus infecting other dogs months later.

Serum and vaccine are available to offer protection. A combination for distemper and hepatitis is now offered.

TURNED-IN OR TURNED-OUT EYELIDS

When the eyelid is inverted, or turned-in, it is technically termed entropion. When the eyelid is turned-out, it is referred to as extropion. Both conditions seem to be found in certain strains of dogs and are classified as being heritable. Both conditions may be corrected by competent surgery. It is possible to operate on such cases and have complete recovery without scar formation. However, cognizance should be taken of either defect in a dog to be used for breeding purposes.

CONJUNCTIVITIS OR INFLAMMATION OF THE EYE

Certain irritants, injuries or infections, and many febrile diseases, such as distemper, produce conjunctivitis, an inflammation of the membranes lining the lids of the dog's eyes. At first there is a slight reddening of the membranes and a watery discharge. As the condition progresses, the conjunctivae become more inflamed looking and the color darkens. The discharge changes consistency and color, becoming muco-purulent in character and yellow in color. The eyelids may be pasted shut and granulation of the lids may follow.

When eye infection persists for an extended period of time, the cornea sometimes becomes involved. Ulcers may develop, eventually penetrating the eyeball. When this happens, the condition becomes very painful and, even worse, often leads to the loss of vision.

Home treatment, to be used only until professional care may be had, consists of regular cleaning of the eye with a 2% boric acid solution and the application of one of the antibiotic eye ointments.

When anything happens to the dog's eye, it is always best to seek professional help and advice.

RABIES

This disease, caused by a virus, is transmissible to all warm blooded animals, and the dog seems to be the number one disseminator of the virus. However, outbreaks of rabies have been traced to wild animals—the wolf, coyote, or fox biting a dog which in turn bites people, other dogs, or other species of animals.

The virus, which is found in the saliva of the rabid animal, enters the body only through broken skin. This usually is brought about by biting and breaking the skin, or through licking an open cut on the skin. The disease manifests itself clinically in two distinct forms. One is called the "furious type" and the other the "dumb type." Both types are produced by the same strain of virus.

The disease works rather peculiarly on the dog's disposition and character. The kindly old dog may suddenly become ferocious; just the reverse may also occur, the mean, vicious dog becoming gentle and biddable. At first the infected dog wants to be near his master, wants to lick his hand or his boots; his appetite undergoes a sudden change, becoming voracious, and the animal will eat anything— stones, bits of wood, even metal. Soon there develops a sense of wanderlust, and the dog seems to wish to get as far away as possible from his owner.

In all rabid animals there is an accentuation of the defense mechanisms. In other words, the dog will bite, the cat will hiss and claw, the horse will bite and kick, and the cow will attack anything that moves.

An animal afflicted with rabies cannot swallow because there is usually a paralysis of the muscles of deglutinition. The animal, famished for a drink, tries to bite the water or whatever fluid he may be attempting to drink. The constant champing of the jaws causes the saliva to become mixed and churned with air, making it appear whipped and foamy. In the old days when a dog "frothed at the mouth," he was considered "mad." There is no doubt but what some uninfected dogs have been suspected of being rabid and shot to death simply because they exhibited these symptoms.

One of the early signs of rabies in the dog is the dropping of the lower jaw. This is a sign of rabies of the so-called "dumb type." The animal has a "faraway" look in his eyes, and his voice or bark has an odd pitch. Manifesting these symptoms, the dog is often taken to the clinic by the owner, who is sure the dog has a bone in the throat. The hind legs, and eventually the whole hindquarters, subsequently become paralyzed, and death ensues.

Many commonwealths have passed laws requiring that all dogs be vaccinated against rabies, and usually, a vaccination certificate must be presented before a dog license may be issued. The general enforcement of this law alone would go a long way toward the eradication of rabies.

Some will ask why a dog must be impounded as a biter when he has taken a little "nip" at someone and merely broken the skin— if this must be done, they cannot understand the "good" of the vaccination. But the vaccination does not give the dog the right to bite. Statistics show that rabies vaccination is effective in about 88% of the cases. All health authorities wish it were 100% effective, thus eliminating a good deal of worry from their minds. Because the vaccination is not 100% effective, we cannot take a chance on the vaccine alone. The animal must be impounded and under the daily supervision of a qualified observer, generally for a period of fourteen days. It is pretty well recognized that if the bite was provocated by rabies, the biting animal will develop clinical symptoms in that length of time; otherwise, he will be released as "clinically normal."

THE SPAYING OF BITCHES

The spaying operation, technically known as an ovariectomy, is the subject of a good deal of controversy. It is an operation that has its good and its bad points.

Spayed bitches cannot be entered in the show ring, and of course can never reproduce their kind. However, under certain circumstances, the operation is recommended by veterinarians. If the operation is to be performed, the bitch should preferably be six to eight months of age. At this age, she has pretty well reached the adolescent period; time enough has been allowed for the endocrine balance to become established and the secondary sex organs to develop.

Mechanical difficulties sometimes arise in the urinary systems of bitches that have been operated on at three or four months of age. In a very small percentage of the cases, loss of control of the sphincter muscles of the bladder is observed. But this can readily be corrected by an injection of the female hormone stilbestrol.

There are many erroneous ideas as to what may happen to the female if she is spayed. Some people argue that the disposition will be changed, that the timid dog may become ferocious, and, strangely enough, that the aggressive animal will become docile. Some breeders say that the spayed bitch will become fat, lazy, and lethargic. According to the records that have been kept on bitches following the spaying operation, such is not the case. It is unjust to accuse the spaying operation when really the dog's owner is at fault—he just feeds the dog too much.

110

THE CASTRATION OF DOGS

This operation consists of the complete removal of the testes. Ordinarily the operation is not encouraged. Circumstances may attenuate the judgment, however. Castration may be necessary to correct certain pathological conditions such as a tumor, chronic prostatitis, and types of perineal troubles. Promiscuous wetting is sometimes an excuse for desexing.

It must be remembered that as with the spayed bitch, the castrated dog is barred from the show ring.

ANAL GLANDS

On either side of the anus of the dog is situated an anal gland, which secretes a lubricant that better enables the dog to expel the contents of the rectum. These glands are subject to being clogged, and in them accumulates a fetid mass. This accumulation is not, strictly speaking, a disease—unless it becomes infected and purulent. Almost all dogs have it, and most of them are neglected without serious consequences. However, they are better if they are relieved. Their spirits improve, their eyes brighten, and even their coats gradually grow more lively if the putrid mass is occasionally squeezed out of the anus.

This is accomplished by seizing the tail with the left hand, encircling its base with the thumb and forefinger of the right hand, and pressing the anus firmly between thumb and finger. The process results in momentary pain to the dog and often causes him to flinch, which may be disregarded. A semi-liquid of vile odor is extruded from the anus. The operation should be repeated at intervals of from one week to one month, depending on the rapidity of glandular accumulation. No harm results from the frequency of such relief, although there may be no apparent results if the anal glands are kept free of their accumulations.

If this process of squeezing out of the glands is neglected, the glands sometimes become infected and surgery becomes necessary. This is seldom the case, but, if needful at all, it must be entrusted to a skillful veterinary surgeon.

METRITIS

Metritis is the acute or chronic inflammation of the uterus of the bitch and may result from any one of a number of things. Perhaps the most common factor, especially in eight- to twelve-year-old bitches, is pseudocyesis, or false pregnancy. Metritis often follows whelping; it may be the result of a retained placenta, or of infection of the uterus following the manual or instrument removal of a puppy.

The term pyometria is generally restricted to cases where the uterus is greatly enlarged and filled with pus. In most such cases surgery must be resorted to in order to effect a cure.

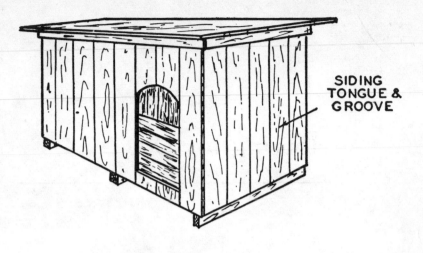

SIDING
TONGUE &
GROOVE

ASSEMBLED VIEW

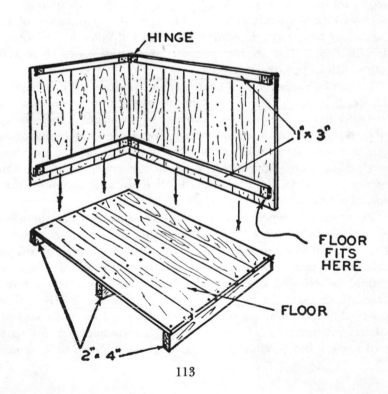

HINGE

1" x 3"

FLOOR
FITS
HERE

FLOOR

2" x 4"

113

Housing for Dogs

EVERY owner will have, and will have to solve, his own problems about providing his dog or dogs with quarters best suited to the dog's convenience. The special circumstances of each particular owner will determine what kind of home he will provide for his dogs. Here it is impossible to provide more than a few generalities upon the subject.

Little more need be said than that fit quarters for dogs must be secure, clean, dry, and warm. Consideration must be given to convenience in the care of kennel inmates by owners of a large number of dogs, but by the time one's activities enlarge to such proportions one will have formulated one's own concept of how best to house one's dogs. Here, advice will be predicated upon the maintenance of not more than three or four adult dogs with accommodations for an occasional litter of puppies.

First, let it be noted that dogs are not sensitive to aesthetic considerations in the place they are kept; they have no appreciation of the beauty of their surroundings. They do like soft beds of sufficient thickness to protect them from the coldness of the floors. These beds should be secluded and covered to conserve body heat. A box or crate of adequate size to permit the dog to lie full length in it will suffice. The cushion may be a burlap bag stuffed with shredded paper, *not straw, hay, or grass*. Paper is recommended, for its use will reduce the possibility of the dog's developing skin trouble.

Most dogs are allergic to fungi found on vegetative matter such as straw, hay, and grass. Wood shavings and excelsior may be used with impunity.

The kennel should be light, except for a retiring place; if sunshine is available at least part of the day, so much the better. Boxes in a shed or garage with secure wire runs to which the dogs have ready access suffice very well, are very inexpensive, and are easy to plan and to arrange. The runs should be made of wire fencing strong enough that the dogs are unable to tear it with their teeth and high enough that the dogs are unable to jump or climb over it. In-turning flanges of wire netting at the tops of the fences tend to obviate jumping. Boards, rocks, or cement buried around the fences forestall burrowing to freedom.

These pens need not be large, if the dogs are given frequent respites from their captivity and an opportunity to obtain needed exercise. However, they should be large enough to relieve them of the aspect of cages. Concrete floors for such pens are admittedly easy to keep clean and sanitary. However, they have no resilience, and the feet of dogs confined for long periods on concrete floors are prone to spread and their shoulders to loosen. A further objection to concrete is that it grows hot in the summer sunshine and is very cold in winter. If it is used for flooring at all, a low platform of wood, large enough to enable the dogs to sprawl out on it full length, should be provided in each pen.

A well drained soil is to be preferred to concrete, if it is available; but it must be dug out to the depth of three inches and renewed occasionally, if it is used. Otherwise, the accumulation of urine will make it sour and offensive. Agricultural limestone, applied monthly and liberally, will "sweeten" the soil.

Gates, hinges, latches, and other hardware must be trustworthy. The purpose of such quarters is to confine the dogs and to keep them from running at large; unless they serve such a purpose they are useless. One wants to know when one puts a dog in his kennel, the dog will be there when one returns. An improvised kennel of old chicken wire will not suffice for one never knows whether it will hold one's dogs or not.

Frequently two friendly bitches may be housed together, or a dog housed with a bitch. Unless one is sure of male friendships, it is seldom safe to house two adult male dogs together. It is better, if possible, to provide a separate kennel for each mature dog. But, if the dogs can be housed side by side with only a wire fence between them, they can have companionship without rancor. Night barking can be controlled by confining the dogs indoors or by shutting them up in their boxes.

Adult dogs require artificial heat in only the coldest of climates, if they are provided with tight boxes placed under shelter. Puppies need heat in cold weather up until weaning time, and even thereafter if they are not permitted to sleep together. Snuggled together in a tight box with shredded paper, they can withstand much cold without discomfort. All dogs in winter without artificial heat should have an increase of their rations—especially as pertains to fat content.

Whatever artificial heat is provided for dogs should be safe, foolproof, and dog-proof. Caution should be exercised that electric wiring is not exposed, that stoves cannot be tipped over, and that it is impossible for sparks from them to ignite the premises. Many fires in kennels, the results of defective heating apparatus or careless handling of it, have brought about the deaths of the inmates. It is because of them that this seemingly unnecessary warning is given.

No better place for a dog to live can be found than the home of its owner, sharing even his bed if permitted. So is the dog happiest. There is a limit, however, to the number of dogs that can be tolerated in the house. The keeper of a small kennel can be expected to alternate his favorite dogs in his own house, thus giving them a respite to confinement in a kennel. Provision must be made for a place of exercise and relief at frequent intervals for dogs kept in the house. An enclosed dooryard will serve such a purpose, or the dog may be exercised on a lead with as much benefit to the owner as to the dog.

That the quarters of the dog shall be dry is even more important than that they shall be warm. A damp, drafty kennel is the cause of much kennel disease and indisposition. It is harmless to permit a dog to go out into inclement weather of his own choice, if he is provided with a sheltered bed to which he may retire to dry himself.

By cleanness, sanitation is meant—freedom from vermin and bacteria. A little coat of dust or a degree of disorder does not discommode the dog or impair his welfare, but the best dog keepers are orderly persons. They at least do not permit bedding and old bones to accumulate in a dog's bed, and they take the trouble to spray with antiseptic or wash with soap and water their dog's house at frequent intervals. The feces in the kennel runs should be picked up and destroyed at least once, and better twice, daily. Persistent filth in kennels can be counted on as a source of illness sooner or later. This warning appears superfluous, but it isn't; the number of ailing dogs kept in dirty, unsanitary kennels is amazing. It is one of the axioms of keeping dogs that their quarters must be sanitary or disease is sure to ensue.

GOOD DOG KEEPING PRACTICES

Pride of ownership is greatly enhanced when the owner takes care to maintain his dog in the best possible condition at all times. And meticulous grooming not only will make the dog look better but also will make him feel better. As part of the regular, daily routine, the grooming of the dog will prove neither arduous nor time consuming; it will also obviate the necessity for indulging in a rigorous program designed to correct the unkempt state in which too many owners permit their dogs to appear. Certainly, spending a few minutes each day will be well worth while, for the result will be a healthier, happier, and more desirable canine companion.

THAT DOGGY ODOR

Many persons are disgusted to the point of refusal to keep a dog by what they fancy is a "doggy odor." Of course, almost everything has a characteristic odor—everyone is familiar with the smell of the rose. No one would want the dog to smell like a rose, and, conversely, the world wouldn't like it very well if the rose smelled doggy. The dog must emit a certain amount of characteristic odor or he wouldn't be a dog. That seems to be his God-given grant. However, when the odor becomes too strong and obnoxious, then it is time to look for the reason. In most cases it is the result of clogged anal glands. If this be the case, all one must do to rid the pet of his odor is to express the contents of these glands and apply to the anal region a little soap and water.

If the odor is one of putrefaction, look to his mouth for the trouble. The teeth may need scaling, or a diseased root of some

117

one or two teeth that need to be treated may be the source of the odor. In some dogs there is a fold or a crease in the lower lip near the lower canine tooth, and this may need attention. This spot is favored by fungi that cause considerable damage to the part. The smell here is somewhat akin to the odor of human feet that have been attacked by the fungus of athlete's foot.

The odor may be coming from the coat if the dog is heavily infested with fleas or lice. Too, dogs seem to enjoy the odor of dead fish and often roll on a foul smelling fish that has been cast up on the beach. The dog with a bad case of otitis can fairly "drive you out of the room" with this peculiar odor. Obviously, the way to rid the dog of odor is to find from whence it comes and then take steps to eliminate it. Some dogs have a tendency toward excessive flatulence (gas). These animals should have a complete change of diet and with the reducing of the carbohydrate content, a teaspoon of granular charcoal should be added to each feeding.

BATHING THE DOG

There is little to say about giving a bath to a dog, except that he shall be placed in a tub of warm (not hot) water and thoroughly scrubbed. He may, like a spoiled child, object to the ordeal, but if handled gently and firmly he will submit to what he knows to be inevitable.

The water must be only tepid, so as not to shock or chill the dog. A bland, unmedicated soap is best, for such soaps do not irritate the skin or dry out the hair. Even better than soap is one of the powdered detergents marketed especially for this purpose. They rinse away better and more easily than soap and do not leave the coat gummy or sticky.

It is best to begin with the face, which should be thoroughly and briskly washed with a cloth. Care should be taken that the cleaning solvent does not get into the dog's eyes, not because of the likelihood of causing permanent harm, but because such an experience is unpleasant to the dog and prone to prejudice him against future baths. The interior of the ear canals should be thoroughly cleansed until they not only look clean but also until no unpleasant odor comes from them. The head may then be rinsed and dried before proceeding to the body. Especial attention should be given to the drying of the ears, inside and outside. Many ear infections arise from failure to dry the canals completely.

With the head bathed and the surplus water removed from that part, the body must be soaked thoroughly with water, either with a hose or by dipping the water from the bath and pouring it over the dog's back until he is totally wetted. Thereafter, the soap or detergent should be applied and rubbed until it lathers freely. A stiff brush is useful in penetrating the coat and cleansing the skin. It is not sufficient to wash only the back and sides—the belly, neck, legs, feet, and tail must all be scrubbed thoroughly.

If the dog is very dirty, it may be well to rinse him lightly and repeat the soaping process and scrub again. Thereafter, the dog must be rinsed with warm (tepid) water until all suds and soil come away. If a bath spray is available, the rinsing is an easy matter. If the dog must be rinsed in standing water, it will be needful to renew it two or three times.

When he is thoroughly rinsed, it is well to remove such surplus water as may be squeezed with the hand, after which he is enveloped with a turkish towel, lifted from the tub, and rubbed until he is dry. This will probably require two or three dry towels. In the process of drying the dog, it is well to return again and again to the interior of the ears.

THE DOG'S TEETH

The dog, like the human being, has two successive sets of teeth, the so-called milk teeth or baby teeth, which are shed and replaced later by the permanent teeth. The temporary teeth, which begin to emerge when the puppy is two and a half to three weeks of age, offer no difficulty. The full set of milk teeth (consisting usually of six incisors and two canines in each jaw, with four molars in the upper jaw and six molars in the lower jaw) is completed usually just before weaning time. Except for some obvious malformation, the milk teeth may be ignored and forgotten about.

At about the fourth month the baby teeth are shed and gradually replaced by the permanent teeth. This shedding and replacement process may consume some three or four months. This is about the most critical period of the dog's life—his adolescence. Some constitutionally vigorous dogs go through their teething easily, with no seeming awareness that the change is taking place. Others, less vigorous, may suffer from soreness of the gums, go off in flesh, and require pampering. While they are teething, puppies should be particularly protected from exposure to infectious diseases and should be fed on nutritious foods, especially meat and milk.

The permanent teeth normally consist of 42—six incisors and two canines (fangs) in each jaw, with twelve molars in the upper jaw and fourteen in the lower jaw. Occasionally the front molars fail to emerge; this deficiency is considered by most judges to be only a minor fault, if the absence is noticed at all.

Dentition is a heritable factor in the dog, and some dogs have soft, brittle and defective permanent teeth, no matter how excellent the diet and the care given them. The teeth of those dogs which are predisposed to have excellent sound ones, however, can be ruined by an inferior diet prior to and during the period of their eruption. At this time, for the teeth to develop properly, a dog must have an adequate supply of calcium phosphate and vitamin D, besides all the protein he can consume.

Often the permanent teeth emerge before the shedding of the milk teeth, in which case the dog may have parts of both sets at the same time. The milk teeth will eventually drop out, but as long as they remain they may deflect or displace the second teeth in the process of their growth. The incisors are the teeth in which a malformation may result from the late dropping of the baby teeth. When it. is realized just how important a correct "bite" may be deemed in the show ring, the hazards of permitting the baby teeth to deflect the permanent set will be understood.

The baby teeth in such a case must be dislodged and removed. The roots of the baby teeth are resorbed in the gums, and the teeth can usually be extracted by firm pressure of thumb and finger, although it may be necessary to employ forceps or to take the puppy to the veterinarian.

The permanent teeth of the puppy are usually somewhat overshot, by which is meant that the upper incisors protrude over and do not play upon the lower incisors. Maturity may be trusted to remedy this apparent defect unless it is too pronounced.

An undershot mouth in a puppy, on the other hand, tends to grow worse as the dog matures. Whether or not it has been caused by the displacement of the permanent teeth by the persistence of the milk teeth, it can sometimes be remedied (or at least bettered) by frequent hard pressure of the thumb on the lower jaw, forcing the lower teeth backward to meet the upper ones. Braces on dog teeth have seldom proved efficacious, but pressure and massage are worth trying on the bad mouth of an otherwise excellent puppy.

High and persistent fevers, especially from the fourth to the ninth month, sometimes result in discolored, pitted, and defective teeth, commonly called "distemper teeth." They often result from maladies other than distemper. There is little that can be done for them. They are unpleasant to see and are subject to penalty in the show ring, but are serviceable to the dog. Distemper teeth are not in themselves heritable, but the predisposition for their development appears to be. At least, at the teething age, the offspring from distemper toothed ancestors seem to be especially prone to fevers which impair their dentition.

Older dogs, especially those fed largely upon carbohydrates, tend to accumulate more or less tartar upon their teeth. The tartar generally starts at the gum line on the molars and extends gradually to the cusp. To rectify this condition, the dog's teeth should be scaled by a veterinarian.

The cleanliness of a dog's mouth may be brought about and the formation of tartar discouraged by the scouring of the teeth with a moist cloth dipped in a mixture of equal parts of table salt and baking soda.

A large bone given the dog to chew on or play with tends to prevent tartar from forming on the teeth. If tartar is present, the chewing and gnawing on the bone will help to remove the deposit mechanically. A bone given to puppies will act as a teething ring and aid in the cutting of the permanent teeth. So will beef hide strips you can buy in pet shops.

CARE OF THE NAILS

The nails of the dog should be kept shortened and blunted right down to the quick—never into the quick. If this is not done, the toes may spread and the foot may splay into a veritable pancake. Some dogs have naturally flat feet, which they have inherited. No pretense is made that the shortening of the nails of such a foot will obviate the fault entirely and make the foot beautiful or serviceable.

It will only improve the appearance and make the best of an obvious fault. Short nails do, however, emphasize the excellence of a good foot.

Some dogs keep their nails short by digging and friction. Their nails require little attention, but it is a rare dog whose foot cannot be bettered by artificially shortening the nails.

Nail clippers are available, made especially for the purpose. After using them, the sides of the nail should be filed away as much as is possible without touching the quick. Carefully done, it causes the dog no discomfort. But, once the quick of a dog's nail has been injured, he may forever afterward resent and fight having his feet treated or even having them examined.

The obvious horn of the nail can be removed, after which the quick will recede to permit the removal of more horn the following week. This process may be kept up until the nail is as short and blunt as it can be made, after which nails will need attention only at intervals of six weeks or two months.

Some persons clip the nails right back to the toes in one fell swoop, disregarding injury to the quick and pain of the dog. The nails bleed and the dog limps for a day or two, but infection seldom develops. Such a procedure should not be undertaken without a general anesthetic. If an anesthetic is used, this forthright method does not prejudice the dog against having his feet handled.

NAIL TRIMMING ILLUSTRATED

The method here illustrated is to take a sharp file and stroke the nail downwards in the direction of the arrow, as in Figure 24, until it assumes the shape in Figure 25, the shaded portion being the part removed, a three-cornered file should then be used on the underside just missing the quick, as in Figure 26, and the operation is then complete, the dog running about quickly wears the nail to the proper shape.

Care for
the Old Dog

First, how old is old, in a dog? Some breeds live longer than others, as a general rule. The only regularity about dog ages at death is their irregularity breed to breed and dog to dog.

The dog owner can best determine senility in his canine friend by the dog's appearance and behavior. Old dogs "slow down" much as humans do. The stairs are a little steeper, the breath a little shorter, the eye dimmer, the hearing usually a little harder.

As prevention is always better than cure, a dog's life may be happily and healthfully extended if certain precautionary steps are taken. As the aging process becomes quite evident, the owner should become more considerate of his dog's weaknesses, procrastinations and lapses. A softer, drier, warmer bed may be advisable; a foam rubber mattress will be appreciated. If a kennel dog has been able to endure record-breaking hot or cold, torrential or desert-dry days, he may in his old age appreciate spending his nights at least in a warm, comfy human house. And if the weather outside is frightful during the day, he should—for minimum comfort and safety—be brought inside before pneumonia sets in.

The old dog should NOT be required or expected to chase a ball, or a pheasant, or one of his species of different sex. The old bitch should not continue motherhood.

If many teeth are gone or going, foods should be softer. The diet should be blander—delete sweet or spicy or heavy tidbits—and there should be less of it, usually. The older dog needs less fat, less carbohydrate and less minerals unless disease and convalescence dictate otherwise. DON'T PERMIT AN OLD DOG TO GET FAT! It's cruel. The special diet known as PD or KD may be in order, if the dog has dietary troubles or a disease concomitant with old age. The veterinarian should be asked about PD or KD diets. Vitamin B-12 and other vitamin reinforcements may help.

The dog diseases of old age parallel many of the human illnesses. Senior male dogs suffer from prostate trouble, kidney disease and cancer. Senior bitches suffer from metritis and cancer. Both sexes suffer blindness, deafness and paralysis. Dogs suffer from heart disease; I know one old dog that is living an especially happy old age through the courtesy of digitalis. If the symptoms of any disease manifest themselves in an old dog the veterinarian MUST be consulted.

Many dog owners are selfish about old dogs. In their reluctance to lose faithful friends, they try to keep their canine companions alive in terminal illnesses, such as galloping cancer. If the veterinarian holds little or no promise for recovery of a pet from an illness associated with old age, or if the pet suffers, the kindest act the owner can perform is to request euthanasia. In this sad event, the kindest step the owner may take in *his* interest is to acquire a puppy or young dog of the same breed immediately. Puppies have a wonderful way of absorbing grief!

Glossary of Dog Terms

Achilles tendon: The large tendon attaching the muscle of the calf in the second thigh to the bone below the hock; the hamstring.

A.K.C.: The American Kennel Club.

Albino: An animal having a congenital deficiency of pigment in the skin, hair, and eyes.

American Kennel Club: A federation of member show-giving and specialty clubs which maintains a stud book, and formulates and enforces rules under which dog shows and other canine activities in the United States are conducted. Its address is 221 Park Avenue South, New York 3, N. Y.

Angulation: The angles of the bony structure at the joints, particularly of the shoulder with the upper arm (front angulation), or the angles at the stifle and the hock (rear angulation).

Anus: The posterior opening of the alimentary canal through which the feces are discharged.

Apple head: A rounded or domed skull.

Balance: A nice adjustment of the parts one to another; no part too big or too small for the whole organism; symmetry.

Barrel: The ribs and body.

Bitch: The female of the dog species.

Blaze: A white line or marking extending from the top of the skull (often from the occiput), between the eyes, and over the muzzle.

Brisket: The breast or lower part of the chest in front of and between the forelegs, sometimes including the part extending back some distance behind the forelegs.

Burr: The visible, irregular inside formation of the ear.

Butterfly nose: A nose spotted or speckled with flesh color.

Canine: (Noun) Any animal of the family *Canidae,* including dogs, wolves, jackals, and foxes.
(Adjective) Of or pertaining to such animals; having the nature and qualities of a dog.

Canine tooth: The long tooth next behind the incisors in each side of each jaw; the fang.

Castrate: (Verb) Surgically to remove the gonads of either sex, usually said of the testes of the male.

Character: A combination of points of appearance, behavior, and disposition contributing to the whole dog and distinctive of the individual dog or of its particular breed.

Cheeky: Having rounded muscular padding on sides of the skull.

Chiseled: (Said of the muzzle) modeled or delicately cut away in front of the eyes to conform to breed type.

Chops: The mouth, jaws, lips, and cushion.

Close-coupled: Short in the loins.

Cobby: Stout, stocky, short-bodied; compactly made; like a cob (horse).

Coupling: The part of the body joining the hindquarters to the parts of the body in front; the loin; the flank.

Cowhocks: Hocks turned inward and converging like the presumed hocks of a cow.

Croup: The rear of the back above the hind limbs; the line from the pelvis to the set-on of the tail.

Cryptorchid: A male animal in which the testicles are not externally apparent, having failed to descend normally, not to be confused with a castrated dog.

Dentition: The number, kind, form, and arrangement of the teeth.

Dewclaws: Additional toes on the inside of the leg above the foot; the ones on the rear legs usually removed in puppyhood in most breeds.

Dewlap: The pendulous fold of skin under the neck.

Distemper teeth: The discolored and pitted teeth which result from some febrile disease.

Down in (or on) pastern: With forelegs more or less bent at the pastern joint.

Dry: Free from surplus skin or flesh about mouth, lips, or throat.

Dudley nose: A brown or flesh-colored nose, usually accompanied by eye-rims of the same shade and light eyes.

Ewe-neck: A thin sheep-like neck, having insufficient, faulty, or concave arch.

Expression: The combination of various features of the head and face, particularly the size, shape, placement and color of eyes, to produce a certain impression, the outlook.

Femur: The heavy bone of the true thigh.

Fetlock or Fetlock joint: The joint between the pastern and the lower arm; sometimes called the "knee," although it does not correspond to the human knee.

Fiddle front: A crooked front with bandy legs, out at elbow, converging at pastern joints, and turned out pasterns and feet, with or without bent bones of forearms.

Flews: The chops; pendulous lateral parts of the upper lips.

Forearm: The part of the front leg between the elbow and pastern.

Front: The entire aspect of a dog, except the head, when seen from the front; the forehand.

Guard hairs: The longer, smoother, stiffer hairs which grow through the undercoat and normally conceal it.

Hackney action: The high lifting of the front feet, like that of a Hackney horse, a waste of effort.

Hare-foot: A long, narrow, and close-toed foot, like that of the hare or rabbit.

Haw: The third eyelid, or nictitating membrane, especially when inflamed.

Height: The vertical distance from withers at top of shoulder blades to floor.

Hock: The lower joint in the hind leg, corresponding to the human ankle; sometimes, incorrectly, the part of the hind leg, from the hock joint to the foot.

Humerus: The bone of the upper arm.

Incisors: The teeth adapted for cutting; specifically, the six small front teeth in each jaw between the canines or fangs.

126

Knuckling over: Projecting or bulging forward of the front legs at the pastern joint; incorrectly called knuckle knees.

Leather: Pendant ears.

Lippy: With lips longer or fuller than desirable in the breed under consideration.

Loaded: Padded with superfluous muscle (said of such shoulders).

Loins: That part on either side of the spinal column between the hipbone and the false ribs.

Molar tooth: A rear, cheek tooth adapted for grinding food.

Monorchid: A male animal having but one testicle in the scrotum; monorchids may be potent and fertile.

Muzzle: The part of the face in front of the eyes.

Nictitating membrane: A thin membrane at the inner angle of the eye or beneath the lower lid, capable of being drawn across the eyeball. This membrane is frequently surgically excised in some breeds to improve the expression.

Occiput or occiputal protuberance: The bony knob at the top of the skull between the ears.

Occlusion: The bringing together of the opposing surfaces of the two jaws; the relation between those surfaces when in contact.

Olfactory: Of or pertaining to the sense of smell.

Out at elbow: With elbows turned outward from body due to faulty joint and front formation, usually accompanied by pigeon-toes; loose-fronted.

Out at shoulder: With shoulder blades loosely attached to the body, leaving the shoulders jutting out in relief and increasing the breadth of the front.

Overshot: Having the lower jaw so short that the upper and lower incisors fail to meet; pig-jawed.

Pace: A gait in which the legs move in lateral pairs, the animal supported alternatively by the right and left legs.

Pad: The cushion-like, tough sole of the foot.

Pastern: That part of the foreleg between the fetlock or pastern joint and the foot; sometimes incorrectly used for pastern joint or fetlock.

Period of gestation: The duration of pregnancy, about 63 days in the dog.

Puppy: Technically, a dog under a year in age.

Quarters: The two hind legs taken together.

Roach-back: An arched or convex spine, the curvature rising gently behind the withers and carrying over the loins; wheel-back.

Roman nose: The convex curved top line of the muzzle.

Scapula: The shoulder blade.

Scissors bite: A bite in which the incisors of the upper jaw just overlap and play upon those of the lower jaw.

Slab sides: Flat sides with insufficient spring of ribs.

Snipey: Snipe-nosed, said of a muzzle too sharply pointed, narrow, or weak.

Spay: To render a bitch sterile by the surgical removal of her ovaries; to castrate a bitch.

Specialty club: An organization to sponsor and forward the interests of a single breed.

Specialty show: A dog show confined to a single breed.

Spring: The roundness of ribs.

Stifle or stifle joint: The joint next above the hock, and near the flank, in the hind leg; the joint corresponding to the knee in man.

Stop: The depression or step between the forehead and the muzzle between the eyes.

Straight hocks: Hocks lacking bend or angulation.

Straight shoulders: Shoulder formation with blades too upright, with angle greater than 90° with bone of upper arm.

Substance: Strength of skeleton, and weight of solid musculature.

Sway-back: A spine with sagging, concave curvature from withers to pelvis.

Thorax: The part of the body between the neck and the abdomen, and supported by the ribs and sternum.

Throaty: Possessing a superfluous amount of skin under the throat.

Undercoat: A growth of short, fine hair, or pile, partly or entirely concealed by the coarser top coat which grows through it.

Undershot: Having the lower incisor teeth projecting beyond the upper ones when the mouth is closed; the opposite to overshot; prognathous; underhung.

Upper arm: The part of the dog between the elbow and point of shoulder.

Weaving: Crossing the front legs one over the other in action.

Withers: The part between the shoulder bones at the base of the neck; the point from which the height of a dog is usually measured.

(End of Part II. Please see Contents page for total number of pages in book.)